THE AI-SAVVY JOB SEEKER

Transform Your LinkedIn Profile and Outshine the Competition

Michelle Dumas

Distinctive Career Publishing
www.distinctiveweb.com/distinctive-career-publishing/

ISBN 13: 979-8-9918916-1-5

Contents

Endorsements

"Michelle Dumas has captured what every job seeker, recruiter, AND job-search coach/resume writer must know to level up job search in today's AI-driven and machine learning-fueled environment. Her book walks readers systematically and pragmatically through the essential steps. She provides the right strategies for differentiating and adding true value to one's LinkedIn. The reader will find unique approaches to personal branding for the professional coupled with must-know techniques to make a LinkedIn profile authentically sizzle. The prompts throughout are incredibly valuable and can best leverage AI in a way that correctly supports the job seeker. I'll be sure to add Michelle's book to my active collection — and incorporate her AI-LI strategies in my work with my clients."

Jan Melnik, MA, MRW, CCM, CPRW
President, Absolute Advantage and Author, Modernize Your Executive Job Search and Resume and LinkedIn Strategies for New College Graduates | www.janmelnik.com

"The AI-Savvy Job Seeker will shift your perspective on career success. It revolutionizes career advice, especially for today's college students–the workforce of tomorrow–by leveraging the power of Artificial Intelligence to empower personal branding, résumé refinement, skill gap analysis, interview preparation, and LinkedIn mastery. This book will help you approach your career as a "Business of One," fully prepared and positioned as the CEO of your own professional journey."

Dr. Cheryl Minnick, Director of Career Success, University of Montana College of Humanities & Sciences

"If you're wondering what AI can do for you and your career, this book has the answers. Offering detailed recommendations and specific prompts, Michelle Dumas clearly explains how to harness the immense power of AI to sharpen every aspect of your LinkedIn profile and other career messages. What's more, she guides you through the many features of LinkedIn with sage advice about how to use every one to your advantage as you conduct a job search and manage your career for the long term. Whether you are a new graduate or an experienced professional, you will benefit from Michelle's expert guidance through the challenging, often stressful process of job search and career management. With AI as your tool and Michelle's expertise guiding your strategy, you will be head and shoulders above most job seekers—while mastering essential skills for your successful future."

Louise Kursmark
President, Best Impression Career Services and Author, Modernize Your Resume and 20+ additional books on resume writing and career management

"I'll be recommending "The AI-Savvy Job Seeker" to all my clients and career industry colleagues. While there has been a lot of talk about how artificial intelligence can help in the job search, this book provides clear, actionable insights. With accessible strategies for everyone from recent college graduates to seasoned executives, the book combines detailed explanations about the WHY of the strategy with the WHAT of how to implement the idea, including specific AI prompts. The blueprints to create an effective "About" section are pure gold for populating this key LinkedIn section. This book is an essential resource for anyone looking to leverage AI in their job search."

Bridget (Weide) Brooks
Owner, Image Building Communications and
Founder, BeAResumeWriter.com

Introduction

I magine walking into a room full of potential employers, colleagues, and industry leaders. Now, picture that room expanding infinitely, accessible 24/7 from anywhere in the world. That's LinkedIn—a digital space where your professional story unfolds before a global audience.

In my 25-plus years in career services, I've watched job searches transform from circling newspaper ads to curating online profiles. Today, your digital footprint isn't just an addition to your professional identity; it's become the cornerstone.

I'm Michelle Dumas, founder and CEO of Distinctive Career Services, and I'm thrilled to guide you through the transformative journey of enhancing your LinkedIn profile using the power of artificial intelligence (AI). But before we delve into the exciting world of AI-powered profile optimization, allow me to share a bit about my background and why I'm passionate about helping professionals like you succeed.

My story begins in 1996 when I founded Distinctive Career Services. From the outset, our mission was clear: to empower as many people as possible with the tools, resources, and confidence they need to pursue and achieve their dream careers. Over the past 25+ years, we've had the privilege of positively impacting the lives and careers of well over 10,000 individuals across all 50 U.S. states and internationally.

As a pioneer in the professional resume-writing industry, I've always been at the forefront of emerging trends and technologies. In fact, I was among the first 150,000 people to join LinkedIn when it launched. Recognizing its potential early on, I began incorporating LinkedIn profile writing into our services, initially by simply adapting the résumés we crafted for our clients.

However, as LinkedIn evolved, so did the art and science of creating compelling profiles. Today, a well-crafted LinkedIn profile is just as crucial as a polished résumé, if not more so. It's your digital calling card, your 24/7 professional showcase, and often the first point of contact between you and potential employers or networking connections.

Throughout my career, I've been driven by a desire to help as many people as possible achieve their highest professional aspirations. While my team and I at Distinctive Career Services offer personalized, expert services in résumé writing and LinkedIn profile optimization, I've always been acutely aware that not everyone can afford professional assistance despite the high return on investment it offers.

This realization was my catalyst for writing "The AI-Savvy Job Seeker: Transform Your LinkedIn Profile and Outshine the Competition." With the advent of sophisticated AI tools, I saw an opportunity to bridge the gap between those who can afford professional services and those who are willing to put in the work themselves but need expert guidance.

This book is my way of democratizing access to high-quality career advice and LinkedIn optimization strategies. By combining my decades of experience with the power of AI, I aim to provide you with a roadmap to create a LinkedIn profile that rivals those crafted by professionals.

But this book isn't just for those new to professional LinkedIn profile creation. If you're a professional who has already worked with us—or with another career services provider—to craft a powerful, compelling, branded LinkedIn profile, this guide is equally valuable to you. As your career evolves, so should your digital presence. This book will empower you with the know-how to refine your "living" profile as your career advances, ensuring it always reflects your current achievements and aspirations. Moreover, you'll discover advanced strategies for leveraging LinkedIn to further your career and build your personal brand in ways you might not have considered before.

What This Book Offers

Whether you're starting from scratch or looking to take an already strong profile to the next level, "The AI-Savvy Job Seeker" is designed to meet you where you are and propel you forward. By harnessing the power of AI, we'll explore how to keep your profile dynamic, engaging, and aligned with your career trajectory—all while saving you time and effort. Here's what you can expect:

- **Step-by-Step Guidance:** I'll walk you through each section of your LinkedIn profile, showing you how to use AI tools to enhance your summary, choose the right keywords, and highlight your skills.

- **AI-Powered Strategies:** I'll show you how to harness AI as a smart assistant, crafting content that not only captivates human readers but also shines in LinkedIn Recruiter searches. You'll learn to strike that perfect balance between engaging storytelling and strategic keyword optimization.

- **Personal Branding:** I'll guide you in infusing your unique professional brand into your profile. You'll learn how to craft a career story that's not just compelling but genuinely reflective of who you are. We'll ensure your authenticity shines through every word.

- **Practical and Actionable Advice:** I've made sure each chapter wraps up with concrete action items. This way, you're not just passively reading – you're actively improving your profile as we go along.

- **Exclusive Online Resources:** I've put together an online treasure trove for you. You'll find all the AI prompts from this book ready for easy copy and paste into your favorite AI tool. I've also included a collection of symbols and emojis to spice up your profile, plus a bunch of other goodies to help you craft the perfect LinkedIn presence. It's all waiting for you at https://www.distinctiveweb.com/linkedin-book-resources. If you're thumbing through a printed copy or reading on your Kindle, don't worry – I've got you covered. Just scan the QR code below with your phone or tablet for instant access to all these resources.

The Ever-Evolving Landscape of AI

As we dive into the world of LinkedIn optimization together, I want to address the elephant in the room - the lightning-fast evolution of artificial intelligence. Trust me, I know it can feel like there's a new AI tool or capability popping up every time you blink. That's why, except in a couple of cases, I've made a deliberate choice not to recommend specific websites or tools that might be outdated before the ink dries on this page.

Instead, I'm equipping you with a Swiss Army knife of versatile prompts. You can use these with whichever AI-powered chatbot you prefer. The good news? Many of these chatbots - think ChatGPT, Claude, Bard (now Gemini), Perplexity, and Bing Chat - still offer free options as of this writing.

For prompts that require access to the latest information, such as recent industry news or trends, I recommend using AI-powered search engines like Perplexity or Bing. These tools can provide up-to-the-minute insights that will keep your LinkedIn profile current and relevant.

The Power of AI in Career Development

Artificial Intelligence isn't just changing the game - it's rewriting the rule-book for career development. While we're focusing on your LinkedIn profile in this book, I want to give you a peek behind the curtain at how AI is reshaping the entire career landscape.

Behind the scenes, AI is transforming how companies recruit, screen résumés, and match candidates to jobs. It's the invisible hand powering applicant tracking systems, crunching labor market trends, and even crystal-balling future skill demands. But what does this mean for you, the job seeker or professional? Let me break down some of the most impactful ways AI is changing the game:

- **Personalized Career Guidance:** AI algorithms can analyze your skills, experience, and interests to suggest tailored career paths and learning opportunities.

- **Résumé Enhancement:** AI-powered tools can help polish your résumé, suggesting tweaks in language, format, and content to make it shine for each job opportunity.

- **Interview Preparation:** Imagine having a tireless interview coach. AI chatbots can run you through interview scenarios, giving you practice and feedback to help you nail the real thing.

- **Skill Gap Analysis:** AI can spot the missing pieces in your professional toolkit by comparing your current skills with what the job market is hungry for.

- **Networking Optimization:** AI can be your eyes and ears in the professional world, suggesting relevant connections and events that align with your career goals and industry.

Now, let's zoom in on how AI can supercharge your LinkedIn game. This platform is a goldmine of opportunities, and AI is the perfect tool to help you strike it rich. Here's how AI can be a game-changer for your LinkedIn experience:

- **Craft compelling headlines and summaries:** AI tools can analyze successful profiles in your field to suggest headlines and summaries that capture attention and effectively reflect your professional brand.

- **Optimize the wording of profile sections:** AI-powered writing assistants can help refine the language in your profile sections, ensuring clarity, professionalism, and impact. They can suggest more powerful verbs, more precise descriptions, and overall improvements that make your profile stand out.

- **Analyze your profile's performance and suggest improvements:** Advanced analytics powered by AI can provide insights into how your profile is performing, including which sections are attracting views and where you can make improvements.

- **Identify trending topics in your industry for thought leadership opportunities:** AI can keep you updated on emerging trends, enabling you to write posts or articles that position you as a thought leader.

- **Optimize your profile for relevant keywords:** By scanning job postings and industry-related content, AI can recommend keywords to include in your profile to increase its visibility to recruiters and hiring managers.

- **Generate ideas for engaging posts and articles:** Writer's block? AI can spark ideas for engaging posts and articles, keeping your content fresh and your network engaged.

- **Draft follow-up messages:** AI can help you maintain engagement with your connections by suggesting personalized follow-up messages after initial interactions.

We'll dive deep into all of these areas and many more as we journey through this book together.

Ethical Considerations in AI-Assisted Profile Optimization

Now, let's talk ethics for a moment. While AI is a powerful ally in enhancing your LinkedIn presence, it's important to use it responsibly. Let's review some essential guidelines for ethical and effective AI use:

- **Keep it Real:** Think of AI as your personal stylist, not your ghost-writer. Use it to polish your professional story, not to spin tall tales about skills or experiences you don't have.

- **Transparency:** If AI is doing a lot of the heavy lifting in your content creation, consider giving it a nod. A little transparency goes a long way in building trust with your network.

- **Human Touch:** Your LinkedIn profile should sound like you at your best, not like a robot. Use AI suggestions as a jumping-off point, then infuse them with your unique personality and flair.

- **Fact-Checking:** Remember, AI isn't infallible. It can slip up or dish out yesterday's news (or worse, sometimes total fabrications). Always double-check any facts or claims before you hit that 'post' button.

- **Fair Use:** When using AI to generate content, make sure you're not accidentally borrowing someone else's work. Respect copyright and intellectual property rights like they're your own.

As you'll discover throughout this book, by keeping these ethical considerations in mind, you can confidently harness AI's power to enhance your LinkedIn profile while staying true to your unique professional story.

Why LinkedIn Matters

Let's face it: in today's hyper-connected world, your LinkedIn profile is often your first opportunity to make a lasting impression on potential employers, clients, or networking contacts. It's more than just an online résumé; it's a dynamic platform where you can showcase your expertise, engage with your industry, and open doors to new opportunities.

A well-optimized LinkedIn profile can:

- **Increase your visibility to recruiters and hiring managers:** Appear in more searches by recruiters and hiring managers, enhancing your chances of being noticed for relevant job opportunities.

- **Facilitate meaningful professional connections:** Connect more easily with industry peers, potential mentors, and other professionals, paving the way for valuable networking opportunities.

- **Provide opportunities for career advancement:** Open doors to new career paths, promotions, and professional growth opportunities by showcasing your potential to current and future employers.

- **Showcase your skills and experiences in a compelling way:** Present your accomplishments and expertise in a format that captures and maintains the attention of key decision-makers..

- **Demonstrate your industry knowledge and thought leadership:** Share insights and contributions, positioning you as a thought leader within your field.

- **Enhance your personal brand:** Clearly establish and communicate your unique professional identity and value proposition, distinguishing you from other professionals in your field.

- **Improve search engine visibility:** Rank your profile well in search engine results, providing an additional channel for professional visibility outside of LinkedIn itself.

- **Attract opportunities for collaboration:** Draw interest not only for job opportunities but also for speaking engagements, partnerships, and other professional projects.

By leveraging AI tools to enhance your LinkedIn profile, you're not just keeping up with the competition – you're positioning yourself to stand out in a crowded digital landscape.

What Sets This Book Apart

While there are many books and resources available on LinkedIn optimization, "The AI-Savvy Job Seeker" is unique in its approach. Here's why:

- **AI-Powered Career Booster:** This isn't just another LinkedIn guide - it's your AI-powered secret weapon for job searching and career advancement. I'll show you how to harness AI tools specifically for LinkedIn, turbocharging your profile in ways most job seekers haven't even thought of yet.

- **Expert Insights:** With over 25 years of experience in the career services industry, I bring a wealth of knowledge and practical insights to this guide. I'm not just sharing theories - I'm giving you real-world strategies that have helped countless professionals land their dream jobs.

- **Holistic Approach:** We're not just polishing individual profile sections here. I'll guide you in weaving all elements of your LinkedIn presence into a compelling professional narrative that showcases your unique value proposition to potential employers.

- **Actionable Strategies:** Each chapter is packed with concrete action steps. By the time you finish this book, you won't just be informed - you'll have a transformed LinkedIn profile that's working overtime for your career.

- **Ongoing Resources:** The online companion reader resources ensure that you have continued support even after you've finished reading the book. Make sure to access and bookmark them, as they will be invaluable to you whenever you work on your profile. To make it easy for you, here is that QR code again:

How to Use This Book

To get the most out of "The AI-Savvy Job Seeker," I recommend the following approach:

- **Read Sequentially:** While each chapter can stand alone, I recommend reading sequentially your first time through, as the book is designed to guide you through a logical process of profile optimization.

- **Complete the Action Items:** Don't skip the action items at the end of each chapter. I created them to help you immediately implement what you've learned.

- **Utilize the Online Resources:** Make sure to make the most of the AI prompts and other online reader resources from the provided link. These will be valuable tools both as you work through the book and whenever you update or edit your profile in the future.

- **Iterate and Refine:** LinkedIn profile optimization is an ongoing process. Don't be afraid to revisit chapters and refine your profile as you gain new experiences or as your career goals evolve.

- **Stay Authentic:** While AI can be a powerful tool, always ensure that your profile accurately reflects your voice and experiences.

While this book is designed to empower you to create a high-quality LinkedIn profile on your own, I want to acknowledge that there's no complete substitute for personalized, professional assistance. If at any point you feel overwhelmed or want an expert touch, don't hesitate to reach out to professional services like Distinctive Career Services (www.distinctiveweb .com). We're always here to help take your profile to the next level.

As we embark on this journey together, I want you to remember that your LinkedIn profile is more than just a digital résumé. It's a powerful tool for career advancement, a platform for professional storytelling, and a gateway to countless opportunities.

Remember, in today's dynamic job market, opportunities don't just find you—you create them. With this book as your guide, you'll be well-equipped to proactively shape your professional journey and unlock exciting new possibilities. Whether you're actively seeking a new position or focused on long-term career growth, the strategies in these pages will empower you to take control of your professional narrative and stand out in the digital landscape.

Are you ready to transform your LinkedIn profile and outshine the competition? Let's get started!

Chapter One

The New Rules of Job Searching

Navigating and Thriving in the Age of Change

Welcome to the new world of work!

Remember the days when a job meant a lifelong commitment to one company, climbing a predictable corporate ladder, and retiring with a gold watch? Those days are long gone. Today's career landscape is more like a wild jungle than a well-trodden path, and it's time to equip yourself with the right tools to navigate it.

Let's kick things off with a trip down memory lane, exploring how job hunting and climbing the career ladder used to work. Then, we'll dive into why these old methods just don't cut it anymore. From the death of lifetime employment to the rise of the gig economy, from rapid technological advancements to increased global competition, we'll explore the forces reshaping the job market.

But don't worry - it's not all doom and gloom. With change comes opportunity, and I'll show you how to seize it. I'll introduce you to the "Business of One" mindset, teaching you to see yourself as the CEO of your own career. I'll cover pitfalls to avoid in this new landscape and provide strategies to adapt your job search for the AI age.

By the end of this chapter, you'll understand why continuous learning, personal branding, income diversification, strategic networking, and an entrepreneurial mindset are your new career superpowers. You'll be ready to embrace the challenges and opportunities of the modern job market, armed with the know-how not just to survive but thrive.

So, are you ready to transform your approach to your career? Let's dive in and discover how to navigate the exciting, sometimes turbulent, but always opportunity-rich waters of today's job market.

A Trip Down Memory Lane

You likely remember your parents or grandparents talking about working for the same company for 30 years, retiring with a gold watch and a cushy pension. That was the old world of work, and believe it or not, many people still cling to these outdated notions. Let's take a trip down memory lane and explore what job searching used to look like - and why some folks are still stuck in this mindset.

The "One and Done" Career Path

Back in the day, choosing a career was like picking a life partner. You'd select a field, settle in, and stay put until retirement. Accountants remained accountants, teachers stayed in the classroom, and engineers kept engineering until their slide rules wore out. It was a world of predictability and stability.

Job Security: The Holy Grail

Imagine that warm, fuzzy feeling of knowing your job was safe. Many workers enjoyed the comfort of job security, believing their loyalty would be rewarded with lifetime employment. It was like having a security blanket for your career - cozy but maybe a little restricting.

Climbing the Corporate Ladder: The Only Way Up

Picture a towering ladder reaching into the clouds. That was the corporate hierarchy, and your job was to climb it, rung by rung. Promotions were linear and often based on seniority. It was a slow and steady ascent, but at least you knew where you were headed.

The Waiting Game: Passive Job Hunting

Job searching? More like job waiting. Many professionals simply sat tight, expecting opportunities to fall into their laps. They'd dust off their résumés once in a blue moon, maybe attend a networking event or two, and hope for the best. It was a bit like fishing without bait - you might catch something, but the odds weren't great.

Skills: Set It and Forget It

Once you had your degree and landed that first job, many people thought they were set for life. The idea of constantly updating your skills to stay relevant wasn't on most people's radars. It was a "learn once, apply forever" mentality.

The New Career Landscape

Now, let's rip off the Band-Aid and face the reality of the work world we live in today: these old-school approaches just don't cut it anymore. The world of work has changed dramatically, and clinging to these outdated methods is like trying to navigate a smartphone with a rotary dial. Here's why:

The Death of Lifetime Employment

Remember when switching jobs was flaky and job security was as cozy as a warm blanket? Those days are as extinct as the dodo. Welcome to the era of career fluidity, where change is the only constant.

The numbers tell the story: As of January 2024, the Bureau of Labor Statistics reports that the average job tenure is just 3.9 years, with the typical professional changing jobs 12 times during their career. This isn't job-hopping; it's strategic career-building in a landscape where companies prioritize flexibility over long-term commitments.

Why the seismic shift?

- Economic volatility has made corporate stability a thing of the past

- Technology advancements (hello, AI!) continually reshape industries

- Workers crave variety, growth, and purpose beyond a single role

Imagine this: John, a mid-level manager at a telecom giant, thought he had it all figured out. Fifteen years of climbing the corporate ladder, a corner office with a view, and a sense of job security as solid as the building he worked in. Then, boom! A merger hit like a corporate tsunami, washing away his position and leaving his carefully honed skills high and dry.

John's story isn't just a cautionary tale - it's a wake-up call echoing through every office cubicle and open-plan workspace. In today's business world, betting on job security is like trying to predict the weather a year in advance. Sure, you might get lucky, but you're more likely to end up caught in an unexpected storm.

Expecting lifelong employment in one company? It's like betting your life savings on a single stock – risky at best, disastrous at worst.

But this new reality isn't just about job-hopping; it's about pivoting industries and even creating entirely new roles. Think about it: How many of today's job titles – Data Scientist, Cloud Architect, AI Ethics Officer – existed a decade ago? Your next position might not even be invented yet!

In this fluid career landscape, here are your new superpowers:

- **Transferable skills:** Your ability to communicate effectively or solve complex problems is valuable across industries.

- **Adaptability:** The most successful professionals can learn, unlearn, and relearn at warp speed.

- **Continuous learning:** It's not just a buzzword; it's your career life-line. If you're not growing, you're falling behind.

The death of lifetime employment doesn't spell doom; it spells opportunity. By embracing change and honing these skills, you're not just keeping up with the evolving job market – you're setting yourself up to excel.

The Gig Economy: Freelance Nation

Gone are the days of the one-size-fits-all career path. The rise of the gig economy has flipped the traditional employment model on its head, transforming the job market from a set menu into a vast, enticing buffet. More workers than ever are either choosing or being nudged towards a portfolio career of freelance, contract, and project-based work. It's a world of endless options, but it comes with a side of uncertainty.

Let's dive into the key ingredients of this gig economy feast:

Flexibility: The New Career Currency

Forget the 9-to-5 grind; flexibility is the new gold standard. And gig workers are cashing in:

- Over two-thirds of full-time gig workers view their flexible arrangements as more secure than traditional jobs. That's right – stability through flexibility!

- Commitment? It's still here. 54% of freelancers dedicate at least five days a week to their craft. They're not just dipping their toes; they're diving in headfirst.

Skills: Your Career's Royal Flush

In this new world, your skill set is like a hand of cards - and trust me, you want to be holding a royal flush. Here's why your skills are the real MVPs in the game of career advancement:

- The tech, business management, and marketing trio are the power players in the freelance world. They're not just popular - they're dominating over half the gig work playground in the U.S. If you've got these skills, you're already ahead of the pack.

- Want to hit the jackpot? Blockchain and AI specialists are the high rollers in the gig economy casino.

- Think of your skillset like a poker hand. Each skill you master is another card in your deck. A pair of data analysis skills here, a trio of project management abilities there, and suddenly, you're not just playing the game - you're controlling the table. The more complementary skills you add, the stronger your hand becomes.

Multiple Income Streams: The New Normal

Why put all your eggs in one basket when you can juggle several?

- By 2023, it was estimated that 17% of U.S. workers were "diversified," blending traditional employment with freelance gigs. It's not just a side hustle; it's a lifestyle.

- As of 2024, some 76.4 million Americans were freelancing. That's nearly a quarter of the U.S. population!

- Globally, the freelance market is a $1.5 trillion behemoth, growing at a staggering 15% annually. It's not just a trend; it's an economic juggernaut.

The gig economy isn't just changing how we work; it's redefining what it means to have a career. It's a world where flexibility reigns supreme, skills are your most valuable currency, and diversification is the name of the game. Sure, it's not without its challenges – the feast can sometimes feel like a famine – but for those willing to adapt, the opportunities are endless.

Tech Advances: The Great Job Disruptor

Technology is evolving faster than you can say "artificial intelligence," and it's not just reshaping industries – it's bulldozing and rebuilding them overnight. Remember those "safe" jobs from a decade ago? Well, they're now playing high-stakes musical chairs with automation and obsolescence. In this tech-driven world, keeping up is old news; it's all about staying light years ahead of the curve.

The AI Revolution

Let's talk numbers, shall we? The impact of artificial intelligence on the global economy is unprecedented. Consider these statistics:

The global AI market is experiencing exponential growth and is projected to expand from \$515.31 billion in 2024 to over \$2 trillion by 2030.

This remarkable trajectory represents more than just market growth—it signals a fundamental transformation in how we work and do business!

Key industries leading this transformation include:

- Manufacturing: As an early adopter of intelligent automation, the manufacturing sector expects to increase its average automation levels from 69% to 79% over the next decade.

- Healthcare: With a 37% annual growth rate since 2022, the AI healthcare market is expected to reach \$188 billion by 2030.

The Great Job Shuffle

The impact of automation on employment is significant and warrants attention.

In the U.S., approximately 25% of jobs face high automation potential, while another 36% fall into the medium-risk category. Global workplace dynamics are shifting, too, with automated systems projected to handle up to 30% of work hours by 2030.

However, this transformation presents opportunities alongside challenges. The World Economic Forum's 2020 report offered a balanced perspective: while it was predicted that 85 million current positions may be displaced by 2025 due to the increasing integration of human-machine collaboration, the same evolution is expected to generate 97 million new roles.

This isn't a story of job loss—it's one of workplace transformation. As artificial intelligence and automation reshape our professional landscape, new opportunities emerge for those who adapt and prepare. The key lies in understanding these changes and positioning yourself for the roles of tomorrow.

Staying Ahead: Your Career Superpower

In this brave new world, adaptability isn't just a good-to-have skill; it's your career lifeline:

- Here's a mind-bender: 85% of the jobs that will exist in 2030 haven't even been invented yet. We're not just talking about new jobs; we're talking about entirely new industries!

- Over half of all employees needed significant reskilling and up-skilling by 2022. If you haven't jumped on that bandwagon yet, you're already playing catch-up.

The New Frontier: Emerging Opportunities

While some jobs are nosediving, others are shooting for the stars:

- **Tech Innovators:** Data science, AI, machine learning, robotics, and software development continue to see rapid expansion. These fields aren't just growing; they're actively shaping our future.

- **Healthcare Professionals:** As our population ages and medical technology advances, healthcare is becoming a powerhouse of job creation. Roles such as nurse practitioners, home health aides, medical managers, and physician assistants are in high demand and show no signs of slowing down.

- **Renewable Energy Experts:** Sustainability is more than a buzzword; it's a growing sector of our economy. Wind turbine technicians and solar panel installers are at the forefront of this green revolution.

- **Virtual and Augmented Reality Specialists:** As our physical and digital worlds continue to merge, we're seeing increased demand for AR and VR experts. These professionals are creating immersive experiences that are transforming industries from retail to education.

- **Biotechnology Pioneers:** From developing new pharmaceuticals to engineering resilient crops, biotechnology is pushing the boundaries of what's possible.

- **3D Printing Innovators:** Additive manufacturing is revolutionizing industries from healthcare to aerospace. Professionals in this field are redefining what's possible in production and prototyping.

- **E-commerce Experts:** As more of our shopping moves online, the demand for e-commerce professionals continues to grow. From user experience designers to logistics specialists, these roles are crucial in our increasingly digital marketplace.

The technological revolution isn't just changing the job market; it's creating an entirely new landscape of opportunities. Yes, it's scary. Yes, it's uncertain. But for those willing to ride the wave, it's the opportunity of a lifetime.

So, here's your mission, should you choose to accept it: Embrace the chaos. Learn voraciously. Adapt relentlessly. In this tech-driven job market, you're either surfing the wave of innovation or you're drowning in obsolescence.

Global Competition: The Worldwide Talent Olympics

The career arena has gone from local league to world championship. Thanks to the internet, remote work revolution, and tech advancements, your competition for that dream job isn't just the guy next door – it's the entire planet!

Global Hiring Explosion: Remote Work Rocks the Boat

Hold onto your résumé because hiring has gone full-on global:

- As of 2024, over 6% of job postings are waving the remote work flag. That's not just a trend; it's a full-blown revolution in the job market landscape!

- By 2024, 16% of companies went full digital nomad, with another 40% rocking the hybrid model. But that's just the tip of the iceberg! A whopping 66% of business executives say having employees scattered across the globe is part of their grand strategy, whether they're remote or not. And for 28%, it's not just a strategy – it's their bread and butter!"

- But here's the kicker: 59% of workers think remote work has cranked up the job competition heat. Your next coworker could be sipping coconut water on a beach in Bali!

This remote work tsunami has turned the talent pool into an ocean. Time to bring your A-game!

The Global Talent Buffet

Companies are now treating the world like an all-you-can-hire buffet:

- They're cherry-picking top talent from every corner of the globe, creating a melting pot of skills, languages, and perspectives.

- Outsourcing and offshoring? It's not just for call centers anymore. High-skill jobs are globe-trotting, too, creating a rollercoaster of challenges and opportunities.

Tech: The Ultimate Matchmaker

AI and tech aren't just changing jobs; they're revolutionizing how we get hired:

- Geographical borders? Please. AI-powered recruitment is connecting employers with talent faster than you can say, "You're hired!"

- A 2024 global workforce study found that 65% of workers now view digital skills as crucial for their career advancement, a dramatic increase from just 37% two years prior. The future is digital, and it's knocking on your LinkedIn profile!

The New Career Superpower: Adaptability

In this global talent show, standing out means constantly upping your game:

- AI-specialist jobs are growing 3.5 times faster than overall job growth.

- Continuous upskilling isn't just nice to have; it's your career lifeline. The skills that landed you your job? They might be obsolete before your next performance review.

The job market has transformed into a worldwide talent Olympics. Your competition isn't just local anymore – it's global, it's fierce, and it's armed with cutting-edge skills. But here's the silver lining: the opportunities are just as boundless as the challenges.

To thrive in this new landscape, you need to think globally, skill up relentlessly, and embrace the digital revolution with open arms. The world is your oyster – but it's also everyone else's.

PRO TIP

The old rulebook has been tossed out the window. Sticking to outdated job search methods and career management strategies isn't just ineffective - it can be career suicide.

The "Business of One" Mindset

The days of paternalistic companies taking care of their employees from cradle to grave are over. Today's relationship between workers and employers is more transactional. It's less "till death do us part" and more "let's see how this goes." This shift requires a whole new mindset about loyalty, career development, and job satisfaction.

Here's a mind-bender: You're not just an employee anymore. You're a one-person business. Does this sound scary? To the contrary, it's actually empowering. Let's break it down:

Every Job is Temporary

Face it: there's no such thing as a "safe" job anymore. Companies merge, downsize, or pivot faster than you can update your LinkedIn profile. But here's the silver lining – when you see every job as temporary, you're always prepared for what's next. It's time to shift your perspective and start viewing your career through an entrepreneurial lens and treat it like a business. So what does this mean for you?

- **Personal Branding:** You're the CEO of You, Inc. What do you stand for? What's your unique value?

- **Skill Development is Your R&D:** Just as companies invest in research, you need to invest in your skills. Learning isn't a luxury; it's a necessity.

- **Networking is Your Marketing:** Your network is your net worth. Every connection is a potential lead for your next opportunity.

Consider Sarah, a forward-thinking marketing professional. Rather than relying solely on her company's development programs, she took charge of her own career growth. Sarah consistently invested in online courses to expand her digital marketing skills, attended industry conferences to stay ahead of trends, and launched a blog to demonstrate her expertise. When her company faced downsizing, Sarah's proactive approach paid off. She had cultivated a strong professional network and acquired cutting-edge skills that made her not just employable but highly sought after in her field.

Sarah's story illustrates a crucial point: in today's rapidly evolving job market, waiting for opportunities isn't enough. The most successful professionals are those who anticipate change and prepare for it. So, how can you navigate this dynamic landscape and position yourself for success?

The good news is that while the challenges are real, so are the opportunities. The key lies in embracing change, adapting your approach, and leveraging new tools - including AI - to your advantage. By taking a proactive stance like Sarah, you can transform potential obstacles into stepping stones for career growth.

Common Mistakes in the New Job Landscape

Now that we've painted a picture of this brave new world, let's talk about the landmines you need to avoid. These are the career missteps that can leave you stuck in the dust while others zoom ahead.

Complacency: The Silent Career Killer

In a world that's moving at warp speed, standing still is actually moving backward. Yet, many professionals fall into the trap of complacency, thinking their current skills and knowledge will carry them through. Danger signs of complacency:

- You can't remember the last time you learned a new skill.

- You're not aware of the latest trends in your industry.

- You think AI and automation won't affect your job (spoiler alert: they will).

Marshall Goldsmith's wisdom rings true: "What got you here won't get you there." In the race against complacency, yesterday's achievements are merely the qualifications for today's starting line. Your next career leap demands a new you—one who's constantly evolving, learning, and embracing change.

Invisibility: Neglecting Your Online Presence

In today's digital age, if you're not online, you might as well be invisible. Yet, many professionals treat their online presence as an afterthought. Common online presence mistakes:

- A LinkedIn profile that reads like a dusty résumé.

- No professional social media activity.

- Lack of thought leadership or industry engagement online.

PRO TIP

Your online presence is your 24/7 personal brand ambassador. Make it work for you, not against you.

The Ostrich Approach: Ignoring Emerging Tech

Burying your head in the sand won't make technological changes go away. Ignoring AI, machine learning, or other emerging tech relevant to your field is like refusing to learn email in the 90s. Tech-avoidance red flags:

- Dismissing new tools as "fads" without investigating them.

- Relying solely on traditional methods when more efficient tech solutions exist.

- Failing to understand how AI might augment (or replace) aspects of your job.

Remember: Technology should be your ally, not your enemy. Embrace it, learn it, and use it to your advantage.

The Hard Skills Tunnel Vision

While technical skills are crucial, focusing solely on them is a recipe for career stagnation. Many professionals neglect the development of soft skills, which are becoming increasingly valuable in the age of automation. Soft skills to cultivate:

- Emotional intelligence

- Adaptability

- Creative problem-solving

- Effective communication

 PRO TIP

According to the World Economic Forum, complex problem-solving, critical thinking, and creativity are among the top skills needed for future jobs.

The "Set It and Forget It" Job Search

Gone are the days when you could dust off your résumé once every few years. Treating job searching as a reactive process only when you're desperate for a change is a surefire way to miss out on opportunities. Signs you're stuck in the old job search mindset:

- Your résumé hasn't been updated in years.

- You only network when you need a job.

- You're not aware of current opportunities in your field.

The best time to look for a job is when you don't need one. Always be open to opportunities, even when you're content in your current role.

Proactive Career Management

Here's the thing: Avoiding these mistakes isn't about paranoia; it's about preparedness. It's about positioning yourself not just for the job market of today but for the one that's coming tomorrow.

Think of your career as a garden. You wouldn't plant seeds and then ignore them, right? You need to water, weed, and nurture your career consistently. Sometimes, you might need to prune; other times, you might need to transplant to new soil entirely. But with constant care and attention, your career can bloom in ways you never imagined.

PRO TIP

Keep your profile updated even when you're not actively job searching. Recruiters often look for passive candidates, and an up-to-date profile ensures you're always presenting your best professional self.

Adapting Your Job Search Strategy

We've covered the new rules and the pitfalls to avoid. Now, let's get into the nitty-gritty of how to play this game and win. It's time to turbocharge your job search strategy for the AI age.

Embrace Lifelong Learning

Welcome to the era of perpetual learning.

Skills now have a shorter shelf life, industries transform at breakneck speed, and employers prize adaptability over static knowledge. To thrive in this environment, you must become a learning machine.

Cultivate a habit of continuous skill development by carving out dedicated time each week for learning. Stay abreast of industry trends by following thought leaders and key publications. Engage actively in your field through webinars, conferences, and workshops—virtual or in-person. Leverage AI tools like ChatGPT to create personalized learning plans, effectively putting a career coach in your pocket.

This proactive approach to learning not only keeps your skills sharp but also demonstrates to employers your commitment to growth and adaptability, key traits in today's dynamic workplace.

AI PROMPTS FOR A CONTINUOUS LEARNING PLAN

"Based on current trends, what are the top 5 emerging skills in [your industry] for the next 3 years? For each skill, please provide a brief explanation of its importance and suggest one reputable online course or resource to start learning it."

- "I'm a [your job title] with [X] years of experience. Can you create a 6-month learning plan for me to stay competitive in my field? Please include a mix of technical and soft skills, and suggest specific learning activities or resources for each month."

- "Analyze the job descriptions for [your dream role] at top companies in [your industry]. What are the most frequently mentioned skills or qualifications? Can you categorize these into must-have skills and nice-to-have skills, and suggest ways to develop the top 3 must-have skills I might be missing?"

- "I want to future-proof my career in [your industry]. Can you identify 3 potential disruptive technologies or trends that might impact my field in the next 5-10 years? For each, explain its potential impact and suggest ways I can start preparing now."

- "Help me create a weekly learning routine that fits into my busy schedule. Assuming I can dedicate 5 hours per week to professional development, how would you break down this time across different learning activities (e.g., online courses, reading industry publications, networking, hands-on projects)? Please provide specific suggestions for each activity type."

Build Your Personal Brand: Stand Out In the Crowd

In a talent tsunami of job applicants, how do you rise above the waves and catch the recruiter's eye? Enter personal branding – your career's secret sauce. Here's the kicker: everyone has a brand, whether they've intentionally established it or not. Your brand is the buzz that follows you, the impression you leave, the story people tell about you when you've left the Zoom room.

Personal branding isn't just about slapping on a fancy label; it's about seizing the narrative of your professional story and turning it into your greatest asset.

So, what's in this secret sauce? It's a unique blend of your skills, experiences, and values, seasoned with a dash of what makes you, well, you. Think of it as your career's DNA – totally unique and impossible to replicate. Here's how to whip it up:

- **Cook up a Killer Value Proposition:** Start with a clear, compelling statement that screams what you bring to the table and why it matters. It's like your professional tagline – short, snappy, and impossible to forget.

- **Consistency is King:** Spread your brand across all platforms like it's the world's best jam. LinkedIn, Twitter, and your personal website should all sing the same tune. This isn't just about looking pretty; it's about being so memorable that recruiters can't get you out of their heads.

- **Get Real with Storytelling:** Ditch the perfect façade and embrace your journey – warts and all. Share those "I can't believe I survived that" moments and the lessons that turned you into the professional powerhouse you are today. It's not about being flawless; it's about being fearlessly authentic.

- **Connect Like a Pro:** Your brand isn't just about you shouting into the void. It's about creating genuine connections. Use your story to resonate with your audience.

- **Position Yourself for the Win:** By actively shaping your brand, you're not just managing your reputation – you're playing 4D career chess. You're positioning yourself as the go-to expert, the problem-solver, the innovator that companies didn't even know they needed.

Remember, in this ever-evolving job market, your personal brand is your ticket to ride. It's how you stand out when everyone else is blending in. By actively shaping your personal brand, you're not just managing your reputation - you're strategically positioning yourself for career opportunities and growth in an ever-evolving job market.

AI PROMPTS FOR PERSONAL BRANDING

"I'm a [your job title] with expertise in [list 2-3 key skills]. Help me craft a compelling personal brand statement that highlights my unique skills and experiences in [your field]. The statement should be concise, memorable, and suitable for use in my LinkedIn headline."

- "Analyze my career journey: [briefly describe your career path and key achievements]. Based on this information, what are 3-5 unique selling points that set me apart in my field? For each point, provide a brief explanation of why it's valuable to potential employers."

- "I want to ensure consistency in my personal brand across different platforms. Given my expertise in [your field] and career goals of [goals], suggest 5 key themes or messages I should consistently communicate. For each theme, provide an example of how I could express it on LinkedIn, in a job interview, and on my résumé."

- "Help me develop an authentic storytelling approach for my personal brand. Based on the following career highlights [list 2-3 significant achievements or challenges you've overcome], craft a brief narrative (200-300 words) that showcases my journey, values, and unique perspective in my field. The story should be engaging and relevant to potential employers or clients."

- "I want to differentiate myself from others in [your field]. Research the common personal branding approaches in my industry, and then suggest 3 innovative ways I could make my personal brand stand out. For each suggestion, explain how it aligns with current industry trends and how I could implement it on my LinkedIn profile."

Diversify: Don't Put All Your Eggs in One Basket

Gone are the days of the one-trick pony career! The smart money's on diversification. We're talking portfolio careers and multiple income streams – your ticket to financial stability. It's not just about earning more (though that's a nice perk); it's about building a stronger safety net.

But it's more than just security. It opens the door to a variety of professional experiences. You get to explore different fields, use a wide range of skills, and stay engaged through continuous learning. In this way, you're shaping a career where each role contributes something unique to your professional journey.

The result? You become the Swiss Army knife of the job market – adaptable, valuable, and ready for whatever curveballs the future throws your way.

Diversifying your career can take many forms. You might start a side hustle that leverages your expertise in new ways, explore freelance opportunities that complement your main job, or invest time in building passive income streams.

Let me share a personal example: writing this book. As a career services professional, I've spent years helping individuals optimize their LinkedIn profiles and navigate their career paths. By channeling this expertise into a book, I'm not only sharing valuable knowledge but also creating a passive income stream. Once published, this book continues to provide value to readers and generate income, even when I'm not actively working on it.

Each of these avenues toward diversification not only bolsters your financial security but also expands your professional network and skill set. In essence, a diversified career portfolio isn't just about money—it's about creating a robust, flexible, and engaging professional life that can weather economic shifts and align with your evolving interests and goals.

AI PROMPTS TO BRAINSTORM SIDE HUSTLES

"I'm a [your profession] with expertise in [list 2-3 key skills]. Generate 5 side hustle ideas that complement my skills. For each idea, provide a brief description, potential target market, and one online platform or tool I could use to get started."

- "Help me identify freelance opportunities in my field of [your profession]. What are the top 3 in-demand freelance services related to my expertise? For each service, suggest how I could package my skills, determine pricing, and find clients. Also, recommend 2-3 reputable freelance platforms where I could offer these services."

- "I want to create passive income streams related to my career in [your field]. Suggest 5 potential passive income ideas that leverage my professional knowledge. For each idea, outline the initial time investment required, potential long-term benefits, and any risks or challenges I should consider. Also, provide one actionable step I can take this week to start exploring each option."

- "Analyze my current career as a [your profession]. Based on my skills and industry, what are 3 complementary fields or industries where I could potentially find part-time or contract work? For each field, explain how it relates to my current profession, what new skills I might need to develop, and suggest one company or organization where I could look for opportunities."

- "I want to monetize my professional knowledge through digital products. Given my background in [your field], suggest 3 types of digital products I could create (e.g., e-books, online courses, templates). For each product type, provide an outline of what the product could cover, who the target audience would be, and how I could market it effectively. Also, recommend one tool or platform I could use to create and sell each type of product."

Think about it: If one income stream dries up, you've got others to fall back on. It's not just smart; it's career insurance.

Network Strategically

Networking in the digital age is both easier and more complex than ever. Networking has gone from schmoozing at cocktail parties to navigating a complex web of online and offline connections. It's a brave new world where your next big break could come from an X thread or a LinkedIn comment.

It's not just about collecting business cards anymore; it's about building meaningful connections across platforms. It's about how many people re-member your name when opportunity comes knocking. Quality over quantity,

Networking power moves:

- Engage regularly on professional social media platforms.

- Attend virtual industry events and actively participate.

- Offer value to your connections; don't just ask for favors.

AI PROMPTS FOR NETWORKING STRATEGY

"I'm a [your profession] looking to expand my network in [target industry]. Draft 3 templates for personalized connection requests on LinkedIn, each with a different approach: a) for someone in a target company, b) for a thought leader in my industry, and c) for a potential mentor. Each template should be concise, engaging, and include a clear reason for connecting."

- "Help me create a strategic networking plan for the next 3 months. Suggest 5 specific actions I can take each month to expand and strengthen my professional network. Include a mix of online and offline activities, and explain how each action contributes to my networking goals. Also, recommend 2-3 AI-powered networking tools I could use to enhance my efforts."

- "I want to offer value to my connections without always asking for favors. Generate 10 ideas for how I can provide value to my professional network. For each idea, explain how it benefits my connections and how it might indirectly benefit my career. Also, suggest how I could use AI tools to help implement each idea efficiently."

- "Analyze my LinkedIn profile: [paste your LinkedIn profile URL or summary]. Based on my background and industry, suggest 5 types of professionals I should aim to connect with to strategically expand my network. For each type, explain why they would be valuable connections and provide a conversation starter I could use to engage with them meaningfully on LinkedIn."

- "I'm planning to attend a virtual industry conference next month. Create a comprehensive networking strategy for me to maximize this opportunity. Include: a) 3 ways to prepare before the event b) 5 engagement tactics to use during the event c) 4 follow-up strategies for after the event d) 2 AI tools I could use to enhance my networking efforts throughout the process For each suggestion, provide a brief explanation of its potential impact on my networking success."

Be the CEO of Your Career

Even if you're not starting a business, thinking like an entrepreneur can skyrocket your career success.

Entrepreneurial traits to cultivate:

- **Proactivity:** Don't wait for opportunities; create them.

- **Resilience:** View setbacks as learning experiences.

- **Innovation:** Always look for better ways to do things.

AI PROMPTS FOR PROFESSIONAL GROWTH

"I'm a [your job title] in the [your industry] sector. Suggest 5 innovative ways I can add value to my current role. For each suggestion, explain how it demonstrates entrepreneurial thinking, potential benefits to the company, and how I could measure its impact. Also, provide one potential challenge I might face in implementing each idea and how to overcome it."

- "Help me develop a 'personal board of directors' to support my career growth. Suggest 5 types of mentors or advisors I should seek out, explaining how each can contribute to my professional development. For each type, provide a strategy to find and approach potential mentors, and 3 specific questions I could ask them to gain valuable insights for my career."

- "I want to cultivate resilience in my career. Describe 3 common professional setbacks in my field as [your job title], and for each: a) Reframe it as a learning opportunity b) Suggest 3 actionable steps to bounce back stronger c) Provide an example of how this setback could lead to future success Also, recommend one book or resource on building career resilience."

- "Generate a 30-day 'Entrepreneurial Mindset Challenge' for me as a [your job title]. For each week, provide 5 small daily actions I can take to develop my proactivity, resilience, and innovation at work. Include a mix of tasks focused on personal development, adding value to my company, and expanding my professional network. Suggest how I could track my progress and reflect on my growth throughout the challenge."

- "I want to apply the concept of 'intrapreneurship' in my role as a [your job title]. Explain what intrapreneurship means and why it's valuable in today's work environment. Then, suggest 3 intrapreneurial projects I could propose in my current job, considering my company's goals and challenges. For each project idea: a) Outline the potential benefits to the company b) Describe how it showcases entrepreneurial thinking c) Suggest how I could pitch the idea to my superiors d) Provide tips on how to execute it successfully while managing my regular responsibilities."

Remember: Entrepreneurial thinking isn't just for startup founders. It's for anyone who wants to take control of their career destiny.

Embracing the New Career Landscape

Look, I get it. All this change can feel overwhelming. You might be thinking, "Do I really need to do all this? Can't I just find a good job and stick with it?"

Here's the truth: The world of work isn't going back to the way it was. But that's not bad news – it's an opportunity. This new landscape offers more freedom, more creativity, and more potential for growth than ever before.

Yes, it requires more effort. Yes, it means stepping out of your comfort zone. But the rewards? They're limitless.

Imagine waking up every day excited about your work, knowing you're constantly growing and evolving. Picture yourself as resilient in the face of economic changes because you've built a diverse skill set and income streams. Envision being in demand, not because you've stuck with one company for years, but because you've consistently invested in your own growth and brand.

That's the potential of embracing these new rules. It's not just about surviving in the new job market – it's about thriving.

In the coming chapters, we're going to dive deep into all of the most essential strategies. By the end of this book, you'll have a comprehensive toolkit for not just surviving but thriving in the AI-driven job market. You'll learn how to make LinkedIn work for you, turning it into a powerful ally in your career journey. So, are you ready to transform your LinkedIn presence and outshine the competition? Let's dive in!

Your Call to Action

As we wrap up this chapter, I want to leave you with a challenge. Pick one area we've discussed – maybe it's updating your LinkedIn profile, setting aside time for learning, or reaching out to a new connection. Choose one small action you can take this week to start adapting to this new landscape.

Because here's the thing: The best time to start was yesterday. The second-best time is now.

You've already taken the first step by reading this chapter. You're aware of the changes happening in the job market, and you're arming yourself with the knowledge to navigate them. That puts you ahead of 90% of professionals out there.

So, are you ready to take control of your career? Are you ready to stop being at the mercy of employers and start being the CEO of your own professional life?

The new world of work is here. It's exciting, it's challenging, and it's full of opportunity for those who are willing to embrace it. And with the strategies I'll cover in this book, along with the power of AI tools at your fingertips, you're going to be more than ready. Let's do this!

Chapter Two

LinkedIn: Your Career Command Center

Mastering the Job Search Revolutionizing Platform

Remember when networking meant awkwardly shuffling around conference rooms, desperately trying to strike up conversations with strangers? Well, those days are as outdated as fax machines and flip phones. Enter LinkedIn, the game-changer that's turned the professional world on its head.

Back in the earliest days of the 21st century, an innovative tech team had a visionary idea: to create a virtual space where professionals could connect. LinkedIn officially launched on May 5th, 2003. Fast forward to today, and that idea has become a global powerhouse with over one billion members in more than 200 countries and territories worldwide. Talk about a growth spurt!

But LinkedIn isn't just a bigger, fancier version of its original self. Oh no, it's evolved into something far more powerful. It's no longer just a place to post your digital résumé and hope for the best. LinkedIn has become the central hub of the professional world - a bustling marketplace of ideas, opportunities, and connections.

Think of LinkedIn as the Swiss Army knife of your career toolkit. It's a job board, a networking platform, a learning center, and a personal branding machine all rolled into one. And in today's hyper-connected, AI-driven job market, it's not just useful - it's essential.

LinkedIn vs. Traditional Job Search Methods

Remember the good old days of job hunting? Pounding the pavement with a stack of résumés, circling classified ads in the newspaper, and hoping your application wouldn't get lost in the black hole of a company's HR department. Those days are as outdated as a flip phone at a tech convention.

Let's break down why LinkedIn is leaving traditional job search methods in the dust.

Wider Reach and Visibility

First up, let's talk reach. Traditional methods? You're limited to your local area and whatever jobs happen to be advertised. LinkedIn? You've got the whole world at your fingertips. We're talking global opportunities! With over 67 million companies on LinkedIn, your next dream job could be halfway across the world - and you wouldn't even need to leave your couch to find it.

But it's not just about quantity - it's about visibility and effectiveness too. On LinkedIn, you're not just another résumé in a stack. Your profile is like a 24/7 professional billboard showcasing your skills and experience to recruiters and hiring managers around the clock. It's like having a permanent booth at a global job fair! And this approach works: every minute, 7 people are hired through LinkedIn. That's not just impressive - it's a testament to the platform's power in connecting talent with opportunities.

Moreover, LinkedIn has become an essential tool for job seekers. In fact, 77% of those who recently changed jobs used LinkedIn to find their new positions. This statistic underscores just how crucial the platform has become in the modern job market. Your profile isn't just a digital résumé; it's your ticket to being part of this dynamic, fast-paced professional marketplace.

Real-time Updates and Interactions

Now, let's chat about the speed of things. Traditional job searching is like sending a message in a bottle - you toss your application out there and then wait...and wait...and wait. LinkedIn? It's more like instant messaging for your career.

You can engage with companies and professionals in real time. See a job posting you like? You can often apply with just a click. Want to know more about a company's culture? Connect with current employees and ask them directly. It's dynamic, it's immediate, and it puts you in the driver's seat of your job search.

Showcasing Skills and Endorsements

Here's where LinkedIn really shines. Your traditional résumé can be tailored, but the moment you submit it, it's static - it's a snapshot of your skills at a moment in time. But your LinkedIn profile? It's a living, breathing testament to your professional growth.

With skills endorsements and recommendations, you're not just telling potential employers what you can do - you've got your network backing you up. It's like having a cheering squad for your career, vouching for your skills and expertise. Try getting that on a paper résumé!

Access to Company Insights and Employee Perspectives

Last but not least, let's talk about insider info. In the traditional job search world, you're often flying blind when it comes to company culture and employee experiences. You might get a glossy brochure or a carefully worded job description, but that's about it.

On LinkedIn, you've got a backstage pass to companies you're interested in. You can follow their updates, see who's coming and going, and even get a sense of their company culture through employee posts and interactions. It's like being a fly on the wall in their office - without the risk of being swatted!

Plus, with LinkedIn's company pages and employee insights, you can get a real sense of what it's like to work somewhere before you even apply. It's like test-driving a car before you buy it but for your career!

So, there you have it. LinkedIn isn't just a modern alternative to traditional job searching - it's a complete career management ecosystem. It's wider, faster, more dynamic, and gives you access to information you could only dream of in the past.

The Power of LinkedIn in Modern Job Searching

Imagine having access to the world's largest professional cocktail party, minus the awkward small talk and soggy hors d'oeuvres. That's LinkedIn in a nutshell - a global network of professionals just a click away. But why is LinkedIn such a big deal in today's job market? Let's break it down:

- **Networking Goldmine:** With millions of professionals from every industry imaginable, LinkedIn is your go-to spot for finding mentors, collaborators, or your next big opportunity.

- **Recruiter's Paradise:** 87% of recruiters regularly use LinkedIn to find candidates. If you're not on LinkedIn or your profile's gathering digital dust, you're practically invisible to a huge chunk of job opportunities.

- **Hidden Job Market Access:** Those juicy positions that never make it to public job boards? They're often first whispered about on LinkedIn. Build a strong network, engage regularly, and you'll be in the know before the masses.

- **Personal Branding Powerhouse:** LinkedIn isn't just about finding jobs - it's your personal marketing campaign. Showcase your skills, share your thoughts, and establish yourself as a go-to expert.

But LinkedIn isn't just a fancy job board - it's a career supercharger. Here's how it can turbocharge your professional journey:

- **Smart Job Search:** LinkedIn uses AI to match you with relevant positions based on your skills and experience. Plus, the "Easy Apply" feature lets you apply for jobs with just a few clicks.

- **24/7 Professional Conference:** Connect with industry leaders, join professional groups, and engage in discussions that matter to your field - all from the comfort of your couch.

- **Industry Insights Goldmine:** Follow companies and thought leaders to stay up-to-date on the latest trends. It's like having a personalized industry newsletter delivered straight to your feed.

- **Built-in Professional Development:** With LinkedIn Learning, you have access to thousands of courses on everything from technical skills to soft skills. Bonus: you can showcase these certifications right on your profile.

- **Thought Leadership Stage:** Share insightful posts, comment on industry trends, and publish articles to establish yourself as an expert in your field. It's your chance to shape the conversation and boost your professional reputation.

Think about it: where else can you job hunt, network, learn new skills, and build your personal brand all in one place? That's the power of LinkedIn. It's not just a platform - it's your career command center.

Consider Tom, a software developer with five years of experience who initially struggled with his job search using traditional methods. He then turned to LinkedIn, optimizing his profile, engaging in tech community discussions, sharing code snippets and project insights, and completing relevant courses on LinkedIn Learning. His strategic activity caught the attention of a Chief Technology Officer at an innovative startup after he provided a thoughtful solution to a coding problem the CTO had shared in a post.

This LinkedIn interaction led to a conversation, then a technical discussion about emerging technologies, and ultimately to a job offer for a senior developer position that wasn't publicly advertised. By using LinkedIn as his career command center - networking, showcasing expertise, and continuously learning - alongside traditional job search tactics, Tom not only landed a new job but also positioned himself as a valuable contributor to the developer community.

But here's the thing - while LinkedIn has all these amazing advantages, it's not about completely abandoning traditional methods. It's about leveraging LinkedIn to supercharge your entire job search strategy. In the following sections, I'll dive into how to do just that at every stage of your career journey.

Leveraging LinkedIn Throughout Your Career

Whether you're a fresh-faced graduate or a seasoned pro, LinkedIn is your career's best friend at every stage. Let's break down how to make the most of this platform no matter where you are on your professional path.

Your Living, Breathing Résumé

First things first - forget the idea that your LinkedIn profile is just an online version of your résumé. Oh no, it's so much more! Think of it as your comprehensive career portfolio, a dynamic showcase of your professional life that evolves as you do.

Unlike the résumé file on your computer, your LinkedIn profile is alive. It grows with you, reflects your latest achievements, and showcases your evolving skill set in real time. It's like having a personal career biographer constantly updating your professional story.

PRO TIP

Make updating your LinkedIn profile a regular habit. Just landed a new project? Add it. Learned a new skill? Showcase it. Your profile should be as current as your coffee order.

Entry-Level: Building Your Network from Scratch

Fresh out of college and feeling like a small fish in a big, professional pond? LinkedIn is your growth accelerator. Here's how to make the most of it:

- **Connect, connect, connect:** Start with classmates, professors, and internship colleagues. Then, branch out to alumni. You'd be surprised how many people are willing to help a fellow alum!

- **Join groups related to your field:** It's like joining professional clubs but without the awkward mixer events.

- **Engage with content:** Like, comment, and share posts relevant to your industry. It's how you get noticed without being that person at the party who won't stop talking about themselves.

Remember, at this stage, it's all about laying the groundwork for your professional network. Think of it as planting seeds for your career garden.

PRO TIP

For entry-level professionals, use LinkedIn's "Career Explorer" tool (https://linkedin.github.io/career-explorer/). It helps you discover how your skills can transfer to other roles you might not have considered.

Mid-Career: Brand Building and Exploring Opportunities

So, you've got a few years under your belt, and you're starting to really know your stuff. Now's the time to flex those professional muscles on LinkedIn:

- **Share your knowledge:** Start creating content. Write articles, share insights, or even create short videos about your industry.

- **Become a connector:** Introduce people in your network who could benefit from knowing each other. It's good karma, and it positions you as a valuable node in your professional network.

- **Keep an eye on new opportunities:** Use LinkedIn's job search features, but also pay attention to what your connections are up to. Sometimes the best opportunities come through your network, not a job board.

This is your time to establish yourself as a go-to expert in your field. Don't be shy - let your professional light shine!

PRO TIP

Mid-career and senior professionals might consider becoming a "LinkedIn Creator" to boost visibility. Consistently posting valuable content can significantly increase your profile views and opportunities.

Senior Professionals: Thought Leadership

You've climbed the mountain, and now it's time to guide others. Here's how to use LinkedIn as a senior professional:

- **Publish long-form content:** Share your years of wisdom through articles and posts. It's your chance to shape industry discussions.

- **Offer mentorship:** Use LinkedIn to connect with up-and-coming professionals in your field. It's rewarding, and it keeps you connected to fresh perspectives.

- **Showcase your legacy:** Highlight major career milestones and the impact you've had in your industry. It's not bragging if it's true!

At this stage, LinkedIn is your platform to leave a lasting mark on your industry. Use it wisely!

Career Changers: Highlighting Transferable Skills

Ready for a new challenge in a different field? LinkedIn is your secret weapon for a smooth transition:

- **Reframe your experience:** Use your profile to highlight how your current skills apply to your target industry. It's all about telling your professional story in a new way.

- **Connect with professionals in your target field:** Don't be afraid to reach out and ask for insights. Most people are flattered to be asked for advice.

- **Show your learning journey:** As you upskill for your new field, showcase your new certifications and courses on your profile. It demonstrates your commitment to your new path.

Remember, changing careers isn't about starting over - it's about applying your unique experience to a new context. Let your LinkedIn profile tell that story!

One of our clients, Mark, a financial analyst with a decade of experience, decided to pursue his passion for technology and marketing. We helped him leverage LinkedIn to make this challenging transition by rewriting his profile to emphasize how his data analysis skills could drive marketing strategies. He also connected with tech marketers, engaging in conversations and seeking advice while completing and showcasing several digital marketing certifications on his profile.

His efforts paid off when a tech startup's CMO, impressed by Mark's unique blend of financial acumen and newfound marketing skills, reached out with a job offer. By strategically using LinkedIn to reframe his experience, network in his target field, and demonstrate his commitment to learning, Mark successfully pivoted to a new career without starting from scratch.

No matter where you are in your career journey, LinkedIn has tools and strategies to help you move forward. It's not just about finding your next job - it's about continuously building your professional brand, expanding your network, and opening doors to opportunities you might not even know exist yet.

So, whether you're just starting out or you're a seasoned pro, it's time to make LinkedIn work for you. Your career will thank you!

Working the LinkedIn Algorithm to Your Advantage

In the vast digital landscape of LinkedIn, there's an invisible force shaping what we see and who sees us - the LinkedIn algorithm. This complex system determines which posts appear in our feeds, whose profiles get highlighted, and ultimately, how visible we are to potential employers and connections.

Understanding how this algorithm works isn't just a matter of curiosity; it's a crucial skill for anyone looking to maximize their professional presence online. Let's unravel the mechanics of this digital gatekeeper and explore how you can work with it to elevate your LinkedIn game.

How the LinkedIn Algorithm Works

Think of the LinkedIn algorithm as a really picky nightclub bouncer. It's constantly deciding what content gets to party on users' feeds and what gets left out in the cold. But unlike that bouncer, the LinkedIn algorithm has some specific criteria it's looking for:

- **Relevance:** The algorithm shows users content it thinks they'll find interesting based on connections, job titles, and past interactions.

- **Engagement:** Posts that get likes, comments, and shares quickly are more likely to be shown to a broader audience.

- **Connection Strength:** Content from people you interact with regularly gets priority.

- **Timeliness:** Recent posts generally get more love than older ones.

But here's where it gets tricky - LinkedIn's algorithm isn't static. It's constantly evolving, like a chameleon in a kaleidoscope. So, while these basics tend to hold true, always be ready to adapt your strategy.

Strategies for Increasing Your Visibility

Now that we know what makes the algorithm tick, let's talk about how to get on its good side:

- **Consistency is Key:** Post regularly, but don't spam. Aim for 2-3 quality posts per week.

- **Timing is Everything:** Experiment with posting at different times to see when your audience is most active.

- **Engage Early and Often:** The first hour after posting is crucial. Respond to comments quickly to boost engagement.

- **Use Rich Media:** Posts with images, videos, or documents tend to perform better than text-only posts.

- **Hashtag Strategically:** While optional, consider using 3-5 relevant hashtags per post. Think of them as signposts guiding people to your content.

Remember, it's not about gaming the system - it's about creating value for your network. The algorithm rewards authentic, engaging content.

Engaging with Content Effectively

Engagement on LinkedIn isn't just about racking up likes - it's about meaningful interactions. Here's how to do it right:

- **Comment Thoughtfully:** Don't just say, "Great post!" Add value to the conversation.

- **Share with Purpose:** When you share someone else's content, add your own insights. Make it a "value-add" for your network.

- **Be a Conversation Starter:** Ask questions in your posts to encourage comments.

- **Engage with Your Network's Content:** The algorithm notices when you're an active participant in your network's discussions.

PRO TIP

Think of engaging on LinkedIn like you're at a professional cocktail party. Be interesting, be interested, and always aim to add value to the conversation.

Building Meaningful Connections

In the eyes of the LinkedIn algorithm, not all connections are created equal. We'll go into detail about building your LinkedIn network in a later chapter, but in the meantime, here are some essentials on how to build connections that matter:

- **Quality Over Quantity:** Don't just connect with everyone. Focus on building a network of people relevant to your professional goals.

- **Personalize Connection Requests:** Always add a note explaining why you want to connect. It's like a digital handshake.

- **Nurture New Connections:** After connecting, engage with their content or send a message to start a conversation.

- **Be a Connector:** Introduce people in your network who could benefit from knowing each other. The algorithm loves a matchmaker!

Remember, the LinkedIn algorithm isn't just about promoting content - it's about fostering meaningful professional relationships. By focusing on building genuine connections and providing value to your network, you're not just working the algorithm - you're building a powerful professional community.

So there you have it - the inside scoop on LinkedIn's algorithm. It might seem like a complex beast, but with these strategies, you'll be taming it in no time. Remember, at the end of the day, the algorithm is designed to reward authentic, valuable interactions. So be yourself, add value, and watch your LinkedIn influence grow!

PRO TIP

When requesting to connect with someone, always include a personalized message. Mention how you know them or why you'd like to connect. This significantly increases the chances of your request being accepted.

LinkedIn Premium: Is It Worth It for Job Seekers?

Now, let's talk about LinkedIn Premium - the turbo boost for your professional networking engine. Here's the scoop: if you can fit it into your budget, Premium versions of LinkedIn are definitely worth considering. Let's break down why.

The Power of LinkedIn Premium

At its core, LinkedIn Premium is about giving you more. More visibility, more information, and more tools to supercharge your job search and career development. While features may evolve, the fundamental promise remains: Premium aims to give you a significant edge in a competitive job market.

Why It's Worth the Investment

- **Enhanced Visibility:** Premium can help you stand out to recruiters and hiring managers. In a sea of candidates, that extra visibility can be a game-changer.

- **In-depth Insights:** Get more detailed information about who's viewing your profile and how you compare to other applicants. Knowledge is power, especially in job searching.

- **Advanced Search and Communication:** Find the right people more easily and reach out directly with InMail credits. It's like having a backstage pass to the professional world.

- **Learning Opportunities:** Many Premium versions include access to LinkedIn Learning, a treasure trove of skill-building courses.

Making the Most of Your Investment

If you do decide to go Premium, here's how to squeeze every drop of value from it:

- **Use It Strategically:** Consider activating Premium only during active job search periods.

- **Explore All Features:** Premium offers a lot. Take time to learn and use all the tools at your disposal.

- **Measure the Impact:** Keep track of how Premium features are benefiting your career goals. Are you getting more profile views? More responses to your outreach?

- **Combine with Best Practices:** Premium works best when combined with an optimized profile, consistent engagement, and strategic networking.

While the free version of LinkedIn is powerful, Premium can take your professional networking and job search to the next level. If it fits your budget, it's an investment worth making in your career.

Remember, though, Premium is a tool, not a magic wand. Its value comes from how effectively you use it. Combine it with authentic engagement, a well-crafted profile, and strategic career moves, and you'll be well on your way to LinkedIn superstardom.

Common Mistakes and How to Avoid Them

Now, let's talk about the landmines you need to avoid on your path to professional networking glory. Even the savviest among us can stumble, so let's shine a light on these common pitfalls and how to sidestep them.

Incomplete or Outdated Profiles

Your LinkedIn profile is your digital first impression. An incomplete or outdated profile is like showing up to a job interview in your pajamas - not a good look. How to avoid this:

- **Regular check-ins:** Schedule monthly profile reviews. It's like a quick, professional mirror check.

- **Use all sections:** From the "About" section to Skills, use every relevant part of your profile.

- **Keep it fresh:** Add new skills, certifications, and accomplishments as you gain them.

Unprofessional Content or Behavior

Remember, LinkedIn isn't Facebook. That hilarious meme might be a hit at the water cooler, but on LinkedIn, it could make your professional image take a nosedive. Instead, share that insightful industry article you just read - your network will thank you, and so will your career. How to avoid this:

- **Think before you post:** Will this content add value to my professional network?

- **Stay positive:** Avoid rants or negative comments about employers or colleagues.

- **Avoid landmines:** Steer clear of divisive topics like politics or controversial social issues.

- **Maintain a professional image:** LinkedIn isn't the place for vacation selfies or party stories.

- **Proofread everything:** Typos and grammatical errors are the arch-nemesis of professionalism.

Ineffective Networking Strategies

Randomly accumulating connections? That's not networking; that's just digital hoarding. How to avoid this:

- **Quality over quantity:** Focus on meaningful connections in your industry or target field.

- **Personalize invitations:** No generic "I'd like to add you to my network" messages, please!

- **Engage authentically:** Comment, share, and interact with your connections' content regularly.

Ignoring Privacy Settings: The Oversharer

LinkedIn offers various privacy settings. Ignoring them is like leaving your professional diary open on the bus. How to avoid this:

- **Regular privacy audits:** Check your privacy settings periodically.

- **Be strategic:** Decide *what* you want visible to *whom*. Your job-seeking status might not be something you want your current boss to see!

- **Use the 'Share profile changes' toggle wisely:** Do you really want to notify your network every time you make a small update?

Remember, avoiding these mistakes isn't about perfection - it's about presenting your best, most authentic professional self. Keep these tips in mind, and you'll be navigating LinkedIn like a pro in no time!

PRO TIP

Don't risk losing your hard-earned connections and carefully crafted profile. Make it a habit to back up your LinkedIn data regularly. Start by going to your LinkedIn Settings, clicking on "Data Privacy," then selecting "Get a copy of your data." But don't stop there – take the extra step of saving your profile as a PDF. To do this, view your profile, click the "More" button below your header, and select "Save to PDF." Consider setting a quarterly reminder for both of these backup tasks. These practices can be lifesavers if LinkedIn experiences technical issues or if you need to recover old information.

Connecting the Dots: Your LinkedIn Strategy

Whew! We've covered a lot of ground, haven't we? Let's bring it all home and recap why LinkedIn isn't just a nice-to-have but a must-have in your career toolkit.

Crucial Role in Modern Career Management

In today's digital-first job market, LinkedIn is your always-on, always-working professional showcase. It's where recruiters hunt for talent, where industry trends emerge, and where your next big opportunity might be just a connection away.

But here's the crucial part: LinkedIn is only as powerful as you make it. It's not enough to simply have a profile. To truly leverage LinkedIn's potential, you need to be an active, engaged participant in this professional ecosystem.

Investing Time in Your LinkedIn Presence

Think of your LinkedIn presence as a professional investment. The time you put into crafting a compelling profile, engaging with your network, and staying active on the platform is an investment in your career growth. And like any good investment, it compounds over time.

But remember, it's not about spending hours every day on LinkedIn. It's about being strategic and consistent. Even 15 minutes a day can make a significant difference if you use that time wisely.

PRO TIP:

Set a 15-minute 'LinkedIn time' in your calendar each day. Use it to make one post, comment on three others, and send one connection request. Consistency is key!

Looking Ahead: Your LinkedIn Optimization Journey

As we wrap up this chapter, you might be feeling a mix of excitement blended with some overwhelm. That's normal! Optimizing your LinkedIn presence is a journey, not a destination.

In the coming chapters, we'll dive deeper into specific strategies for making your LinkedIn profile shine. We'll explore how to craft a compelling headline, write an engaging "About" section, showcase your experience effectively, and much more.

Remember, every professional journey is unique, and your LinkedIn strategy should reflect that. Take the insights from this chapter and the ones to come, and adapt them to your career goals.

PRO TIP

Don't let perfectionism paralyze your profile progress. Start building your profile now, even if it's not flawless. Remember, LinkedIn allows for continuous editing, so you can always refine and improve later. Taking action today puts you ahead of those still waiting for the "perfect" moment.

Your Call to Action

As we close this chapter, I want to challenge you to take one action right now to improve your LinkedIn presence. Maybe it's updating your headline, reaching out to a new connection, or sharing an industry article with your thoughts. Whatever it is, take that step. Because in the world of career management, the best time to start was yesterday, and the second-best time is now.

So, are you ready to transform your LinkedIn presence from good to great? Let's do this! Your AI-powered LinkedIn journey is just beginning, and the possibilities are endless. Onward to LinkedIn greatness!

Chapter Three

Decoding the Recruiters' Playbook

Your Guide to LinkedIn Success

Your LinkedIn profile is more than just an online résumé—it's a beacon in a vast sea of professional talent. Every day, countless recruiters navigate this ocean, armed with powerful tools and finely tuned instincts, searching for the ideal candidates to fill coveted positions. But what exactly catches their eye? With more than 49 million people actively job searching on LinkedIn each week, the competition is fierce. What makes recruiters pause, lean in, and reach out to one profile over another?

This chapter unveils the often mysterious world of LinkedIn recruiting. We'll step into the shoes of these modern-day talent scouts, exploring their methods, understanding their challenges, and uncovering the subtle signals that can make your profile stand out from the crowd. By the end, you'll view your LinkedIn presence through a new lens—the perspective of a recruiter.

Whether you're actively job hunting or simply looking to optimize your professional presence, understanding the recruiter's perspective is key to success on LinkedIn. Let's decode the intricate dance between the seekers and the sought-after in the world's largest professional network.

The Role of LinkedIn in Modern Recruiting

LinkedIn has become the recruiter's primary hunting ground. It's a vast, ever-expanding talent pool, and recruiters are constantly fishing for their next great hire. In fact, according to Zippia, by 2023, 90% of recruiters were regularly using LinkedIn to find candidates for jobs. While you're updating your status or browsing your feed, recruiters are actively searching for professionals like you.

Why should you care about recruiters' activities on LinkedIn? Simply put, knowledge is power. Understanding how recruiters think and operate on this platform gives you a significant advantage. It allows you to position yourself effectively, increasing your visibility to recruiters and showcasing your professional value. And the payoff can be substantial: 67% of recruiters believe that professionals hired through LinkedIn are of higher quality compared to those found through other methods. This perception can work in your favor, potentially giving you an edge in the job market.

By recognizing the weight that recruiters place on LinkedIn profiles, you can tailor your presence to meet their expectations. When you align your profile with what recruiters are looking for, you're not just another candidate – you're a high-quality prospect in their eyes. This understanding can be the key to unlocking new career opportunities and standing out in a competitive job market. Let's peek behind the recruiter curtain and see what magic they're working.

Running Targeted Job Ads

Recruiters leverage LinkedIn's sophisticated targeting options to place job ads in front of the most relevant candidates. They can target based on location, industry, job function, seniority level, and even specific skills. This precision is paying off: based on LinkedIn's own numbers, over 540,000 job applications are submitted per hour on LinkedIn, resulting in 7 hires every minute. In fact, over 3 million new hires are made annually through the platform.

This targeted approach ensures that job postings reach the most qualified candidates, streamlining the hiring process for both recruiters and job seekers. It's a testament to the power of LinkedIn's algorithms and the importance of optimizing your profile to align with these targeted searches.

Proactively Searching for Candidates

Beyond running targeted ads, many recruiters take a proactive approach to talent acquisition. They utilize LinkedIn Recruiter, a powerful tool that enables them to search for and identify potential candidates, including those who may not be actively job hunting. This tool provides recruiters with a comprehensive view of the talent landscape, allowing them to identify ideal candidates with precision.

LinkedIn Recruiter offers over 40 advanced filters, including location, industry, job function, and skills. Recruiters can use keywords and Boolean search strings to pinpoint specific skills, job titles, or qualifications. This sophisticated search capability transforms the recruitment process into a highly targeted operation akin to a professional matchmaking service for careers.

Recruiters can also filter candidates based on their previous employers. If you have experience with a company known for excellence in your field, it's advisable to highlight this prominently in your profile.

Moreover, recruiters can identify candidates who are "engaged with your talent brand" - in other words, people who have applied to jobs, followed company pages, or interacted with company posts. Your LinkedIn activity, including likes and comments, could potentially catch a recruiter's attention.

Leveraging LinkedIn's Algorithm to Find Top Matches

LinkedIn's algorithm isn't just for deciding what shows up in your feed. Recruiters are best friends with this algorithm, using it to surface the most relevant candidates for their open positions. The algorithm takes into account factors like your skills, experience, location, and even how complete your profile is. It's like a matchmaking service, but for jobs!

Assessing Candidates Through Profile Activity

Last but not least, recruiters are playing detective with your LinkedIn activity. They're not just looking at your job titles and education. They're checking out your posts, your comments, and the articles you share. They're trying to get a sense of who you are professionally, what you know, and how you communicate. Your LinkedIn activity is like your professional DNA, and recruiters are sequencing it!

PRO TIP

When updating your profile, focus on incorporating industry-specific keywords, especially in your headline, summary, and experience sections. This increases your visibility in recruiter searches.

The LinkedIn Recruiter's Workflow

Now, let's put on our recruiter hats and walk a mile in their LinkedIn shoes. Understanding their process is like getting a backstage pass to your own hiring show. Ready? Let's delve into their day-to-day operations and uncover the key factors that influence their decisions.

Setting Up Search Parameters and Filters

Recruiters don't just dive into the LinkedIn ocean without a game plan. They're more like skilled fishermen, carefully choosing their bait and fishing spot. They set up specific search parameters and filters based on the job they're trying to fill.

Think location, job title, years of experience, and specific skills - - recruiters can fine-tune their search with remarkable precision. It's comparable to a chef carefully selecting ingredients for a gourmet dish. They might specify, "I need a candidate in Seattle with 5+ years in software development, proficient in Python, and experienced in AI." This level of specificity allows them to hone in on the most suitable candidates for the role.

Quickly Scanning Search Results and Profiles

Now, here's where it gets interesting. Once they've cast their net, recruiters aren't leisurely reading through every profile that pops up. Oh no, they're speed-dating their way through search results.

We're talking seconds per profile. Six to nine seconds, on average, to be exact. That's about the time it takes to read a couple of sentences in this book or to scan the headlines of a news article quickly. It's a remarkably brief window of opportunity to make an impression. Your profile needs to be the equivalent of a neon sign in Times Square - impossible to miss.

In those precious few seconds, here's what catches their eye:

- Your headline (more on this goldmine in the next chapter)

- Current role and company

- Previous roles and companies

- Skills section

- Education

Think of these as the chapter titles in your career story. If they're intriguing enough, the recruiter will want to read more.

Consider the case of Maria, a registered nurse with 10 years of experience in pediatric care. Maria was one of our clients who had been casually exploring new job opportunities for several months without much success. After working with us to understand how recruiters use LinkedIn, we supported her in transforming her online presence.

We crafted a compelling headline that highlighted Maria's specialization in pediatric oncology and her certification in pain management. Together, we reorganized her experience section to showcase her leadership in implementing a new patient care protocol, which significantly improved recovery times. We also ensured her skills section was rich with relevant keywords like "pediatric care," "patient education," and "family-centered nursing."

Within a month of these changes, Maria received a message from a recruiter at a prestigious children's hospital in a major city. He was seeking an experienced pediatric nurse with leadership experience and the specialized skills that Maria offered. This initial contact led to a series of interviews where Maria was able to elaborate on the experiences highlighted in her profile. Ultimately, she received a job offer for a senior nursing position that not only advanced her career but also allowed her to make a bigger impact in pediatric healthcare.

Identifying Potential Matches Based on Key Criteria

As they're zipping through profiles, recruiters are playing a high-stakes game of "Hot or Not" with your career information. They're looking for specific keywords, job titles, and experiences that match their criteria. It's like a professional version of swiping right or left.

In-depth Review of Promising Candidates

If your profile survives the initial scan, congratulations! You've advanced to the "potential match" category. This is where recruiters invest more time - up to 20 minutes - to explore your professional journey thoroughly.

They'll scrutinize your career progression, achievements, and how well you align with their open role. It's akin to moving from a quick elevator pitch to a more comprehensive boardroom presentation. You've caught their attention; now it's time to showcase the depth and breadth of your professional expertise.

Reaching Out to Promising Candidates

Finally, for those select profiles that have made it through the rigorous screening process, it's time for direct communication. Recruiters will initiate contact through LinkedIn messages, InMail, or even traditional email if you've made that information available.

However, it's important to remember that initial contact from a recruiter doesn't guarantee a job offer. This is often just the beginning of a more thorough vetting process. Think of it as passing the first round of interviews

- you've demonstrated potential, but there are still more opportunities ahead to prove your fit for the role. The real challenge of impressing your potential employers is just beginning.

PRO TIP

Enable the "Open to Work" feature on your LinkedIn profile, but customize it to be visible only to recruiters. This way, you can discreetly signal your availability without alerting your current employer.

What Recruiters Look For

With the recruiter's workflow in mind, let's zoom in on their specific criteria. What exactly makes a profile stand out in their search? It's time to decode the recruiter's wish list!

- **Relevance to Job Openings:** First and foremost, recruiters are looking for candidates who closely match the requirements of the position they're trying to fill. It's like a puzzle - they're looking for the piece that fits just right.

- **Work Experience and Job Titles:** Current and previous job titles are weighted heavily in LinkedIn's search algorithms and recruiter behavior. Recruiters often start their search with job titles. So, make sure your titles accurately reflect your roles and responsibilities.

- **Skills and Qualifications:** Approximately 40% of recruiter searches start with skills. Your skills section is like your professional toolbox - recruiters want to see if you have the right tools for the job.

- **Tenure and Career Progression:** Recruiters aren't just interested in what you're doing now - they want to see where you've been and where you're headed. They're looking at how long you've stayed in roles and whether your career trajectory is pointing up.

- **Location:** A candidate's location plays a significant role in determining profile rank in searches. Make sure your location is accurate and up-to-date.

- **Profile Completeness:** A thoroughly completed profile signals to recruiters that you take your professional presence seriously. Each completed section provides another opportunity to showcase your qualifications and helps recruiters understand your full potential.

- **Network Size and Engagement:** The number of connections and level of activity on LinkedIn can indicate a candidate's engagement. It's like being at a networking event - recruiters are more likely to notice the person actively mingling than the wallflower.

- **Recommendations and Endorsements:** These provide social proof of a candidate's skills and work quality. It's like having references built right into your profile.

PRO TIP

If you are planning to relocate with your next job change, set your LinkedIn location to where you want to move rather than your current location. This strategic move can help you appear in searches for your desired area, increasing your chances of connecting with recruiters and opportunities in that location.

Common Recruiter-Repelling Blunders

We've explored what catches a recruiter's eye, but what about the things that make them scroll right past your profile?

Incomplete or Outdated Profiles

Picture this: A recruiter discovers your profile and is intrigued by your current job title. But their interest quickly fades when they find sparse details about your experience or, worse, outdated information showing you're still in a role you left long ago.

An incomplete or outdated profile is like showing up to a job interview in your pajamas. It signals a lack of professional investment. Remember, if you don't take the time to maintain your profile, recruiters won't take the time to consider you.

Lack of Relevant Keywords in Key Sections

Remember our recruiter friends and their love for search parameters? Well, if your profile is keyword-poor, you're essentially playing hide-and-seek with recruiters - and winning in the worst way possible.

Not including industry-specific terms, job functions, or skills in your profile is like having a website that isn't indexed by search engines. You might have an impressive online presence, but if you're missing the key terms people are searching for, you're essentially invisible to those who are looking for exactly what you offer. Just as a website needs the right keywords to appear in relevant search results, your LinkedIn profile needs industry-specific language to show up in recruiters' targeted searches.

Insufficient Detail About Skills and Experiences

So, your profile says you "increased company revenue" at your last job. Great! But by how much? When? How did you do it?

Vague statements don't provide concrete evidence of your capabilities. Recruiters need specific metrics and examples that demonstrate your ability to deliver measurable results. These numbers serve as proof points of your success and show potential employers the tangible value you can bring to their organization.

Poor Profile Organization, Making it Hard to Scan Quickly

Remember the initial first scan? A dense, cluttered, disorganized profile is like trying to speed-read "War and Peace." It's not going to happen.

If your most impressive achievements are buried under a mountain of text, or if your profile reads like a stream-of-consciousness novel, recruiters are likely to move on before they strike gold.

The key takeaway here? Don't make recruiters work hard to figure out how awesome you are. Because guess what? They won't.

These common profile organization mistakes can significantly impact your visibility and success on LinkedIn. But they're also completely fixable. If you've recognized your profile in any of these examples, you're already ahead of the game—awareness is the first step toward improvement. In the following sections, we'll explore exactly how to transform your profile into one that recruiters can't resist.

Optimizing for Both Human Readers and AI Tools

Now that we've covered what recruiters look for and the mistakes to avoid, let's talk about how to make your profile irresistible to both human recruiters and their AI sidekicks.

Understand How Humans Read Profiles

Remember the 6-9 second scan? That's where your profile needs to shine for human readers. Make those seconds count by ensuring your key information is easy to spot and digest.

Use clear, concise language. Break up text with bullet points. Make your achievements pop with numbers and results. Think of it like creating a movie trailer for your career - highlight the most exciting parts that will make them want to see more!

Understand How AI-powered Tools Analyze Profiles

But it's not just human eyes you need to impress. LinkedIn's AI algorithms play a huge role in determining whether your profile shows up in a recruiter's search results.

- **Keyword density and placement:** AI tools scan your profile for relevant keywords. They're looking at how often these words appear and where they're placed.

- **Skills matching:** The algorithm compares your listed skills against job requirements. This is why your skills section is so crucial.

- **Experience relevance:** AI tools analyze your work history to determine how relevant your experience is to the job at hand.

Strategies for Appealing to Both Humans and AI

So, how do you please both humans and AI? Here's your strategy:

- **Strategic keyword placement:** Use relevant keywords naturally throughout your profile. Don't just stuff them in - weave them into your career story.

- **Using industry-specific language:** Show you're in the know by using terms and phrases common in your field.

- **Quantifying achievements:** Numbers catch both human eyes and AI attention. "Increased sales by 50%" is more impactful than "Increased sales significantly."

- **Storytelling elements:** While AI looks for keywords, humans connect with narratives. Find a balance between being searchable and being engaging.

Key Profile Elements to Focus On

Now that we've covered the why and how, let's zoom in on the what. Here are the key elements of your profile that deserve your attention. We'll cover each of these in more detail later in this book.

- **Clearly state your career goals and interests.** Don't make recruiters play guessing games. If you're open to new opportunities, say so! Use the 'Open to Work' feature or mention your career aspirations in your summary. It's like putting a "For Sale" sign on a house - it tells people you're on the market!

- **Make your contact information easily accessible.** Don't make recruiters search for ways to reach you. Make sure your email is visible to your connections, or better yet, include it in your About section.

Remember, a recruiter who can't contact you quickly might move on to the next candidate.

- **Craft a compelling headline.** Your headline is prime real estate. It's the first thing recruiters see, and it plays a big role in LinkedIn's search algorithm. Don't just list your job title - use this space to showcase your value proposition. Instead of "Marketing Manager," try "Results-Driven Marketing Manager | Specializing in Digital Campaigns That Drive 200% ROI"

- **Optimize your About section.** Use this to give a quick overview of your professional brand. It's your elevator pitch - make it count!

- **Showcase your experience effectively.** This is where you get to showcase your achievements. Don't just list job duties - highlight your wins. Use action verbs, quantify your results, and show how you've grown in each role.

- **Highlight relevant skills and endorsements.** Your skills section is more important than ever, given the trend towards skills-based recruiting. List skills that are relevant to your target roles, and don't be shy about asking for endorsements.

- **Leverage recommendations.** Recommendations are like having your biggest fans write glowing reviews about your professional blockbuster. A solid recommendation can be the cherry on top of your profile sundae.

- **Complete other important sections.** Don't neglect areas like Education and Volunteer Experience. They round out your professional story and can set you apart from other candidates.

Beyond the Profile: Engagement and Visibility

Your perfectly optimized profile is just the beginning. To really catch a recruiter's eye, you need to be an active LinkedIn citizen.

- **Build and engage with your network.** Comment on posts, share interesting articles, and join in discussions. It's like being the life of the LinkedIn party - it gets you noticed.

- **Interact with company pages.** Remember that recruiters can filter for candidates who engage with their company. Use that to your advantage! Follow companies you're interested in, like, and comment on their posts.

- **Use the "Open to Work" feature strategically.** LinkedIn offers an "Open to Work" feature that can signal to recruiters that you're open to new opportunities. Use it strategically - you can make it visible to all LinkedIn members or only to recruiters.

- **Keep your profile updated.** Your LinkedIn profile isn't a "set it and forget it" deal. It's more like a garden - it needs regular tending to truly flourish. Make profile updates a habit. As your career grows, make sure your LinkedIn grows with it.

A great example of this is the story of Ethan, a civil engineer with a passion for urban planning. Ethan was looking to pivot his career towards sustainable city development. Rather than simply updating his profile, he decided to become an active participant in LinkedIn's professional community.

Ethan began by following urban planning experts and joining groups focused on sustainable development. He didn't just lurk, though. He actively participated in discussions, sharing his engineering insights on how infrastructure could be adapted for more sustainable cities. He also wrote articles about innovative solutions he'd researched, such as green stormwater management systems and energy-efficient building designs.

His consistent, thoughtful engagement caught the eye of a city planner working on a major eco-city project. Impressed by Ethan's innovative ideas and clear passion for sustainable urban development, the planner reached out to Ethan directly through LinkedIn. This initial connection led to a series of discussions about the challenges of implementing sustainable practices in urban environments. Ethan's unique perspective as an engineer with a keen interest in sustainability proved valuable, and he was eventually invited to join the eco-city project team as a sustainability consultant.

Ethan's story demonstrates that LinkedIn isn't just a platform for passive job searching. By actively engaging in relevant discussions, sharing knowledge, and demonstrating expertise, professionals can create opportunities that align with their career aspirations. It's about being a visible and valuable contributor to your professional community.

Building Relationships with Recruiters on LinkedIn

Now, let's focus on an essential aspect of your LinkedIn strategy: transforming recruiter connections into meaningful professional relationships. Because in the world of job searching, it's not just about what you know; it's also about who knows you!

- **Engage with recruiter content professionally.** Think of a recruiter's content as a professional party. Don't just stand in the corner - get involved! Like their posts, comment thoughtfully, and share insights. But remember, this isn't your college friend's Facebook page. Keep it professional, relevant, and insightful.

- **Provide value through thoughtful interactions.** Here's a secret: Recruiters are people too! They appreciate genuine interactions. Don't just reach out when you need something. Share articles they might find interesting, congratulate them on their work anniversaries, or offer insights on industry trends.

- **Follow up appropriately after initial contact.** So, a recruiter reached out? Great! But your work isn't done. Follow up like a pro. Respond promptly, show enthusiasm, and always follow through on any next steps.

- **Maintain long-term connections for future opportunities.** Keep those recruiter relationships warm even when you're not actively looking. A quick check-in every few months can keep you on their radar. Think of it as watering a plant - a little attention over time can yield great results down the line.

Assembling Your Lure: Putting Knowledge into Action

By now, you should have a good understanding of how recruiters use LinkedIn and what they're looking for.

Remember, optimizing your LinkedIn profile is an ongoing process. It's not about tricking the system - it's about presenting your best professional self in a way that's easy for recruiters to find and understand.

Your mission, should you choose to accept it (and let's face it, you're reading this book, so you totally do), is to start looking at your LinkedIn profile with fresh eyes. Pretend you're a recruiter with only 6 seconds to spare. What stands out? What could be clearer or more compelling?

Make one improvement today. Just one. Maybe it's tweaking your headline, adding a key skill, or reaching out to a connection for a recommendation. Whatever it is, take that step.

Remember, each recruiter-friendly tweak you make to your profile is another step toward your dream job. You're not just updating a profile - you're investing in your future.

Chapter Four

Sharpening Your Professional Edge

Crafting a Focused LinkedIn Profile and Irresistible UVP

Y ou've got a LinkedIn profile. Great! But let's be real - so do 1 billion other people. The question is: Does yours stand out in the crowd, or is it just another face in the digital sea?

Think of your LinkedIn profile as your professional alter ego. It's not just an online résumé; it's your chance to shine, to tell your unique story, and to catch the eye of that dream employer.

But here's the kicker: a generic, one-size-fits-all approach is about as effective as shouting into the void. Let's dive into why laser-focusing your LinkedIn profile is your secret weapon and how it can supercharge your job search.

Why Generic Profiles Fall Flat

Picture this: A recruiter is searching LinkedIn for the perfect candidate. YOU are the perfect candidate. You have precisely the mix of experience and skills they are seeking. But here's the twist - your profile might not even make it to their shortlist if it's not optimized for their search terms.

Now, let's say your profile does pop up. The recruiter is sifting through hundreds of results. Would they be more likely to click on a profile that vaguely mentions "experienced professional with diverse skills" or one that boldly states "Marketing Manager with 7+ years of experience driving ROI through data-driven campaigns"?

Generic profiles are like wallflowers at a networking event – they blend into the background, failing to make an impression. Even worse, they might not even get invited to the party. They lack the specific keywords to show up in searches and the punch needed to grab a recruiter's attention in those crucial first few seconds. Why? Because they don't speak to the specific needs of the employers you're targeting.

In essence, a generic profile faces two major hurdles:

1. It might not even appear in recruiter searches due to a lack of relevant keywords.

2. If it does appear, it fails to stand out among the other candidates.

By focusing your profile, you're not just improving your chances of making a good impression - you're increasing the likelihood of being found in the first place. It's about being both visible and memorable in the vast LinkedIn landscape.

The Power of a Targeted Approach

Now, let's flip the script. A focused, targeted profile acts like a beacon, drawing the right eyes to your professional story. Here's how it can supercharge your LinkedIn presence:

Increased Visibility in Search Results

LinkedIn's algorithm isn't just a mysterious black box – it's your potential ally. When you pepper your profile with industry-specific keywords and phrases, you're essentially speaking the language of both the algorithm and recruiters. This means when they search for candidates with your skills, you're more likely to pop up on their radar.

For example, if you're a project manager in the tech industry, using phrases like "Agile methodology," "Scrum master," or "product roadmap" can significantly boost your searchability.

Stronger Appeal to Specific Employers

Imagine you're a marketing director looking to hire a content strategist. You come across two profiles:

> **Profile A:** "Experienced writer with strong communication skills."

> **Profile B:** "Content Strategist specializing in SEO-optimized blog content that increased organic traffic by 150% for B2B SaaS companies."

Which one would you be more excited to reach out to? Profile B speaks directly to the employer's needs, showcasing relevant experience and tangible results.

Clearer Professional Narrative

A focused profile tells a cohesive story about who you are professionally. It's not just a list of jobs and skills – it's a narrative that shows your career progression, your specialties, and where you're headed next.

This clarity helps recruiters and potential connections understand your professional identity at a glance. It answers the crucial question: "What makes this person unique and valuable?"

Zeroing In: How to Define Your Career Focus

Now that we've established why a focused profile is crucial, you might be wondering, "How do I actually define my focus?" Great question! Let's break it down into a simple, actionable process.

Think of defining your career focus like creating a recipe for your dream job. You need the right ingredients in the right proportions. Here's how to mix it up:

Start With Your Core Function

What's the main dish you want to serve up professionally? Is it marketing magic, sales sorcery, or perhaps product development wizardry? Pick your primary job function – this is your base ingredient. Consider:

- What specific role or set of responsibilities do you excel in?

- Which of your skills are most in demand in your industry?

- What type of work energizes you the most?

Example: A marketing professional might specify "Digital Marketing Strategy" or "Content Marketing Leadership" as their core function.

Sprinkle in Your Professional Level

Are you a fresh-faced rookie ready to take on entry-level challenges or a seasoned mid-manager looking to level up? Maybe you're eyeing that corner office at the executive level. Whatever your flavor, add it to the mix. Reflect on:

- How many years of relevant experience do you have?

- What level of responsibility are you prepared to take on?

- Are you looking for lateral movement or career advancement?

Example: "Mid-level Marketing Manager with 5-7 years of experience, seeking Senior Manager roles."

Toss in Your Geographical Preferences

Where do you want your career to bloom? Are you a city slicker or a small-town enthusiast? Maybe you're open to remote work from a beachside hammock? Pin down your ideal location(s). In today's global job market, location can be a critical factor. Consider:

- Are you open to relocation, or do you prefer to stay local?

- How do you feel about remote work opportunities?

- Are there specific cities or regions where your industry thrives?

Example: "Seeking roles in the Greater Boston area, open to remote positions with occasional travel."

Now, here's where it gets interesting. To really make your career focus pop, add one or more of these special ingredients:

A Dash of Company Culture

Do you thrive in a fast-paced, innovative environment or prefer a more structured, traditional setting? Are you looking for a workplace that emphasizes collaboration, or do you excel in more independent roles? Company culture can significantly impact your job satisfaction and performance. Reflect on:

- What type of work environment brings out your best performance?

- What company values align with your personal beliefs?

- How important is work-life balance to you?

Example: "Seeking a collaborative, innovation-driven culture with a strong emphasis on sustainability."

A Pinch of Industry Spice

Which industry (or industries) gets your professional taste buds tingling? Tech? Healthcare? Green energy? Your industry focus can significantly impact your career trajectory. Ask yourself:

- In which industries do your skills and experience best align?

- Are there emerging industries that excite you?

- How transferable are your skills across different sectors?

Example: "Specializing in B2B SaaS marketing, with a growing interest in HealthTech."

A Sprinkle of Company Size

Do you thrive in the intimacy of a small business or get energized by the resources of a Fortune 500 giant? The size of an organization can greatly influence your role and growth opportunities. Consider:

- Do you thrive in the dynamic environment of startups or prefer the structure of larger corporations?

- How important is having access to extensive resources and established processes?

- Are you comfortable with the ambiguity often present in smaller companies?

Example: "Interested in mid-sized companies (50-500 employees) with a startup mindset"

A Zest of Product or Service

What kind of products or services do you want to be involved with? Software? Luxury goods? Life-saving medical devices? Ask yourself:

- What types of products or services are you most passionate about?

- Where does your expertise add the most value?

- Are there emerging technologies or services that interest you?

Example: "Focused on marketing cloud-based collaboration platforms."

A Hint of Business Model Flavor

B2B or B2C? E-commerce or brick-and-mortar? Subscription-based or consulting? Pick the business models that align with your skills and interests. Consider:

- Do you prefer B2B or B2C environments?

- Are you interested in subscription-based services, e-commerce, or traditional retail models?

- How do you feel about consulting or agency work versus in-house roles?

Example: "Specializing in B2B marketing for SaaS subscription models."

Just a Bit of Company Stage and Challenge

Are you energized by the rapid growth and constant change of a startup, or do you prefer the stability and established processes of a mature corporation? Perhaps you're excited by the prospect of helping a company navigate a significant transition or turnaround. The stage and current challenges of a company can greatly influence your role and the type of work you'll be doing. Consider:

- Do you thrive in the dynamic, all-hands-on-deck environment of a startup?

- Are you more comfortable with the defined roles and structures of an established company?

- Does the idea of contributing to a company's turnaround or major transformation excite you?

How do you feel about the different risks and rewards associated with each stage?

Example: "Interested in early-stage startups in the growth phase, where I can contribute to scaling operations and building foundational processes."

A Garnish of Specific Companies

Have a few dream companies in mind? Go ahead and name them. It's like telling the universe exactly what you want on your plate. Reflect on:

- Which companies are leaders in your field?

- Are there organizations whose mission particularly resonates with you?

- Which companies are known for innovation in areas that interest you?

Example: "Targeting innovative tech companies like Salesforce, HubSpot, or similar growth-oriented organizations."

Voila! Mix all these ingredients together, and you've got yourself a well-defined career focus. Here's what it might look like:

> "Mid-level marketing manager specializing in data-driven campaigns for B2B SaaS companies, preferably in a fast-growing startup environment in the San Francisco Bay Area. Particularly interested in companies focused on AI and machine learning applications, such as TechCo and InnovateAI."

Remember, the more specific you are, the easier it becomes to tailor your LinkedIn profile. It's like giving GPS coordinates to recruiters – you're making it incredibly easy for them to find exactly where you fit in the professional landscape.

Balancing Focus with Versatility

Now, you might be thinking, "But wait, won't a super-specific profile limit my options?" It's a valid concern, but here's the truth: a focused profile doesn't mean pigeonholing yourself. It means highlighting your core strengths and the value you bring to your target roles or industries.

Think of it like a spotlight on a stage. The spotlight doesn't diminish the rest of your skills or experiences – it simply draws attention to your star qualities. You can still mention your diverse skills and experiences but frame them in a way that supports your primary professional narrative.

For instance, if you're a marketing professional targeting content strategy roles, you might highlight your content creation skills prominently. However, you can also mention how your experience in data analysis informs your content strategies, showcasing your versatility within your focused area. Here's how this could look in your profile:

> Leveraging 8+ years of experience in content creation and an-
> alytics to craft engaging narratives that resonate with target
> audiences and drive measurable results. Skilled in using data
> insights to optimize content performance, resulting in a 40%
> increase in engagement rates.

Leveraging AI to Refine Your Focus

Feeling overwhelmed about how to focus your profile? This is where AI can
be your secret weapon.

AI PROMPTS TO SHARPEN YOUR CAREER FOCUS

"I'm currently a [Your Current Role] with experience in [Key
Skills/Industries]. I'm interested in transitioning to [Desired
Role/Industry]. Based on my background, what are the top 3
transferable skills I should emphasize, and what are 2 potential
job titles I should target in my LinkedIn profile?"

- "Analyze my work history: [Brief summary of past 3 jobs]. What
  common themes or strengths emerge? How can I frame these to
  appeal to [Target Industry/Role], and what are 3 specific achievements I should highlight in my LinkedIn summary?"

- "I'm passionate about [Your Interests, e.g., sustainability, AI,
  healthcare innovation]. Given my background in [Your Field],
  what are 5 emerging job roles or niche areas within [Target
  Industry] that could align with my interests and skills? How
  should I describe my career aspirations in my LinkedIn headline
  to attract these opportunities?"

- "Based on current trends in [Your Industry], what are the top

5 in-demand skills for [Your Target Role] that I should aim to develop or highlight? For each skill, suggest a concise way to showcase it in my LinkedIn profile, either through job descriptions or the skills section."

- "I'm torn between focusing on [Industry A] and [Industry B] in my job search. Compare these industries in terms of growth potential, required skills, and typical career paths. Then, suggest how I could position my LinkedIn profile to appeal to both while still maintaining a clear focus. Include a sample headline and summary opening that bridges both industries."

Remember, AI tools are here to assist, not replace your unique voice. Use AI suggestions as a starting point, then refine and personalize the replies to truly reflect your professional identity.

Developing Your Unique Value Proposition (UVP)

Now that you've identified your career focus, it's time to address a crucial question: What distinguishes you in the professional landscape? This is where your Unique Value Proposition (UVP) comes into play – think of it as a concise, powerful encapsulation of your professional worth.

Your UVP is the distinctive combination of skills, experiences, and qualities that make you an ideal candidate for your target roles. It's not merely a list of qualifications; rather, it's a compelling answer to why an employer should choose you over other qualified candidates.

Consider your UVP as your professional signature – the unique mark you leave in your field. It's what makes potential employers take notice and think, "This is exactly the kind of talent we need on our team."

Let's explore how to craft a UVP that effectively communicates your professional value and sets you apart in a competitive job market.

Cooking Up a Killer UVP

Start by taking stock of your professional pantry:

- **Key Strengths:** What are you naturally good at? Maybe you're the spreadsheet whisperer or the team conflict resolver.

- **Unique Skill Combo:** Think about your unusual skill pairings. Are you a data analyst with killer presentation skills? A software developer with a knack for user psychology?

- **Experiences That Set You Apart:** Did you lead a project that saved your company millions? Or maybe you started a successful side hustle that taught you valuable entrepreneurial skills?

Scope Out the Market's Cravings

Now, put on your detective hat and investigate what employers in your target field are hungry for:

- Scour job postings in your desired roles. What skills and qualities keep popping up?

- Follow industry leaders and companies on LinkedIn. What challenges are they talking about?

- Attend industry events or webinars. What's keeping professionals in your field up at night?

Find the Sweet Spot

Your UVP lives at the intersection of what you're great at and what employers desperately need. It's like finding the perfect flavor combination that makes taste buds sing.

Craft Your UVP Statement

Now, distill all of this into a clear, punchy statement. Here's a simple formula to get you started:

- *"I help [target audience] to [solve this problem/achieve this goal] through my [unique skill set/approach]."*

For example:

"I help tech startups skyrocket user engagement by crafting data-driven marketing strategies that blend creativity with analytical rigor."

or

"I transform complex financial data into actionable insights, enabling C-suite executives to make confident decisions that drive growth."

Sprinkling Your UVP Throughout Your Profile

Your UVP isn't just for your "About" section. It should be the secret sauce that flavors your entire LinkedIn profile. Here's how to spread it around:

- **Headline:** Give a taste of your UVP right off the bat.

- **About Section:** Dive deeper into your UVP, backing it up with concrete examples.

- **Experience:** Show your UVP in action through your job descriptions and achievements.

- **Skills & Endorsements:** Prioritize skills that support your UVP.

- **Recommendations:** Ask for recommendations that highlight aspects of your UVP.

Your UVP in Action: Before-and-After

Before (Generic Profile):

"Experienced marketing professional with strong communication skills."

After (UVP-Infused Profile):

"Data-driven marketing strategist who turns user insights into
campaigns that boost engagement by an average of 150%. I
blend creative storytelling with analytical precision to help
SaaS companies connect with their audience and drive sustainable growth."

See the difference? The second one doesn't just tell. It shows. It's specific, it's results-oriented, and it speaks directly to what SaaS companies are
looking for.

Avoiding the "Jack of All Trades" Trap

Now, you might be tempted to list every skill you've ever acquired, thinking
it'll make you appealing to more employers. Resist that urge! A focused
UVP doesn't mean you're one-dimensional. It means you're strategic about
presenting your most valuable assets. Let's look at two examples:

What not to do: "Versatile professional with experience in
software development, project management, customer service,
graphic design, and data analysis. Also skilled in social media
marketing, technical writing, and public speaking."

This approach tries to cover too many bases, potentially diluting your
core strengths and leaving employers unsure of your primary value.

What to do instead: "Innovative software engineer specializing in AI-driven solutions for healthcare. Combine deep learning expertise with a background in biomedical engineering
to develop predictive diagnostic tools that improve patient
outcomes and streamline clinical workflows."

This version presents focused expertise while hinting at interdisciplinary knowledge that adds unique value to a specific field.

Remember, you're not trying to be all things to all employers. You're positioning yourself as the go-to person for specific, high-value problems in your field. It's about quality, not quantity.

Evolving Your UVP

Your UVP isn't set in stone. As you grow in your career, take on new challenges, and as the industry evolves, your UVP should evolve, too. Make it a habit to revisit and refine your UVP regularly. It's like updating your wardrobe - what worked for you five years ago might not be your best look today.

Leverage AI to Craft Your UVP

Feeling stuck? AI can be your brainstorming buddy.

AI PROMPTS TO CRAFT YOUR UVP

"I'm a [Your Role] with [X] years of experience in [Your Industry]. My top 3 skills are [Skill 1], [Skill 2], and [Skill 3]. I've recently achieved [Major Achievement]. Analyze this information and provide: a) 3 potential UVP statements tailored for [Target Industry/Role] b) A list of 5 key phrases I should incorporate into my LinkedIn profile to support each UVP c) A suggestion for how to quantify my impact in each UVP"

- "Compare these two industries: [Current Industry] and [Target Industry]. Based on my background as a [Current Role], please provide: a) A list of 5 transferable skills that are highly valued in my target industry b) 3 potential UVP statements that highlight how my experience in [Current Industry] brings unique value to [Target Industry] c) A brief explanation of how each UVP addresses a specific pain point in the target industry"

- "I want to position myself as a [Desired Role] specializing in

[Niche Area]. My background includes [Brief Career Summary]. Please help me craft a UVP by: a) Identifying 3 emerging trends or challenges in [Niche Area] b) Suggesting how my experience aligns with addressing these trends/challenges c) Providing 2 UVP statements that emphasize my forward-thinking approach d) Recommending 3 specific metrics or achievements I should highlight to support each UVP"

- "Analyze these elements of my professional brand: [List 3-5 key projects, achievements, or unique experiences] Based on this information: a) Identify an overarching theme or unique strength that sets me apart b) Suggest how this strength addresses a critical need in [Target Industry/Role] c) Craft a UVP statement that showcases this unique strength d) Provide 3 bullet points I can use in my LinkedIn 'About' section to support this UVP e) Recommend how to adapt this UVP for my LinkedIn headline (under 220 characters)"

- "I'm targeting roles at the intersection of [Industry 1] and [Industry 2]. My background includes [Your Relevant Experience]. To create a compelling UVP: a) Identify 3 unique challenges faced by companies operating in both these industries b) Suggest how my cross-industry experience can address these challenges c) Provide 2 UVP statements that position me as a valuable asset for companies in this intersection d) Recommend 5 industry-specific keywords or phrases to incorporate into my LinkedIn profile e) Suggest a creative way to visualize my cross-industry value proposition (e.g., a Venn diagram or infographic concept) that I could include in my LinkedIn featured section"

These detailed prompts are designed to help you dig deeper into your unique professional attributes, align them with market needs, and craft a compelling UVP that resonates with your target audience. But remember, whatever AI provides you is a starting point. Your final UVP should be uniquely you – polished and professional, but with your authentic voice shining through.

Creating an Attention-Grabbing Headline

Your LinkedIn headline is prime real estate – it's your first impression, your digital handshake, and your chance to make recruiters stop scrolling and start reading. With 220 characters at your disposal, you've got room to pack a punch. Let's make every character count!

The Power of Your Headline

Think of your headline as the trailer for your professional blockbuster. It needs to be catchy and informative and leave them wanting more. But most notably, it also needs to be searchable. Remember, recruiters aren't just browsing – they're hunting for specific skills and roles.

Key Elements of a Stellar Headline

1. **Your Target Job Title:** This is your headline's backbone. It's often the first thing recruiters search for. If you're gunning for a specific role, make it crystal clear.

2. **Your UVP:** Showcase what makes you unique. This is where you differentiate yourself from the crowd.

3. **Key Skills or Expertise:** Pepper in those juicy keywords that recruiters are salivating over.

4. **Industry or Specialty:** If you're targeting a specific sector, make it known.

5. **Achievements or Credentials:** Got an impressive stat or certification? Flaunt it!

5 Headline Formulas to Rock Your Profile

- *The Classic:* [Job Title] | [Key Skill] | [Notable Achievement] | [Industry] Expert in [Skill 1], [Skill 2], [Skill 3]

Example: "Marketing Director | Digital Strategy Expert | Drove 200% ROI on Campaigns | SaaS Specialist in SEO, PPC, Content Marketing"

- *The Aspiring Professional: [Target Job Title] | [Current Role] with [Key Skill] | [Relevant Certification] | Proficient in [Skill 1], [Skill 2], [Skill 3]*

Example: "Aspiring Data Scientist | Analytics Manager with Machine Learning Expertise | AWS Certified | Proficient in Python, R, SQL, Tableau"

- *The Career Pivoter: [Target Industry] [Target Role] Candidate | Leveraging [Transferable Skill] from [Current Industry] | Key Skills in [Skill 1], [Skill 2], [Skill 3]*

Example: "FinTech Product Manager Candidate | Leveraging UX Design Expertise from E-commerce | Key Skills in Agile, Data Analysis, User Research"

- *The Problem Solver: [Job Title] | Helping [Target Companies] [Solve Specific Problem] through [Expertise] | Expert in [Skill 1], [Skill 2], [Skill 3]*

Example: "UX Consultant | Helping SaaS Startups Boost User Retention through Data-Driven UX Optimization | Expert in A/B Testing, User Journey Mapping, Wireframing"

- *The Value Proposition: [Job Title] | Delivering [Key Benefit] through [Your Expertise] | [Industry] Specialist in [Skill 1], [Skill 2], [Skill 3]*

Example: "Business Analyst | Delivering Data-Driven Insights

to Optimize Operations | Manufacturing Specialist in Process
Improvement, KPI Development, Predictive Analytics"

Symbols: Yay or Nay?

Using symbols like | • ▯ ▯ ◆ → ▯ can make your headline pop visually. But use
them judiciously – you're a professional, not an emoji artist.

A few well-placed symbols can organize information and draw the eye.

- The vertical pipe (|) and bullet point (•) are classic choices for sepa-
  rating information.

- Arrows (▯ →) can indicate progression or direction.

- Stars (▯ ▯) can highlight key achievements or skills.

- Diamonds (◆) offer a subtle way to break up text.

Overdo it, and you risk looking gimmicky. Remember, the goal is to enhance readability and visual appeal, not to create a symbol-laden distraction.

Keywords: Your Headline's Secret Weapon

Remember, your headline isn't just for human eyes – it's also for LinkedIn's
search algorithm. Incorporate relevant keywords, especially those common
in job postings for your target role. But don't just stuff keywords – weave
them in naturally.

PRO TIP

While LinkedIn doesn't reveal its algorithm, it is widely believed that it gives extra weight to the first few words in your headline.
So, front-load it with your most crucial keyword(s) (usually your target
job title).

Headline Hacks for Career Transitions

- Use "Aspiring [Job Title]" to signal your career goal while being transparent.

- Try "[Industry] [Role] Candidate" to show you're actively seeking opportunities.

- Highlight transferable skills that bridge your current experience with your target role.

Examples of Scroll-Stopping Headlines

"Artificial Intelligence Engineer | Turning Data into Business Intelligence | Patent Holder in Machine Learning"

"Aspiring Chief Sustainability Officer | Environmental Scientist | Helping Companies Achieve Net-Zero Goals"

"Sales Enablement Manager | Bridging the Gap Between Marketing & Sales | 150% Team Performance Boost"

"Human Resources Director Candidate | Culture Champion | Transforming Employee Experience in Tech Startups"

"Content Strategist | SEO Wizard • Storyteller • Lead Generator | Driving 10M+ Monthly Organic Views"

Remember, your headline is a living entity. Test different versions, monitor your profile views, and don't be afraid to iterate. Your perfect headline is out there – let's find it!

AI PROMPTS TO CRAFT YOUR HEADLINE

"I'm targeting a role as [Desired Job Title] in the [Target Industry]. My current title is [Current Job Title], and my top 3 skills are [Skill 1], [Skill 2], and [Skill 3]. My biggest career achievement is [Achievement]. Please provide: a) 3 headline options that incorporate my target role and current experience b) A list of 10 relevant keywords for my target role, ranked by likely search volume c) 2 versions of each headline: one with symbols and one without d) Suggestions for how to quantify my impact in the headline"

- "I'm transitioning from [Current Industry] to [Target Industry]. My target role is [Desired Job Title], and I want to highlight my transferable skills of [Skill 1], [Skill 2], and [Skill 3]. Please create: a) 4 headline options that position me as a strong candidate for my target role b) A list of 5 industry-specific buzzwords or trends I should consider including c) 3 ways to phrase my transition without using the word 'aspiring' d) A brief explanation of how each headline addresses potential employer concerns about my industry switch"

- "I'm a [Current Job Title] with [X] years of experience, targeting a [Desired Job Title] role. My UVP is [Your UVP]. Please provide: a) 5 headline options that showcase my UVP and target role b) Suggestions for 3 achievements or metrics I could include to strengthen each headline c) A list of 7 action verbs that would resonate in my target role d) 2 'outside-the-box' headline ideas that could help me stand out in my industry e) Advice on whether to include my current job title, and how to phrase it if so"

- "I'm a recent graduate seeking my first role as a [Target Entry-Level Position]. My degree is in [Your Degree], and I have internship experience in [Relevant Experience]. Create: a) 4 headline options that position me as a promising entry-level candidate b) A list of 6 skills or qualities employers typically seek in entry-level [Target Position] roles c) 3 ways to highlight my internship experience without explicitly using the word 'intern' d) Suggestions for how to incorporate my academic achievements into my headline e) Advice on whether to mention 'recent graduate' in my headline, with pros and cons"

- "I'm a [Current Job Title] looking to highlight my expertise in [Niche Skill/Technology]. I want to target roles that specifically utilize this skill. Please provide: a) 5 headline options that position me as a specialist in my niche b) A list of 10 related technologies or skills that could strengthen my headline c) 3 ways to quantify my expertise or impact in this niche area d) Suggestions for how to balance highlighting my niche skill with maintaining broader appeal e) Advice on whether to include my current job title, and how to phrase it if so"

Your Action Plan to Craft Your Brand

Knowledge is the seed, but action is the water that helps it grow. You've now learned the essential elements of focusing your LinkedIn profile, developing your unique value proposition, and creating an attention-grabbing headline. It's time to transform these insights into a powerful professional brand that resonates with your target audience. Don't wait for the 'perfect' moment - the best time to refine your LinkedIn presence is right now. Let's turn your knowledge into a compelling professional narrative!

Ready to elevate your LinkedIn profile? Here's your action plan:

- Conduct a thorough review of your career goals and target roles. Define your carer focus as precisely as possible.

- Related to your career focus, list your key strengths, unique skill combinations, and standout experiences. Research your target industry to identify current needs and challenges.

- Craft your Unique Value Proposition (UVP) statement using the provided formula. Utilize the AI prompts to generate alternative UVP ideas and refine your statement. Incorporate it throughout your profile, especially in your About section.

- Select a headline formula that best suits your career situation. Incorporate your target job title, UVP, and key skills. Experiment with appropriate symbols to enhance your headline's readability. Ensure it's keyword-rich for searchability.

- Create 3-5 variations of your headline and plan to test them over time. Use the AI prompts to generate headline ideas tailored to your specific situation.

- Conduct a comprehensive profile audit. Read through your entire profile with your new focus, UVP, and headline in mind. Note any possible improvements. You will revisit these notes later.

- Join 2-3 relevant LinkedIn groups in your industry or related to your target roles. Engage in discussions at least once a week to increase your visibility.

Congratulations! You've just taken a giant leap towards transforming your LinkedIn profile from a digital wallflower into a recruiter magnet. By focusing your profile, crafting a compelling UVP, and creating an attention-grabbing headline, you're well on your way to standing out in the vast LinkedIn landscape.

Remember, in the world of LinkedIn, generics don't cut it. Your focused profile tells recruiters exactly where you fit in their puzzle. Your UVP showcases why you're not just a good fit but the best fit. And your headline? It's your professional hook, reeling in the right opportunities.

But don't stop here. Your LinkedIn journey is an ongoing process of refinement and optimization. As your career evolves, so should your profile. Keep experimenting, keep refining, and most importantly, keep being authentically you. After all, that's your true unique value proposition.

Chapter Five

Keyword Mastery

Cracking the Code of Recruiter Searches on LinkedIn

Keywords are the bridge between your LinkedIn profile and the recruiters who are searching for candidates just like you. Let's dive into how mastering these keywords can dramatically increase your visibility to recruiters.

The Role of Keywords In Recruiter Searches

Imagine your LinkedIn profile as a beacon in a vast digital ocean. Keywords—the specific terms and phrases that describe your skills, experiences, and qualifications—are the light that makes your beacon shine brighter, guiding recruiters directly to you.

In the enormous pool of LinkedIn profiles, the right keywords can make the difference between being overlooked and being discovered.

LinkedIn's search capabilities have become increasingly sophisticated over time. Today's LinkedIn Recruiter offers advanced tools that allow hiring professionals to quickly filter through millions of profiles with great precision.

While AI enhances these capabilities, perhaps more than any other element, it's the keywords in your profile that determine your visibility in these searches. Understanding how to leverage these keywords has become more important than ever in standing out to recruiters.

How LinkedIn Recruiter Processes Profiles

Let's pull back the curtain and see how LinkedIn Recruiter, the powerful tool used by hiring professionals, actually works.

Introduction to LinkedIn's Recruiter Tools

LinkedIn Recruiter is a sophisticated platform that allows hiring professionals to search for, filter, and organize candidates efficiently. It's designed to help recruiters quickly identify the most promising profiles from LinkedIn's vast user base.

Here are some of the key factors LinkedIn Recruiter considers in a profile:

Skills Matching

Here's a juicy tidbit for you: according to LinkedIn, 40% of recruiter searches now begin with skills rather than job titles. That's right, your ability to wrangle Python or master project management might be more important than your fancy job title.

In fact, LinkedIn has upped the ante, allowing you to list up to 100 skills on your profile now (previously, they allowed for 50 skills). That's 100 chances to catch a recruiter's eye!

Keyword Relevance and Density

LinkedIn Recruiter doesn't just count keywords; it analyzes their relevance and context. It's looking for the right keywords in the right places, used in a way that makes sense for your profession.

Experience Alignment

LinkedIn Recruiter doesn't just look at your current role. It's piecing together your entire career story, looking for a narrative that aligns with the job at hand. Your past roles, responsibilities, and achievements all play a part in determining your relevance to a recruiter's search.

Profile Completeness and Engagement

A complete profile gives recruiters more information to work with. Your activity on the platform – comments, likes, shares, and posts – also factors into your visibility. An active, complete profile signals to recruiters that you're an engaged professional in your field.

How LinkedIn's Search Algorithm Works

LinkedIn's search algorithm is complex and multifaceted. It considers everything from the keywords in your profile to your connections, your activity, and even how closely you match the searcher's network. The algorithm also values recency, so regular updates to your profile can boost your visibility in search results.

It's important to note that the algorithm is dynamic, constantly refining its understanding of what makes a good match based on user behavior. This means that optimizing your profile is an ongoing process, not a one-time task.

PRO TIP

LinkedIn's algorithm has a recency bias. This means that newer content and profile updates are given more weight in search results. To take advantage of this, update your profile regularly - even small changes can boost your visibility in search results.

Identifying The Most Important Keywords

Now that we understand how LinkedIn Recruiter works, it's time to arm ourselves with the right keywords. But how do we find these magical words that will make recruiters sit up and take notice? Don't worry, you don't need a crystal ball or a degree in SEO. Let's dive into some free, effective techniques to uncover the keywords that will make your profile shine.

Become a Job Description Detective

One of the most potent techniques is to analyze job postings for positions you're eyeing. Think of job descriptions as your personal keyword treasure map. Here's how to crack the code:

- Find 6-12 job listings that match your target role or industry.

- Copy and paste the text from these listings into a word cloud generator like Wordle or WordCloud.

- The words that appear largest are your keyword goldmine. These are the terms recruiters use most frequently.

For example, if you're a marketing professional and see "content strategy," "SEO," and "social media analytics" popping up in large font in your word cloud, you know these are hot keywords to include in your profile.

Analyze Top-Performer Profiles

Put on your analyst hat and examine the profiles of professionals in roles similar to your target position. Here's your research plan:

- Search for people with your desired job or in your target industry.

- Review their profiles, noting commonly used terms and phrases.

- Pay special attention to their headlines, summaries, and experience sections.

What patterns do you see? Are there specific skills or achievements that stand out? If you notice that successful professionals in your field consistently mention "agile methodologies," "cross-functional team leadership," or "data-driven decision making," it's a good bet these are keywords you should consider incorporating.

Leverage LinkedIn's "Skills" Section

LinkedIn's "Skills" section isn't just a list – it's a keyword goldmine. Here's how to strike it rich:

- When adding skills to your profile, LinkedIn suggests related skills.

- These suggestions often reflect industry-standard terms and in-demand skills.

- Don't be shy – LinkedIn now allows you to list up to 100 skills. That's 100 chances to catch a recruiter's eye!

If you add "project management" as a skill, and LinkedIn suggests "Scrum," "Agile," and "JIRA," these are likely valuable keywords in your industry.

Think Like Your Target Audience

Put yourself in the shoes of the people you want to find your profile. What terms would they use to search for someone with your expertise? Consider:

- Who is your target audience? Recruiters? Clients? Industry peers?

- What problems do they need solved?

- What terms would they use to describe the ideal candidate?

If you're a UX designer, your target audience might search for terms like "user research," "prototyping," or "usability testing."

Speak the Language of Your Industry

Every industry has its own jargon, and in the world of LinkedIn, that jargon can be your secret weapon. Here's how to leverage it:

- Use industry-specific terms relevant to your work.

- Include certifications, methodologies, or tools you're proficient in.

- Don't shy away from technical terms, but make sure you can back them up!

For instance, if you're in IT, terms like "cloud computing," "cybersecurity," or "DevOps" might be crucial keywords.

Become a Keyword Thesaurus

One keyword is good, but several related keywords are better. Here's how to expand your keyword vocabulary:

- Use tools like a thesaurus or AI to generate alternative phrases.

- For example, "software development" could include variations like "software engineering" or "application development."

- This helps diversify your keyword usage and increases your chances of being discovered.

Harness the Power of AI for Keyword Research

ChatGPT can be your personal keyword consultant.

AI PROMPTS FOR KEYWORD RESEARCH

"I'm updating my LinkedIn profile for a [your job title] position in the [your industry] industry. Can you analyze this job description and provide: a) A list of 10-15 essential keywords and skills, b) 5 industry-specific buzzwords or phrases, and c) 3 emerging trends or technologies mentioned? Here's the job description: [paste job description]"

- "Based on current market trends, what are the top 20 skills and keywords for a [your job title] in [your industry] for [year]? Please categorize them into technical skills, soft skills, and industry-specific knowledge. Also, suggest 5 certifications or qualifications that would be valuable to mention."

- "I want to optimize my LinkedIn headline and summary. My current role is [your current job title], but I'm targeting positions as a [your target job title]. Can you provide: a) 5 powerful headline options incorporating relevant keywords, b) A list of 10 must-include keywords for my summary, and c) 3 achievement-focused statements using these keywords?"

- "Help me craft keyword-rich bullet points for my experience section. My role is [your job title] at [company name], and my main responsibilities include [list 3-5 key responsibilities]. Can you generate 5-7 impactful bullet points that incorporate relevant industry keywords and highlight measurable achievements?"

- "I'm transitioning from [current industry] to [target industry] as a [target job title]. Can you identify: a) 10 transferable skills and keywords that bridge these industries, b) 5 keywords specific to my target industry that I should familiarize myself with, and c) 3 ways to describe my experience that would appeal to recruiters in my target industry?"

- "Analyze the LinkedIn profiles of these three industry leaders in my field: [paste URLs of 3 LinkedIn profiles]. Can you identify: a) Common keywords and phrases they use, b) Unique or standout terms in each profile, and c) Suggestions for how I can incorporate similar high-impact keywords in my own profile?"

- "I'm targeting multinational corporations in the [your industry] sector. Based on this, can you provide: a) 15 globally recognized keywords and skills for my field, b) 5 phrases that demonstrate international or cross-cultural experience, and c) 3 examples of how to phrase my achievements to appeal to global companies?"

- "As a [your job title] with [X] years of experience, I want to emphasize my leadership and strategic skills. Can you suggest: a) 10 leadership-focused keywords relevant to my industry, b) 5 ways to describe strategic initiatives using industry-specific language, and c) 3 examples of how to quantify leadership achievements using these keywords?"

- "I'm interested in highlighting my expertise in [specific area, e.g., 'data-driven marketing' or 'sustainable engineering']. Can you provide: a) A list of 20 niche-specific keywords and phrases, b) 5 cutting-edge tools or methodologies in this area, and c) 3 ways to demonstrate thought leadership in this specialization on my LinkedIn profile?"

- "Based on my background as a [your job title] in [your industry], what are 10 adjacent roles I could potentially transition into? For each role, please provide: a) 5 key skills or keywords I should emphasize, b) 2 industry-specific certifications that would be valuable, and c) 1 example of how to reframe my current experience to appeal to recruiters for this adjacent role."

Remember, ChatGPT is a tool, not a magic wand. Always review and personalize its suggestions to ensure they accurately reflect your experience and skills.

Keep Your Finger on the Pulse

The business world is constantly evolving, and so should your keywords. Stay up-to-date with industry trends:

- Follow thought leaders in your industry on LinkedIn.

- Join relevant professional groups and participate in discussions.

- Attend webinars and conferences (virtual or in-person) in your field.

- Regularly check job postings, even if you're not actively job hunting.

The hot keyword today might be old news tomorrow. For example, a few years ago, "big data" was the buzzword. Now, it's all about "artificial intelligence" and "machine learning."

Quality Over Quantity

Keyword density matters in LinkedIn's search algorithm, but balance is key. You want to optimize your profile without sacrificing readability. Think of it as seasoning a dish - the right amount enhances the flavor, but too much overpowers it. Here are some tips to help you strike that perfect balance:

- Use keywords naturally throughout your profile.

- Focus on the headline, skills, summary, and experience sections.

- Avoid keyword stuffing, which can make your profile seem inauthentic or spammy.

- If a keyword doesn't genuinely reflect your skills or experience, leave it out.

- Choose the most important and relevant 10-12 keywords and repeat them across various parts of your profile.

Remember, your profile should read like it was written by a human, for humans. After all, while algorithms might find you, it's people who will read your profile and decide to reach out.

Test and Refine

Not seeing the results you want? Don't be afraid to experiment with different keywords. Here's how to refine your approach:

- Monitor your profile views. If they increase after adding certain keywords, you're on the right track.

- Pay attention to the roles you're being contacted about. Do they align with your goals?

- Don't be afraid to experiment with different keywords.

- Regularly update your profile with new skills and experiences.

Remember, your LinkedIn profile is a living document. As your career evolves, so should your keywords.

But knowing the right keywords is just the first step. In the next section, we'll explore how to strategically incorporate these keywords throughout your profile without sounding like a robot.

PRO TIP

Boost your keyword presence by creating content on LinkedIn. Use LinkedIn's article publishing feature or create posts that incorporate your target keywords. This not only increases your visibility but also reinforces your expertise in specific areas to both the LinkedIn algorithm and potential recruiters.

Strategically Incorporating Keywords

Think of keywords as the breadcrumbs that lead recruiters directly to your profile. They're the magic words that make LinkedIn's algorithm sit up and take notice, whispering, "Hey, this person is exactly who that recruiter is looking for!"

But here's the thing: it's not just about peppering your profile with buzz-words. It's about weaving these keywords into your professional narrative in a way that resonates with both the AI-powered search algorithms and the humans who'll ultimately read your profile. It's a delicate balance of art and science, showcasing your authenticity while also speaking the language of your industry.

In this section, we're going deep into the strategy of keyword placement. We'll explore how to sprinkle these magic words throughout your profile for maximum impact. We'll look at each section of your profile and discuss how to optimize them for search without sacrificing your unique voice.

Headline: Your Professional Tagline

Your headline is prime real estate on LinkedIn. It's your first impression and a crucial spot for keywords. Remember, the most important keyword here is the job title you're targeting.

For detailed strategies for crafting a compelling, keyword-rich headline, refer back to Chapter 4. We've covered this topic in-depth there, including formulas and examples to help you create a headline that grabs attention and ranks well in searches.

As a reminder, here's the golden rule: Start with the job title you're targeting. For example,

> "Marketing Director | Brand Strategist | Digital Campaign Expert".

See what I did there? Job title first, followed by areas of expertise.

PRO TIP

You can now associate skills with specific experiences on your profile. This adds context and credibility to your skill claims. Be strategic - only associate the most relevant 5-10 skills with each experience.

Job Titles: Your Career Milestones

LinkedIn allows up to 100 characters for each job title. Use this space wisely! Start with your official title, then use the pipe symbol (|) to separate it from descriptive keywords. For example:

> "Senior Project Manager | Agile & Scrum Expert | IT Implementation Specialist"

This approach serves two purposes: it adds keywords and provides clarity about your role. Remember, job titles can vary across companies, so these additional terms help recruiters understand your specific responsibilities.

AI PROMPT TO KEYWORD-OPTIMIZE JOB TITLES:

"My official job title is [your title], and I have [X] characters remaining. My key responsibilities include [list 2-3 main duties]. Can you suggest 5 ways to expand my job title using the pipe symbol (|) to include relevant keywords that will clarify my role and catch a recruiter's attention?"

"Skills" Section: Your Professional Toolkit

The "Skills" section is a recruiter's best friend when narrowing down candidates.

AI PROMPTS TO REFINE LINKEDIN SKILLS

"I'm a [your job title] in the [your industry] industry. Can you generate a list of 100 relevant skills I should consider adding to my LinkedIn profile? Please include both technical and soft skills, and group them by category."

- "Based on the following job description for a [target job title], can you identify the top 20 skills I should prioritize in my LinkedIn profile? [Paste job description]"

- "I want to associate skills with my experiences on LinkedIn. For my role as [job title] at [company], where I was responsible for [list key responsibilities], what are the 10 most relevant skills I should associate with this experience?"

You can list up to 100 skills. Here's how to maximize its impact:
- Use as many relevant skills as possible. More skills mean more chances to appear in searches.

- Stick to LinkedIn's suggested skills. As you type, LinkedIn will offer recommendations. It is always best to choose from these rather than creating custom phrases.

- Prioritize your skills. Put the most relevant and in-demand skills at the top of your list.

- Include both hard and soft skills. Technical skills are crucial but don't forget transferable skills like leadership or communication.

- Keep it updated. Review and refresh your skills every 6-12 months.

- Seek endorsements, especially for your top 3 skills, which are displayed prominently.

- Use LinkedIn's skill suggestions to add synonyms and related terms. This broadens your profile's visibility in searches.

About/Summary Section: Your Professional Story

This section is your chance to weave keywords into your career narrative. A powerful technique to showcase your most significant accomplishments while optimizing with keywords is to pair a keyword phrase with an accomplishment that demonstrates it. For example:

> "**PROJECT MANAGEMENT:** Served as project lead on Institutional Renewals of 130+ organizations. Streamlined process by consolidating renewals and ensured efficiency and accuracy of data reported and analyzed."

and

> "**CUSTOMER SERVICE:** Solicited feedback from organizations to identify strengths and areas of improvement, and partnered with underwriting team to improve physician application and process. Adhered to response time for all requests and received high marks on customer survey."

Along with the rest of your About content (which we'll cover in Chapter 7), consider including 3-5 of these keyword-accomplishment pairings to highlight your most impressive and relevant achievements.

AI PROMPT TO KEYWORD-OPTIMIZE ACCOMPLISH-MENTS

"I'm a [your job title] with [X years] of experience in [your industry]. My key skills include [list 3-4 key skills]. Can you create 5 keyword-accomplishment pairings for my LinkedIn About section, following this format: [KEYWORD PHRASE IN CAPS]: Brief description of a relevant accomplishment that demonstrates this skill."

Experience Descriptions: Your Career Highlights

Your experience section is a goldmine for keyword optimization. Here's how to make it shine:

- Use the keyword-accomplishment pairing technique in your job descriptions to front-load your bulleted accomplishments with keywords (see the tip for your About section above).

- Use industry-specific terminology and acronyms (but explain them if they're not widely known).

- Include relevant projects, tools, and technologies you've worked with.

- Tailor your descriptions to align with your target roles.

Remember, it's not just about stuffing keywords. Each experience description should tell a mini-story of your impact and value.

Other Sections: The Supporting Cast

While your headline, skills, about section, and experience are the stars of your LinkedIn profile, don't underestimate the power of the supporting cast. These additional sections provide more opportunities to showcase your skills, experiences, and, yes, those all-important keywords. Let's explore how to leverage these sections:

- **Education:** Beyond listing your degrees, use this section to highlight relevant coursework, projects, or thesis topics that align with your target industry. Include industry-specific terminology and skills gained during your studies.

- **Licenses & Certifications:** This section is a goldmine for industry-specific keywords. List all relevant certifications using the official titles and acronyms. Include the issuing organization and date of certification.

- **Volunteer Experience:** Volunteer work can demonstrate soft skills and industry involvement. Use relevant keywords to describe your roles and achievements in volunteer positions.

- **Publications:** Using industry-specific titles and descriptions, list any articles, papers, or books you've authored.

- **Patents:** If applicable, include patents with relevant technical terms.

- **Courses:** Using industry terminology in the descriptions, list any additional classes you've taken.

- **Projects:** Describe significant projects, incorporating relevant keywords and technologies used.

- **Honors & Awards:** Mention awards using industry-specific award names and including keyword-rich descriptions.

- **Test Scores:** If relevant to your field, include scores from professional tests or exams.

- **Languages:** List language proficiencies, which can be important keywords for international roles.

- **Organizations:** Mention professional memberships, using official organization names and your roles within them.

- **Recommendations:** While you can't directly control the content, recommendations often naturally include industry-specific language and skills.

- **Featured:** Use this section to showcase your best work. Add articles, links, media, or documents that demonstrate your expertise, ensuring descriptions are keyword-rich.

- **Interests:** Following relevant companies, groups, and thought leaders can indirectly support your keyword strategy by associating your profile with industry-specific entities.

Strategies for Keywords in Supporting Sections

Optimizing keywords in your LinkedIn profile's supporting sections is a multifaceted strategy that can significantly boost your visibility to recruiters.

Start by being comprehensive - fill out as many relevant sections as possible, viewing each as an opportunity to showcase your professional story through carefully chosen keywords. However, relevance is key; focus on information that aligns with your current career goals and target roles.

When listing certifications, organizations, or courses, use official names and recognized acronyms to ensure accuracy and searchability.

In sections that allow descriptions such as "Projects" or v"Volunteer Experience," weave in industry-specific terms and skills to paint a vivid picture of your capabilities.

Remember, your profile is a living document - update it regularly with new certifications, skills, or volunteer roles to keep it current and keyword-rich. Don't overlook the power of multimedia; in sections like "Featured," use keyword-optimized captions for any uploaded media.

Finally, ensure consistency across your profile by cross-referencing keywords between supporting and main sections. This comprehensive approach not only enhances your searchability but also presents a well-rounded view of your professional expertise to potential employers and connections.

By optimizing these additional sections, you create a comprehensive, keyword-rich profile that presents a full picture of your professional capabilities. This makes your profile a powerful tool in your career arsenal, improving both your searchability and the depth of information available to those viewing your profile.

Mastering the Keyword Symphony

Let's step back and examine your LinkedIn profile from a more comprehensive perspective. Crafting an effective profile requires a strategic and holistic approach to keyword usage. Your profile should be a carefully curated representation of your professional identity, skillfully designed to appeal to both LinkedIn's algorithms and discerning human recruiters.

By striking this balance, you can create a profile that not only ranks well in search results but also resonates with potential employers. Let's explore how to optimize your entire profile to ensure it stands out in the competitive landscape of professional networking.

- **Structure your keyword strategy purposefully.** Start with primary keywords in your headline and "About" section, expand in "Experience" descriptions, and reinforce in the "Skills" section.

- **Diversify your keywords.** Blend industry-specific terms with broader professional competencies. Balance technical jargon with accessible language. Include a mix of job titles, tools, methodologies, and soft skills.

- **Integrate keywords seamlessly.** Ensure your narrative flows naturally, avoiding forced insertions. Refine if content feels disjointed or repetitive. Aim for a profile that's engaging to humans and optimized for algorithms.

- **Know your audience.** Consider recruiters and industry peers when selecting keywords. Use terminology that resonates with your target roles. Craft your profile for *both* AI searches and human evaluation.

- **Stay adaptable.** Regularly update your keyword strategy to reflect industry trends. Incorporate new skills and experiences as you grow professionally.

- **Monitor performance.** Track your search result appearances and engagement from recruiters. Reassess and refine your keyword selection if you are not seeing the desired results.

- **Learn and iterate.** Study successful profiles in your industry. Continuously improve your approach. Balance strategic keyword usage with authentic storytelling to create a compelling, search-optimized profile.

Common LinkedIn Keyword Mistakes to Avoid

While keywords are crucial for optimizing your LinkedIn profile, it's easy to fall into common traps that can undermine your efforts. Let's explore these pitfalls and how to avoid them:

Keyword Stuffing

- **The Mistake:** Overloading your profile with keywords, making it read unnaturally.

- **The Fix:** Use keywords judiciously and in context. If it doesn't sound natural when you read it aloud, it's probably too much.

Claiming Unverified Skills

- **The Mistake:** Including keywords that represent skills or expertise you don't actually possess.

- **The Fix:** Only list skills that you can confidently demonstrate or discuss in an interview. Focus on accurately representing your true abilities and experiences, even if it means using fewer buzzwords.

Ignoring Context

- **The Mistake:** Using keywords without considering their relevance to your experience or the role you're targeting.

- **The Fix:** Ensure each keyword is supported by your actual experience or skills. Don't claim expertise in areas where you have little to no background.

Neglecting Long-Tail Keywords

- **The Mistake:** Focusing only on broad, generic terms and missing out on more specific phrases.

- **The Fix:** Include longer, more specific keyword phrases that are highly relevant to your niche or target roles.

Overlooking Industry Jargon

- **The Mistake:** Using overly simplified terms when industry-specific language would be more appropriate.

- **The Fix:** Incorporate relevant industry jargon and acronyms, but be sure to spell out acronyms at least once for clarity.

Ignoring Semantic Variations

- **The Mistake:** Using only one version of a keyword, missing out on potential matches due to slight variations in terminology.

- **The Fix:** Include different forms or synonyms of key terms. For example, use both "project management" and "managing projects" or "data analysis" and "analyzing data" to capture a broader range of search queries.

Focusing on Outdated Skills

- **The Mistake:** Emphasizing outdated skills or technologies that are no longer in demand.

- **The Fix:** Stay current with industry trends and focus on skills that are currently valued in your field.

Ignoring Location-Based Keywords

- **The Mistake:** Neglecting to include location-specific terms if you're targeting roles in particular areas.

- **The Fix:** If location is relevant to your job search, include city, state, or region names where appropriate.

Using Subjective Descriptors

- **The Mistake:** Relying on vague, subjective terms like "innovative," "creative," or "expert" without context.

- **The Fix:** Back up such claims with specific examples or achievements that demonstrate these qualities.

Copying and Pasting from Job Descriptions

- **The Mistake:** Directly copying keywords from job postings without tailoring them to your actual experience.

- **The Fix:** While job descriptions are great sources for keywords, always adapt them to reflect your own skills and experiences accurately.

Neglecting to Update Keywords

- **The Mistake:** Setting and forgetting your keywords, even as your career evolves.

- **The Fix:** Regularly review and update your profile keywords to reflect your current skills, experiences, and career goals.

Overlooking Keywords in URL and File Names

- **The Mistake:** Using generic names for your LinkedIn URL or uploaded documents.

- **The Fix:** Customize your LinkedIn URL with your name and include relevant keywords in the file names of any documents you upload to your profile.

Focusing Only on Hard Skills

- **The Mistake:** Neglecting soft skills in favor of technical keywords.

- **The Fix:** Include a balance of both hard and soft skills. Many recruiters search for candidates with specific soft skills like "leadership" or "communication."

Remember, the goal is to create a profile that is both keyword-optimized and authentically representative of your professional brand. By avoiding these common mistakes, you'll create a LinkedIn presence that appeals to both the platform's algorithm and the human recruiters who will ultimately read your profile.

Your Action Plan to Unlock the Power of Keywords

In the realm of LinkedIn, keywords are the secret ingredients that can transform your profile from invisible to irresistible. You've now learned the crucial role keywords play in making your profile discoverable and appealing to both algorithms and human recruiters. But knowledge alone isn't enough - it's time to put these insights into action. Don't let your profile languish in obscurity when it could be shining brightly in search results. Let's harness the power of keywords to elevate your LinkedIn presence!

Ready to supercharge your LinkedIn profile with strategic keywords? Here's your action plan:

- Conduct comprehensive keyword research. Analyze job postings for your target role, review profiles of professionals in your desired position, and explore LinkedIn's "Skills" section suggestions. Use AI tools to generate industry-specific keyword lists.

- Create a master list of keywords, categorizing them into technical skills, soft skills, and industry-specific terms (AI can help with this task). Optimize your "Skills" section by adding up to 100 relevant skills, balancing hard and soft skills to reflect your target role requirements.

- Enhance your job titles using the full 100-character limit. Associate key skills with each of your work experiences and ensure consistency in formatting across all positions.

- Begin to consider how you might leverage primary sections such as "About" and "Experience," as well as supporting sections like "Education," "Licenses & Certifications," and "Volunteer Experience" for additional keyword placement. Make notes on your ideas. We will revisit this later in this book.

- Review your headline and, if necessary, revise it to include your target job title and key skills, aligning with your identified keywords.

- Set up a system for maintaining and updating your keyword strategy. Plan to review and update your skills section every 6 months and reassess your overall keyword strategy quarterly to stay current with industry trends.

- Engage with your network to seek endorsements for your top skills. Aim for at least 5 endorsements on your most crucial skills to boost credibility and searchability.

Remember, keyword optimization is an ongoing process, not a one-time task. Your goal is to create a profile that speaks fluently to *both* algorithms *and* humans, positioning you as the ideal candidate for your target roles. Each keyword is a stepping stone toward greater visibility and opportunity.

Chapter Six

The Art and Science of Building Your Profile

Best Practices for Weaving Your Professional Narrative

A s we've already established, your LinkedIn profile isn't just another online presence - it's your professional storefront, your digital handshake, and, often, the first impression you'll make on potential employers or networking connections. An engaging LinkedIn profile can be the difference between landing your dream job and getting lost in the sea of applicants.

But what makes a LinkedIn profile truly engaging? It's not just about listing your job titles and education. It's about telling your professional story in a way that captures attention, showcases your unique value, and leaves a lasting impression. It's about creating a profile that not only informs but also intrigues and inspires.

The Dual Purpose of a LinkedIn Profile

Your LinkedIn profile serves two crucial purposes, and striking the right balance between them is key to your success on the platform.

Attract Recruiters and Succinctly Convey Your Qualifications

Think of your profile as a lighthouse in the vast ocean of professionals but with an intelligent beacon system. It needs to shine bright enough to catch the eye of recruiters and employers while also speaking their language through strategic keyword placement. This keyword optimization acts like a homing signal, guiding recruiters to your shore of expertise.

But it's not just about being found - it's about being understood. Once recruiters land on your profile, it should quickly and clearly communicate your qualifications, experiences, and the unique value you bring to the table. Your profile is both your beacon and your welcome mat, optimized to attract and then impress.

Invite Connections and Foster Networking

At the same time, your LinkedIn profile is your networking hub. It's not just a static document; it's a living, breathing representation of your professional self. It should invite connections, spark conversations, and foster meaningful professional relationships. Your profile should be approachable and engaging, encouraging others to reach out and connect.

Comparing Résumés and LinkedIn Profiles

While your LinkedIn profile and your résumé might contain similar information, they're far from identical twins. Let's break down the key differences:

Purpose and Scope

- **Résumé:** A detailed overview of your career and professional credentials focused for a specific goal. Individual career stories illustrate your personal brand and unique value offerings.

- **LinkedIn Profile:** Helps build connections and foster networking while providing space to create a "living" multimedia career portfolio. Infused with your personal brand and personality.

Writing Style

- **Résumé:** Written in the implied first-person (as if you are writing about yourself but without any pronouns such as "I" or "me").

- **LinkedIn Profile:** Written in the first person with a conversational tone. Pronouns are both acceptable and expected as they promote you as an approachable individual open to networking.

Headshots

- **Résumé:** Never include a photo of yourself (this might not always be true outside of the North American job market).

- **LinkedIn Profile:** You should include a professional and on-brand photo of yourself.

Personal Information

- **Résumé:** Never include information about your family and personal hobbies (unless those hobbies directly support your target goal).

- **LinkedIn Profile:** A peek into your volunteer activities, community work, passions, brand values, vision, mission, and hobbies can help you build meaningful connections and can be conversation starters. Include them prudently.

Content Depth

- **Résumé:** Typically concise and focused on professional achievements directly relevant to the job application.

- **LinkedIn Profile:** While content should be succinct and readable, a robust profile with multimedia content and complete sections will stand out.

Length and Format

- **Résumé:** Usually limited to 1-2 pages, with a clear, professional format. Often tailored for each job application.

- **LinkedIn Profile:** There is no strict length limit. This allows for a more comprehensive career history and achievements. LinkedIn provides a standard format.

Accessibility

- **Résumé:** Typically shared directly with potential employers or recruiters. It is not publicly accessible unless you choose to publish it.

- **LinkedIn Profile:** Public and searchable (unless you adjust privacy settings). Accessible to a wide network of professionals, recruiters, and potential employers.

Updates and Maintenance

- **Résumé:** Updated periodically and (ideally) tailored when applying for new positions. But once submitted, it is a static document.

- **LinkedIn Profile:** It can be updated in real time and allows for regular updates on current projects, achievements, and career milestones.

Recommendations and Endorsements

- **Résumé:** May include references, but typically, these are provided separately upon request.

- **LinkedIn Profile:** LinkedIn includes features for recommendations from colleagues and endorsements for specific skills, providing social proof of your abilities.

Think of your résumé as a formal business suit tailored for a specific job interview. Your LinkedIn profile, on the other hand, is more like your favorite smart casual outfit - professional but with a touch of personality that makes you approachable at a networking event.

Fundamental Best Practices for Profile Writing

Now that we understand the unique nature of a LinkedIn profile, let's explore the best practices for crafting one that stands out and gets results.

Maintain Consistency With Your Résumé

While your LinkedIn profile allows for more personality, it's crucial to maintain consistency with your résumé. Think of them as two instruments in your career orchestra - they should be playing the same tune, just in different styles.

Ensure that key details like job titles, dates of employment, and significant achievements (especially any numbers you've used to illustrate results) align across both platforms. Your personal branding - the unique combination of skills, experiences, and qualities that make you stand out - should be consistent too. And most importantly, your Unique Value Proposition (UVP) - the core message about what you offer - should shine through in both.

For example, if you're a marketing manager who specializes in turning around underperforming teams, this should be clear in both your résumé and your LinkedIn profile. The difference? On LinkedIn, you might tell a brief story about how you did this, complete with your thought process and the personal satisfaction you derived from the achievement.

This consistency ensures that whether a potential employer encounters you first on LinkedIn or through your résumé, they're getting a coherent picture of who you are professionally.

Adopt a Conversational Tone

Unlike your résumé, your LinkedIn profile should sound like you're having a conversation with the reader. Use "I" and "my" freely. This isn't the time for stuffy, formal language - imagine you're explaining your career to a respected colleague over coffee.

Instead of: *"Responsible for leading a team of 10 in developing innovative software solutions."*

Try: *"I lead a talented team of 10, and together, we cook up innovative software solutions that make our clients' lives easier."*

The second version gives a sense of your personality and leadership style, making you more relatable and memorable.

Infuse With Personality and Personal Touches

Your LinkedIn profile is your chance to let your professional personality shine. Are you known for your quick wit? Your calm under pressure? Your ability to explain complex concepts simply? Weave these qualities into your profile.

Don't be afraid to mention relevant personal interests or experiences that make you unique. Maybe your hobby as a weekend rock climber has taught you valuable lessons about risk assessment that apply to your work in finance. Or perhaps your volunteer work at a local animal shelter has honed your patience and problem-solving skills.

Remember, these personal touches can be great conversation starters and help you build more meaningful connections. Just be sure to keep it professional and relevant.

Utilize Storytelling Techniques to Engage Readers

Humans are wired for stories. We remember them better than dry facts and figures. So, turn your professional experiences into mini-stories that engage and inform.

Instead of simply listing your achievements, frame them as challenges you overcame or goals you pursued. What was the situation? What action did you take? What was the result? For instance:

"When I joined XYZ Corp, our customer satisfaction scores were at an all-time low. I spearheaded a company-wide initiative to overhaul our customer service approach. Within six months, we saw our satisfaction scores jump by 40%, and customer retention improved by 25%."

This brief story gives context to your achievement, demonstrates your problem-solving skills, and provides concrete results - all in a way that's much more engaging than a simple bullet point.

PRO TIP

Stories in your LinkedIn profile help make your experience more relatable. Stories help recruiters and hiring managers envision how you might perform in their organization by illustrating how you've handled challenges in the past.

Emphasize and Reinforce Your UVP

Your UVP is the golden thread that should run through your entire profile. It's not just something you state once and forget - it should be reinforced throughout your profile.

In your Headline, summarize your UVP in a punchy statement. In your "About" section, expand on it. In your "Experience" section, provide examples that demonstrate it. In your "Skills" section, list the abilities that support it.

For example, if your UVP is being a "data-driven marketer who turns numbers into narratives," you might:

- Include "Data Storyteller" in your Headline

- Discuss your passion for finding the stories behind the numbers in your About section

- Highlight projects where you used data to drive successful marketing campaigns in your Experience section

- List skills like data analysis, data visualization, and content marketing in your Skills section

Incorporate Keywords Naturally

Keywords are the secret sauce that makes your profile discoverable by recruiters and hiring managers. But here's the tricky part - you need to use them naturally, not force them in awkwardly.

Start by identifying the key skills and terms relevant to your industry and target roles. Then, weave these naturally into your profile. Use them in your Headline, sprinkle them throughout your "About" section, and incorporate them into your job descriptions in the "Experience" section.

For instance, if you're in IT project management, keywords might include "Agile methodology," "Scrum," "JIRA," "risk management," and "stakeholder communication." You might write something like:

> "As a certified Scrum Master, I lead cross-functional teams using Agile methodology. I'm passionate about clear stakeholder communication and effective risk management, which I've found are key to delivering successful IT projects on time and within budget."

This paragraph naturally incorporates several key terms while still sounding conversational and authentic.

Remember, the goal is to create a profile that's optimized for search but written for humans. If it sounds forced or unnatural when you read it aloud, it probably needs some tweaking.

Be Thorough But Maintain Clarity and Readability

Balance is key when crafting your LinkedIn profile. While you want your profile to be comprehensive, you also need it to be concise and engaging. Think of it as creating a professional highlight reel rather than a documentary of your career.

A complete profile serves multiple purposes:

- It gives LinkedIn's algorithm more data to match you with relevant opportunities

- It provides recruiters with a clear picture of your professional journey and capabilities

- It demonstrates your attention to detail and professional commitment

- It helps you appear in more relevant searches for skills and experience you possess

In fact, a study conducted by ResumeGo found that job seekers with comprehensive profiles have a 71% higher chance of getting a job interview.

But remember, completeness doesn't mean verbosity. Your profile should be informative yet scannable, as recruiters often skim quickly. Think of it as writing a compelling short story, not a novel. Provide comprehensive information without overwhelming your readers.

Here are some tips to achieve this balance:

- Use bullet points for key achievements or skills to break up text and highlight important information.

- Keep paragraphs short - aim for 2-3 sentences each.

- Use strong, action-oriented language to convey information concisely.

- Leverage LinkedIn's various sections (Skills, Accomplishments, Volunteer Experience, etc.) to organize information logically.

- Regularly update your profile to ensure it remains current and comprehensive.

By creating a profile that's both complete and concise, you're not just ticking boxes—you're crafting a powerful professional narrative that's primed for discovery and engagement. Remember, in the world of LinkedIn, completeness equals visibility, and visibility can lead to opportunity.

PRO TIP

Don't underestimate the impact of white space on your LinkedIn profile's readability. Strategic use of line breaks, short paragraphs, and bullet points can significantly improve the visual appeal and scannability of your content. Aim for 2-3 sentence paragraphs and use bullet points for key achievements or skills.

This approach not only makes your profile more inviting to read but also helps key information stand out. Remember, a well-structured profile with ample white space can keep a recruiter engaged longer, increasing your chances of making a lasting impression.

The Name Game: Optimizing Your Digital Identity

Let's talk about your name. Sounds simple, right? Well, not so fast!

Your name is the cornerstone of your LinkedIn profile, and it deserves careful consideration. It's often the first thing recruiters and potential connections see. Here's how to make it work for you:

- **Consistency is key:** Match your LinkedIn name with your résumé and other professional documents.

- **Stand out from common names:** Consider using a middle initial or full middle name.

- **Showcase credentials:** Add relevant qualifications (like MBA or CPA) after your name.

- **Name changes:** Include your former name in parentheses if it's still professionally relevant.

- **Pronunciation help:** For challenging names, add phonetic spelling or use a common nickname.

Examples:
- "Elizabeth J. Smith" instead of "Liz Smith"

- "John Doe, MBA, PMP"

- "Sarah Smith (Johnson)"

- "Siobhan O'Sullivan (She-vawn)" or "Xiao 'Sean' Chen"

Remember, your name sets the tone for your entire profile. Keep it professional, consistent, and informative to make a strong first impression.

PRO TIP

LinkedIn's name pronunciation feature allows you to record a 10-second audio clip of your name, helping others say it correctly. To add this, use the LinkedIn mobile app: go to your profile, tap the edit icon near your name, and select "Add name pronunciation." Record your name clearly, and consider using the full 10 seconds to add a brief personal branding message. This feature not only ensures proper pronunciation but also adds a personal touch to your profile, making you more approachable to recruiters and connections.

A word of caution: Avoid the temptation to add job titles or industry descriptors to your name field. Not only does this violate LinkedIn's user agreement, but it can also harm your profile's credibility. Save these details for your headline and summary, where they can shine without compromising your profile's integrity.

Remember, your name on LinkedIn is more than just an identifier—it's the beginning of your professional narrative. Keep it clean, keep it professional, and let it set the tone for the impressive profile that follows.

It's a small detail with a big impact, so give it the attention it deserves.

Building Your Profile: A Synthesis of Best Practices

Crafting an engaging LinkedIn profile is both an art and a science. It requires a delicate balance of professionalism and personality, showcasing your achievements while remaining approachable and relatable.

As you write your profile, keep these best practices in mind, but don't let them stifle your unique voice. Your LinkedIn profile is your chance to stand out in a sea of professionals - to tell your unique story in a way that resonates with potential employers, clients, and connections.

Remember, your LinkedIn profile is a living document. Don't be afraid to experiment, tweak, and refine your profile over time. Pay attention to which parts of your profile get the most engagement and adjust accordingly.

In the following chapters, we'll dive deeper into each section of your LinkedIn profile, with specific strategies and examples to help you make each part shine. But for now, focus on these overarching principles. They're the foundation upon which you'll build a LinkedIn profile that truly represents you - your skills, your achievements, your personality, and your professional brand.

Your LinkedIn profile is more than just a digital résumé. It's your professional story, your personal brand, your networking hub, and your career showcase all rolled into one. Make it count. Make it you. And most importantly, make it work for your career goals.

Chapter Seven

Your Digital First Impression

Strategies and Formulas for a Standout "About" Section

I magine that a recruiter lands on your LinkedIn profile, drawn in by a standout headline. What's the next stop? Your "About" section. This is where the magic happens. Think of it as your digital elevator pitch, the moment you grab their attention, share your professional story, and spark curiosity. But here's the challenge—you have just seconds to make that impression count.

Shining a Spotlight on Your Professional Story

Your "About" section isn't just a summary; it's the heart of your personal brand. It's where you show what sets you apart and makes your unique value clear. In today's world of short attention spans and fast scrolling, this is your moment to captivate, to tell your story in a way that sticks.

LinkedIn About vs. A Traditional Résumé Summary

Think of your résumé summary as a formal handshake at a job interview—it's polished, professional, and to the point. But your LinkedIn "About" section? That's more like a conversation at a networking event—still professional but also personal, engaging, and, yes, maybe even a little fun.

Unlike a résumé—which should still reflect your personal brand and give glimpses of your authentic style and approach to your work—your "About" section offers even more room to build on that, injecting it with personality. It allows you to dive deeper into your professional journey and to highlight the unique value you bring. It's not just about listing achievements; it's about revealing who you are as a professional and where you're headed next.

Character Limit and Visibility: Making Every Word Count

Here's where things get interesting. LinkedIn gives you up to 2,600 characters—roughly 370 to 460 words—to tell your story. Sounds like plenty, right? But there's a catch: only the first 300 characters or so are visible before LinkedIn hits your reader with a "See more" prompt. This means you have to pack the most compelling information into those opening lines to entice people to keep reading.

The Networking Power of Your "About" Section

Your "About" section isn't just for recruiters—it's a networking powerhouse. It's where you start conversations, find common ground, and inspire people to reach out. A well-crafted "About" section can open doors you didn't even know existed, sparking connections that could lead to opportunities.

How Your "About" Section Impacts LinkedIn's Algorithm

While LinkedIn's exact algorithm might remain a mystery, one thing is clear: it rewards complete, keyword-rich profiles. Your "About" section is prime real estate for those keywords that boost your visibility in searches. But here's the trick—we're writing for humans first, algorithms second. The goal is to naturally weave those keywords into your professional story so they blend seamlessly, like a secret ingredient in your career recipe.

Crafting Your Story: Optimizing Your "About" Section

Ready to make your "About" section truly resonate? Let's get to work.

Essential Components for a Compelling "About" Section

Crafting a standout "About" section is like assembling a powerful personal branding toolkit. Each element is a vital tool, working together to construct a profile that captures attention and leaves a lasting impression.

Now, let's break down the key components that will transform your "About" section from something easily overlooked to truly unforgettable. Each piece adds a new layer to your professional narrative, working together to build a profile that stands out in today's competitive landscape.

Paint a Picture of Your Professional Future

Your "About" section isn't just a look back at where you've been—it's a roadmap to where you're headed. So, what's the next exciting chapter in your career story? Instead of merely recounting past achievements, frame them as stepping stones toward your future goals.

Are you leveraging your startup experience to step into a corporate innovation role? Or maybe your years in finance have prepared you to disrupt the fintech industry?

Whatever your next move, show how each experience has equipped you for it. This forward-looking approach helps recruiters, potential employers, and networking connections see exactly how you fit into their plans. It's not just about where you've been—it's about where you're going and why you're the perfect person to lead the way.

Remember, your LinkedIn profile isn't set in stone—it's a living, breathing document that evolves with your career. Make it crystal clear how your unique combination of skills, experiences, and vision positions you as the ideal candidate for the next step in your journey.

Promote Your Superpower (aka UVP)

What sets you apart from the crowd? Maybe you're the wizard who turns struggling teams into high-performers, or perhaps you're the data whisperer who transforms complex numbers into crystal-clear strategies. Whatever your superpower, make it unmissable. This is your chance to answer the question every recruiter is asking: "Why you?"

Prove Your Worth: Achievements That Speak Volumes

Actions always speak louder than words, so let your accomplishments do the talking. Instead of claiming you're "innovative," include an example that explains how you increased company revenue by 150% with your ground-breaking strategies. Concrete examples and hard data add weight to your words and credibility to your claims.

Provide a Human Touch: Your Professional Journey

Here's where you breathe life into your professional persona. Perhaps your background in improv comedy makes you a master of thinking on your feet in high-pressure business situations. Or maybe your experience as a volunteer firefighter has honed your crisis management skills. These personal insights don't just make you relatable—they make you memorable.

Add Your Professional Call-to-Action

Don't leave your readers hanging - guide them to the next step. Whether you want them to reach out for networking or consider you for opportunities, make your desired action clear and accessible. Include your professional email or a link to your calendar for a seamless connection.

Hook, Line, and Sinker: Craft a Compelling Opening

Imagine your LinkedIn "About" section as a book in a bookstore. Now, picture only the first paragraph visible, with the rest hidden behind a "Read More" flap. That's exactly what you're dealing with on LinkedIn - your professional story, with just 300 characters on display before LinkedIn truncates it with a "...see more" link. This means you've got roughly 2-3 sentences to capture your audience's attention and entice them to click for more.

Why is this 300-character limit so crucial? Because in our fast-scrolling, information-saturated digital world, those first visible characters can make or break your chances of engagement. They're your digital storefront, your professional teaser trailer.

A compelling opening within these 300 characters can:

- Pique curiosity and encourage readers to click "See more"

- Immediately communicate your Unique Value Proposition (UVP)

- Set the tone for your professional brand

- Differentiate you from others in your field

- Encourage further engagement with your profile

Think of these 300 characters as your professional "elevator pitch" - concise, impactful, and designed to leave your audience wanting more. They should give a tantalizing glimpse of your full story, compelling viewers to click that "...see more" link and dive deeper into your professional narrative.

Remember, while your entire opening can certainly extend beyond 300 characters, those first visible characters are your golden opportunity to hook your audience. They need to be crafted with precision, offering just enough information to intrigue while creating a curiosity gap that can only be satisfied by reading more.

So, how do you make those 300 characters work overtime for your professional brand? Let's explore some strategies and examples from clients who have worked with our team of professional writers at Distinctive Career Services...

Be the Solution They Seek

Try leading with a sentence that makes it immediately clear to the reader that you understand their problems, challenges, and needs and are the ideal person to solve them. Here is an example from the "About" section of an executive who was targeting leadership roles with small and mid-size companies:

> Leading small-to-mid-size companies to a better tomorrow than today. That is the motivating goal that drives my executive leadership. Combined with my overarching belief that so-called business problems and challenges are just opportunities in disguise, requiring strategic and visionary leadership to recognize and capitalize on those opportunities, my career record is one of repeated and continuous success... *(353 characters)*

Open With a Defining Personal Belief

Lead with a statement that captures the essence of your value and sets the tone for everything that follows. Here is another example from the "About" section of a healthcare industry executive:

> With more than 20 years of executive leadership in healthcare, I offer a time-tested and proven record of innovation, inspirational leadership, and growth. Recognized as a visionary strategist who passionately energizes the organizations I lead, I possess a special talent for engaging stakeholders at all levels and driving through internal and external barriers to exceed corporate objectives where others have failed before. My definition of 'No' is different. No is just an opportunity to invite more people into the conversation, to find your way to Yes.... *(473 characters)*

Showcase What Others Say About You

A quote that another person has said or written about you can sometimes be an attention grabber. Here is an example of this strategy in action (this was the opening of the "About" section of a hospitality industry executive):

> Often referred to as a hospitality "Renaissance Man" by my friends and colleagues, I have dedicated my career to the craft of developing and managing top-rated boutique resort and hotel developments in business, vacation, and experiential de stinations....(251 characters)

Tell Your Origin Story

If you have an especially compelling "origin" story that explains what has shaped you into the leader you are today, you could try leading with that, as in this example executive's professionally written "About" section:

> As a first-generation American with immigrant parents, I grew up believing that with hard work and perseverance, no dream was beyond reach. My father came to America with just $50 borrowed dollars and a desire to pursue the American Dream. Working two full time jobs while he took classes and earned his master's degree, my father became a pharmacist and a real estate investor. It was from watching this journey that I was inspired to pursue my own career with such fervor, a career that has taken me in even more uncommon directions than my father's mix of the pharmaceutical industry and real estate....(499 characters)

Start with a Provocative Statement or Claim

An opening that surprises or challenges the reader can grab immediate attention. This could be a bold claim about your value proposition or a statement that demonstrates confidence in your abilities. It works well when you have a strong track record to back it up.

I don't believe in limits—only opportunities. For over two decades, I've transformed struggling businesses into market leaders, proving that no challenge is too great when met with bold strategy and decisive action...*(183 characters)*

Pose a Thought-Provoking Question

A question relevant to the reader's pain points or challenges draws them in by encouraging them to reflect. This approach works particularly well for profiles targeting a specific audience, especially if you're positioning yourself as a solution to their problem.

What if your business could not only survive but thrive in today's unpredictable market? For the last 18 years, I've helped organizations across five continents do exactly that, leveraging global experience to drive sustainable growth...*(200 characters)*

Share a Surprising Statistic or Fact

Starting with a relevant statistic can be an eye-opener for your audience and immediately make your profile more engaging, especially if you can tie it into your own experience or achievements.

Did you know that about 65% of new businesses fail within their first decade? My mission is to change that. With two decades of business development and strategic growth experience, I've helped startups not only survive but thrive, guiding them to become industry leaders within their first five years - a critical period when nearly half of new businesses typically fail.... *(371 characters)*

Start with a Strong Value Proposition

Lead with a direct statement of the value you offer, focusing on how you can solve the reader's problems or challenges. This strategy works well when you have a clear and compelling value proposition to convey right from the start.

> I specialize in helping businesses break into new markets, grow revenue streams, and establish lasting partnerships. Over my 18 years in global business development, I've consistently delivered results that exceed expectations, whether it's doubling revenue in underperforming regions or spearheading multimillion-dollar expansions...*(290 characters)*

Highlight an Unexpected or Unique Skill

If you have a unique skill or approach that sets you apart from others in your field, lead with it. This strategy works especially well if you can link it directly to a business outcome.

> Fluent in the language of global markets, I don't just speak English, Spanish, and French—I speak the language of business growth. My expertise in market expansion and cross-cultural collaboration has helped businesses thrive across Latin America, Asia, and Europe...*(227 characters)*

These examples are just the tip of the iceberg when it comes to crafting compelling openings. As you read through them, did any particular approach resonate with you? Perhaps you've been inspired to tell your own origin story or share a powerful statistic that encapsulates your impact.

Jot down any ideas that sparked your interest - we'll circle back to these when we pull everything together at the end of the chapter. Remember, the best opening is one that authentically represents you while immediately capturing your audience's attention.

Structuring Your Story for Impact

Your "About" section isn't just about what you say—it's also about how you present it. In today's fast-paced digital world, attention spans are shorter than ever, and first impressions are made in seconds. A well-structured "About" section can be the difference between a casual glance and an engaged read. By thoughtfully organizing your content, you're not just sharing information—you're crafting an experience that guides your reader through your professional narrative.

Let's explore some strategies to transform your "About" section from a dense block of text into an inviting, easily digestible showcase of your professional brand.

Bite-sized Brilliance

Break your content into easily digestible morsels. Aim for crisp, short paragraphs (2-3 sentences max) and punchy bullet points to make your "About" section scannable and reader-friendly. Consider these strategies:

- **Use topic sentences:** Start each paragraph with a clear, impactful statement that summarizes the main point.

- **Employ the "one idea per paragraph" rule:** This helps maintain focus and clarity.

- **Use white space:** Don't be afraid of breaks between paragraphs. They give the eye a rest and make your content less intimidating.

- **Craft concise bullet points:** Use them to highlight key skills, achievements, or unique selling points. Keep each point short, between 1-3 lines, if possible.

Visual Flair: Beyond Basic Bullets

Enhance your "About" section's visual appeal with unique elements. This can help your profile stand out and make key information more memorable.

Consider these techniques:

- **Use distinctive symbols:** Replace standard bullet points with arrows (⊠), stars (⊠), or checkmarks (√) to draw attention to important points.

- **Incorporate symbols strategically:** A single, relevant symbol can add personality to section headers. For example, use a ⊠ for "Career Goals" or a ⊠ for "Achievements".

- **Create visual breaks:** Use horizontal lines (⊠⊠⊠) to separate sections clearly.

- **Employ text formatting:** While LinkedIn doesn't allow for much text formatting, you can use ALL CAPS (very selectively, please) or "quotation marks" to emphasize select key phrases.

Remember, the goal is professional intrigue, not visual overload. Use these elements sparingly and consistently.

Signposts for Your Professional Journey

Guide your readers through your story with clear section headers. This enhances readability and helps your audience quickly locate the information that intrigues them most. Here's how to make the most of this strategy:

- **Choose clear, descriptive headers:** Use phrases that immediately convey what the section is about.

- **Keep headers consistent:** Use the same formatting for all headers (e.g., ALL CAPS or Symbol + Bold Text).

- **Order strategically:** Place your most compelling or relevant sections near the top.

- **Consider your audience:** Think about what information your target readers (e.g., recruiters, potential clients) would be most interested in, and create headers accordingly.

What do I mean by section headers? Here are some possibilities (you'll find many more in our online resources for readers). These headings are designed to be flexible, depending on your focus—whether you want to emphasize your leadership, problem-solving abilities, or personal passions. But please use them as inspiration. The sky is the limit.

WHAT I DO
HOW I ADD VALUE
MY LEADERSHIP STYLE
WHAT DRIVES ME
AREAS I EXCEL IN
WHAT MAKES ME DIFFERENT
MY UNIQUE APPROACH
PROBLEMS I SOLVE
MY CAREER JOURNEY
HOW I MAKE A DIFFERENCE
MY PASSION
WHAT YOU SHOULD KNOW ABOUT ME
CAREER HIGHLIGHTS
HOW I CAN HELP YOU
WHAT I'M KNOWN FOR
WHAT INSPIRES ME
WHAT I BELIEVE
MY CORE VALUES
WHERE I SEE MYSELF IN 5 YEARS
THE VALUE I BRING
MY FAVORITE QUOTE
HOW I APPROACH CHALLENGES
WHAT'S NEXT FOR ME
THE IMPACT I MAKE
MY GLOBAL PERSPECTIVE
WHY I LOVE WHAT I DO
WHAT SUCCESS MEANS TO ME
MY PROFESSIONAL MISSION
HOW I DRIVE RESULTS
INDUSTRIES I SPECIALIZE IN
MY BIGGEST ACHIEVEMENTS
WHAT I STAND FOR
WHAT EXCITES ME
MY VISION FOR THE FUTURE

SKILLS THAT SET ME APART
MY PERSONAL VALUES
HOW I SOLVE COMPLEX PROBLEMS
LESSONS I'VE LEARNED
WHAT SUCCESS LOOKS LIKE TO ME
HOW I APPROACH LEADERSHIP
MY STRATEGIC FOCUS
WHY I DO WHAT I DO
WHAT MOTIVATES ME
MY APPROACH TO TEAMWORK
CHALLENGES I'VE OVERCOME
HOW I EMPOWER OTHERS
AREAS I'M PASSIONATE ABOUT
THE RESULTS I DELIVER
WHAT YOU CAN EXPECT FROM ME
HOW I FOSTER GROWTH

By implementing these structuring techniques, you transform your "About" section from a wall of text into an engaging, easily navigable presentation of your professional brand. Remember to review your profile on both desktop and mobile devices to ensure your formatting looks good across all platforms.

Sealing the Deal: Crafting a Compelling Call-to-Action

Your "About" section isn't just a showcase—it's an invitation to engage. A strong closing with a clear Call-to-Action (CTA) can transform passive readers into active connections.

Your CTA should be concise, specific, and aligned with your professional goals. Whether you're seeking new opportunities, looking to expand your network, or offering your expertise, make it easy for readers to take the next step.

Including your professional email address in your "About" section can significantly boost engagement. It allows potential connections to reach out directly, bypassing LinkedIn's InMail limits and reducing barriers to communication. Remember, every profile view is an opportunity—your CTA is how you capitalize on it.

Here are a few example closings to inspire you.

"I'm always open to connecting with other professionals to discuss industry trends, innovations, and best practices. Feel free to reach out to me here on LinkedIn or via email at [email]."

"If you're interested in exploring ways we can collaborate or share insights, don't hesitate to get in touch. I'm available to connect at [email]."

"Building meaningful professional connections is important to me. I invite you to reach out to exchange ideas or discuss mutual interests. I can be reached at [email]."

"I'm always eager to connect with like-minded professionals for knowledge-sharing and networking. You can reach me at [email], and I look forward to hearing from you."

"I'm open to new opportunities for collaboration and professional growth. Feel free to reach out at [email] if you'd like to discuss how we can work together."

"I'm always interested in growing my network and exploring new ideas. Please connect with me here on LinkedIn or email me at [email] for a confidential conversation."

Remember, your "About" section is a living, breathing representation of your professional self. It should evolve as your career progresses and your goals shift. Don't shy away from experimenting with different structures and content to find what resonates best with your audience.

Steering Clear of Profile Pitfalls

Even the most seasoned professionals can stumble when it comes to crafting their LinkedIn "About" section. Let's shine a light on some common missteps so you can ensure your profile stands out for all the right reasons.

The Jargon Jungle: Overusing Industry Lingo and Buzzwords

While we've touched on this before, it's worth emphasizing again: keywords are crucial, but use them wisely. Your "About" section should read naturally, not like a laundry list of buzzwords. Aim to communicate your expertise clearly and engagingly, not to win at industry bingo.

Avoid turning your "About" section into a tag cloud or a mere list of "key skills." Instead, weave relevant keywords naturally into your narrative. When using specialized terms, provide context. This approach makes your profile more readable and positions you as an expert who can translate complex ideas into accessible language.

Remember, the goal is to tell your professional story, not just to be found in searches. Strike a balance between optimization and authenticity.

PRO TIP

After writing your "About" section, read it aloud. If it sounds like natural speech and effectively conveys your professional journey and value proposition, you've struck the right balance between keyword optimization and authentic communication.

The Corporate Robot: Being Too Formal or Impersonal

Your "About" section shouldn't read like a corporate memo, but it's not a casual social media post, either. The goal is to find that sweet spot between professionalism and personality. While it's essential to maintain a polished image, don't fall into the trap of sounding like an impersonal press release.

A common mistake is writing your "About" section in the third person, as you might for a formal bio. On LinkedIn, this can come across as stiff and disconnected. Remember, you're not introducing a stranger—you're presenting yourself. Writing in the first person helps create a direct, engaging connection with your reader.

That said, LinkedIn is still a professional platform. Unlike Facebook or Instagram, it's important to strike a balance between showing your personality and staying on topic. Share anecdotes and insights that highlight your professional life and goals, but avoid oversharing or using overly casual language that might fit better on other social platforms.

Aim for a conversational yet polished tone, as if you're speaking directly to a respected colleague or potential client. This makes you more relatable and memorable while maintaining the professionalism expected on LinkedIn. Your goal is to sound like the best, most articulate version of yourself—authentic, engaging, and credible.

The Wallflower: Failing to Differentiate Yourself

In a sea of professionals, what makes you unique? Avoid generic statements that could apply to anyone in your field. Instead, focus on your specific achievements, a unique combination of skills, or a particular approach to your work. Share the perspective or expertise that only you can offer.

For example, consider these two statements:

> Generic: "Experienced marketing professional with a passion for driving results."

> Differentiated: "As a marketing strategist with a background in behavioral psychology, I specialize in crafting campaigns that not only capture attention but also trigger action. My unique approach has led to an average 40% increase in customer engagement for B2B tech companies, turning casual browsers into loyal brand advocates."

The generic statement could apply to almost any marketing professional. The differentiated version, however, highlights a unique combination of skills (marketing and behavioral psychology), specifies a niche (B2B tech companies), and provides a concrete achievement (40% increase in customer engagement). It also gives a sense of the individual's particular approach to their work, making them stand out in a crowded field.

Remember, your goal is to paint a picture that only you can paint. What's your unique professional fingerprint? That's what will make recruiters, potential clients, or networking connections sit up and take notice.

The Ghost: Skipping the Section or Skimping on Content

Leaving your "About" section blank or providing only a sentence or two is a missed opportunity. This section is your chance to tell your professional story and make a strong first impression. Take full advantage of the 2,600-character limit to paint a comprehensive picture of who you are and what you bring to the table.

Let's address some common excuses for neglecting this crucial section:

"My experience speaks for itself."

Counter: While your work history is important, the "About" section is where you can provide context, highlight key achievements, and showcase your unique perspective. It's your chance to connect the dots of your career in a way that a simple list of jobs can't.

"I'm not a writer."

Counter: You don't need to be Shakespeare to write an effective "About" section. Focus on being clear and authentic. If you're really struggling, consider asking a trusted colleague for feedback or using AI tools to help generate ideas. The formulas provided in this chapter will be invaluable for breaking through writer's block.

"I'm not looking for a job right now."

Counter: Your LinkedIn profile isn't just for job hunting. It's a networking tool, a way to establish thought leadership and a platform for professional growth. A well-crafted "About" section can lead to speaking opportunities, collaborations, or clients, even if you're not actively job-seeking.

"I don't want to brag."

Counter: There's a difference between bragging and confidently stating your achievements. Your "About" section is the place to highlight your successes. Frame them in terms of the value you've provided to employers or clients.

"I don't know what to say."

Counter: Start with the basics: your current role, your key skills, and what you're passionate about professionally. Then add details about major achievements, your unique approach to your work, or your career goals. Remember, this is your professional story - you're the expert on you!

A blank or sparse "About" section can signal a lack of effort or engagement with your professional community. By taking the time to craft a comprehensive "About" section, you're investing in your professional brand and opening doors to new opportunities.

The Copy-Paste Trap: Duplicating Your Résumé Summary

While your LinkedIn profile and résumé may contain similar information, they serve different purposes. Simply copying your résumé summary into your "About" section misses the mark. Your LinkedIn About should be more personal, more detailed, and more engaging. It's an opportunity to expand on your experiences, share your professional philosophy, and connect with your audience in a way that a résumé summary simply can't.

Remember, your "About" section is often the first (and sometimes only) part of your profile that people read in detail. By avoiding these common mistakes, you're ensuring that this crucial section is working hard to present you in the best possible light. Take the time to craft an "About" section that is uniquely you - professional, engaging, and authentic.

"About" Section Blueprints for Success

Creating a compelling "About" section can feel like a daunting task, especially when you're staring at a blank page. Think of it like an architect using blueprints to guide construction - this section offers a set of formulas to help you build a standout "About" section.

These aren't rigid rules but rather flexible frameworks that you can adapt to your unique professional story. Each approach is designed to highlight different aspects of your career and personality, allowing you to choose the one that best aligns with your goals and style.

These formulas, inspired by successful profiles created at Distinctive Career Services, are designed to highlight different aspects of your career and personality. They're starting points - feel free to adapt them to your unique professional story.

Formula 1: The Value Proposition Focus

This formula emphasizes what you offer and the impact you create.

Opening: Start with a bold statement, a thought-provoking question, or a quick overview of your value proposition.

WHAT I DO / THE VALUE I BRING:
Outline your core expertise in 3-5 bullet points or short paragraphs, focusing on what you do and how it benefits others.

CAREER HIGHLIGHTS / KEY ACCOMPLISHMENTS:
Summarize a few of your top achievements or notable projects. Use bullet points for quick impact.

MY APPROACH / WHAT MAKES ME DIFFERENT:
Share a few sentences about your personal philosophy or approach to your work, showcasing your unique style.

CALL TO ACTION:
Close with an invitation to connect, keeping it discreet.

Example "Value Proposition" Profile:

What if your brand could expand globally and double its market share in just two years? That's exactly the kind of growth I help companies achieve. With 15+ years of experience in global marketing strategy, brand management, and digital transformation, I specialize in creating marketing plans that drive immediate results and long-term success.

WHAT I DO

I work with organizations looking to expand, build strong brands, and capture new audiences in competitive markets. My expertise lies in crafting tailored strategies that connect with consumers and drive revenue growth.

☒ GLOBAL MARKETING STRATEGY: I design and execute campaigns that align with both corporate goals and local market needs.
☒ BRAND DEVELOPMENT: I help businesses define their voice and build brands that resonate across cultures.
☒ DIGITAL MARKETING: I leverage data-driven insights to optimize SEO, content marketing, social media, and paid ads.
☒ MARKET EXPANSION: I guide companies in entering new international markets, adapting strategies to local environments.
☒ TEAM LEADERSHIP: I lead cross-functional teams focused on growth, collaboration, and problem-solving.

CAREER HIGHLIGHTS

My track record includes leading successful marketing initiatives for Fortune 500 companies and innovative start-ups. Notable achievements:

☒ Doubled market share in Europe for a major CPG brand by launching a targeted digital campaign.
☒ Led rebranding for a global tech company, increasing engagement by 30% and conversions by 25%.
☒ Expanded products into Latin America, driving $10M in new revenue

in one year.

⊠ Developed a digital marketing plan that tripled lead generation and increased web traffic by 150%.

MY APPROACH

I believe marketing is about building authentic connections. I lead with a collaborative approach that blends creative thinking with analytical precision. By aligning strategies with business objectives, I help brands resonate with their audiences.

WHY WORK WITH ME?

I bring global experience, strategic vision, and hands-on execution that consistently delivers growth. Whether you're looking to expand into new markets, enhance your brand, or optimize your digital presence, I have the expertise to help.

⊠ LET'S CONNECT

Interested in discussing marketing strategies or potential collaborations? Connect with me here on LinkedIn or reach out via email at [email].

Formula 2: The Storyteller Approach

This formula incorporates storytelling and personal elements to create a narrative flow.

Opening: Start with a personal story, career journey, or an attention-grabbing anecdote.

MY JOURNEY / CAREER HIGHLIGHTS:
Provide a brief overview of your professional journey, touching on key milestones.

WHAT I DO / THE PROBLEMS I SOLVE:
Highlight what you do and the key problems you solve for your clients or employers.

WHAT MAKES ME DIFFERENT / MY LEADERSHIP STYLE:
Describe your unique approach to work and what sets you apart.

CALL TO ACTION:
End with an invitation to connect.

Example "Storyteller" Profile:

> I grew up fascinated by how technology could reshape businesses, and that fascination turned into a career dedicated to helping companies evolve. Over the past 18 years, I've partnered with organizations across industries, guiding them through digital transformations that boost efficiency, reduce costs, and unlock new opportunities.
>
> ⬚ MY JOURNEY
>
> From startups to Fortune 500 companies, I've worked with leaders to help them reimagine processes and adopt technologies that move their businesses forward. I've navigated complex change initiatives, collaborated across departments, and empowered teams to embrace innovation.
>
> Along the way, I've built a reputation for being a problem-solver who turns challenges into opportunities. Whether it's revamping outdated systems or implementing cutting-edge solutions, I thrive on finding the right strategy to drive results.
>
> ⬚ WHAT I DO
>
> I specialize in digital transformation and business consulting, working with companies to:
>
> ⬚ OPTIMIZE OPERATIONS: Streamline processes to enhance efficien-

cy and reduce operational costs.

⬚ IMPLEMENT NEW TECHNOLOGIES: Help businesses integrate AI, automation, and data analytics into their operations.

⬚ LEAD CHANGE MANAGEMENT: Guide teams through organizational change, fostering buy-in and long-term success.

⬚ ENHANCE CUSTOMER EXPERIENCE: Improve customer engagement through innovative digital solutions.

⬚ CAREER HIGHLIGHTS

⬚ Revamped legacy systems for a global retail chain, reducing operational costs 25% and improving process efficiency.

⬚ Led a major automation project that saved a manufacturing firm over $5M annually and reduced production times 40%.

⬚ Guided the digital transformation of a mid-sized tech company, resulting in a 30% increase in customer satisfaction and a 20% boost in revenue.

⬚ MY APPROACH

I'm passionate about collaborating with teams to deliver tangible results. I believe that innovation happens when creativity meets practicality. My approach combines visionary thinking with a hands-on, results-oriented execution style. I guide businesses through change, ensuring solutions are sustainable and scalable.

⬚ WHY I'M DIFFERENT

I don't just implement new technologies—I help businesses rethink how they work. My goal is to ensure that every solution leads to meaningful, measurable improvements that drive growth and efficiency. I tailor every strategy to fit the specific needs of each organization I work with.

⬚ LET'S CONNECT

Interested in exploring how digital transformation can reshape your business? Let's connect here on LinkedIn, or feel free to reach out via email at [email].

Formula 3: The Expertise-Driven Formula

This formula emphasizes core skills and expertise to position the professional as a subject-matter expert.

Opening: Lead with a bold statement about your expertise.

AREAS OF EXPERTISE:
Use bullet points to list your key skills and areas of expertise.

CAREER MILESTONES:
Highlight a few key accomplishments to showcase your track record.

WHAT I BRING TO THE TABLE:
Explain how your skills directly benefit your clients or employers.

CALL TO ACTION:
Wrap up with a professional and discreet invitation to connect.

Example "Expertise-Driven" Profile:

With over a decade of experience in data science, machine learning, and advanced analytics, I specialize in turning complex data into actionable business insights that drive growth. I'm passionate about leveraging AI and predictive analytics to solve real-world business problems, optimize operations, and uncover hidden opportunities.

AREAS OF EXPERTISE

☑ Data Science & Machine Learning: Expertise in building predictive models, machine learning algorithms, and AI systems to improve decision-making and efficiency.

☑ Advanced Analytics: Skilled in data mining, statistical analysis, and developing analytical frameworks to generate insights that guide strategy and drive performance.

☑ Big Data Solutions: Proficient in big data technologies like Hadoop, Spark, and cloud-based analytics platforms, helping companies harness large datasets.

☑ Business Intelligence (BI): Strong focus on developing BI dashboards and reports to visualize key metrics and drive data-driven decisions.

☑ Team Leadership & Collaboration: Proven ability to lead cross-functional teams, working closely with stakeholders across departments to deliver tailored data solutions.

CAREER HIGHLIGHTS

☑ Led the development of a machine learning model for a major retail company, which reduced inventory costs by 20% through predictive demand forecasting.

☑ Designed and implemented a real-time data pipeline for a financial services firm, reducing data processing times by 50% and enabling faster decision-making.

☑ Drove a 30% increase in sales for a consumer goods company by developing a customer segmentation model that targeted high-value audiences.

☑ Launched a BI initiative that integrated data from multiple sources, improving reporting accuracy and reducing manual processing time by 40%.

HOW I ADD VALUE

I'm passionate about solving business problems through data and analytics. I bring a combination of technical expertise and business acumen to deliver solutions that drive measurable impact. My approach involves collaborating with teams across functions to ensure solutions align with business goals and are scalable for future growth.

MY APPROACH TO LEADERSHIP

I believe in fostering a collaborative team environment where creativity and innovation can thrive. I encourage my team to take ownership of their work, think strategically, and always consider the business impact of every solution we develop.

WHY WORK WITH ME?

I bring a unique blend of technical expertise and strategic insight, allowing me to build solutions that deliver real business value. Whether you need to optimize operations, enhance customer insights, or leverage AI for predictive analytics, I'm here to help.

⬜ LET'S CONNECT

If you're interested in discussing data science strategies, AI solutions, or how analytics can enhance your business, feel free to connect with me here or reach out at [email].

Formula 4: The Leadership-Focused Formula

This formula is ideal for senior executives or leaders looking to showcase their leadership philosophy.

Opening: Begin with a leadership philosophy or a quote that defines your leadership style.

MY LEADERSHIP STYLE:

Describe how you lead teams and what your leadership values are.

KEY ACCOMPLISHMENTS / TRANSFORMATIONAL LEADERSHIP:
Highlight leadership wins or major accomplishments.

HOW I MAKE A DIFFERENCE:
Focus on the specific impact you've had on organizations and teams.

CALL TO ACTION:
Finish with a discreet call to action for connecting.

Example "Leadership-Focused" Profile:

Great leaders don't just set goals—they inspire teams to exceed them. With over 20 years of leadership experience, I specialize in transforming organizations by streamlining operations, improving efficiency, and building high-performance teams that drive sustained success.

• MY LEADERSHIP STYLE
I believe that leadership is about empowering others to achieve their best. My approach centers on transparency, collaboration, and fostering an environment where innovation thrives. By focusing on strategic alignment and clear communication, I ensure that every member of the team understands their role in driving the company forward.

• AREAS OF EXPERTISE

⬚ OPERATIONAL EXCELLENCE: Expert in refining processes and implementing systems that boost efficiency, cut costs, and increase output.

⬚ ORGANIZATIONAL TRANSFORMATION: Proven track record of leading change initiatives that turn underperforming teams into high-functioning units.

⬚ LEAN SIX SIGMA: Certified in Lean Six Sigma methodologies, driving continuous improvement and waste reduction.

⬚ TEAM LEADERSHIP & DEVELOPMENT: Experienced in building, mentoring, and leading cross-functional teams to achieve both individual and organizational goals.

⬚ STRATEGIC PLANNING: Skilled in long-term planning that aligns operations with business goals to maximize productivity and profitability.

• CAREER HIGHLIGHTS

⬚ Turned around an underperforming division of a manufacturing company, increasing productivity by 40% and reducing operational costs by 25%.
   ⬚ Led the integration of operations during a major acquisition, ensuring smooth transitions and alignment of processes across multiple regions.

⬚ Implemented Lean Six Sigma practices that reduced waste by 30% and improved overall operational efficiency.

⬚ Mentored and developed future leaders within the organization, creating a pipeline of talent that has continued to drive success long after my direct involvement.

• HOW I LEAD CHANGE
Change is inevitable, but it's how you navigate it that makes the difference. My leadership style combines visionary thinking with practical, results-driven execution. I focus on understanding the needs of the business, rallying teams around shared goals, and driving initiatives that produce measurable, lasting improvements.

• WHY WORK WITH ME?
I bring decades of leadership experience, a proven record of transforming teams and processes, and a passion for driving operational excellence. If your organization is looking to streamline operations, implement new strategies, or navigate a major transformation, I can help guide the way.

> • LET'S CONNECT
> I'm always open to discussing leadership strategies and opportunities for collaboration. Reach out to me here on LinkedIn or via email at [email] to connect.

Formula 5: The Global Perspective Formula

Ideal for professionals with international experience or any individual with a global outlook.

Opening: Start by referencing your global experience or perspective.

GLOBAL EXPERIENCE / CAREER HIGHLIGHTS:
List your key international experiences or successes.

HOW I LEVERAGE MY GLOBAL EXPERIENCE:
Explain how your international experience benefits organizations or clients.

WHAT MAKES ME UNIQUE:
Highlight any language skills, cultural understanding, or other factors that set you apart globally.

CALL TO ACTION:
Close with a call to action for professional networking.

Example "Global Perspective" Profile:

> Growing up in a military family and living on four continents has shaped my global perspective and fueled my passion for international business. As I prepare to graduate with a B.S. in International Business, I'm excited to begin my career in a field that aligns with my love for cross-cultural communication, global markets, and strategic growth.
>
> GLOBAL EXPERIENCE & EXPERTISE

⬚ CULTURAL ADAPTABILITY: Having lived in Europe, Asia, and South America, I've developed an innate ability to navigate diverse cultural environments, bridging communication gaps and building relationships across borders.

⬚ INTERNATIONAL COURSEWORK: Through my academic studies, I've gained a deep understanding of global trade, international finance, and the complexities of entering new markets.

⬚ VOLUNTEER EXPERIENCE ABROAD: Volunteering in communities across Southeast Asia and Latin America has sharpened my leadership and collaboration skills in dynamic, multi-cultural settings.

⬚ CROSS-BORDER COLLABORATION: Skilled in fostering relationships with diverse groups, from classmates to colleagues in international projects, ensuring alignment and shared success.

⬚ STRATEGIC THINKING: Adept at analyzing global market trends and identifying opportunities for business expansion, driven by both classroom and hands-on experience.

KEY ACHIEVEMENTS

⬚ Led a student consulting project that analyzed market entry strategies for a U.S. company expanding into Southeast Asia, resulting in actionable recommendations presented to business leaders.

⬚ Volunteered in Peru for six months, working alongside local communities to improve small-scale agricultural business practices and foster sustainable growth.

⬚ Completed coursework in international business law, global supply chain management, and emerging market economies, gaining a holistic view of the factors influencing global trade.

MY GLOBAL PERSPECTIVE

Having moved and traveled extensively with my military family, I learned early on that understanding and respecting cultural differences is key to thriving in international environments. These experiences, coupled with my academic background and volunteer work, have prepared me to navigate the complexities of global business and contribute to organizations aiming for cross-border success.

WHY WORK WITH ME?
I offer a unique blend of international experience, academic knowledge, and cultural adaptability that positions me well to succeed in the global business arena. Whether working on market expansion strategies or fostering cross-cultural partnerships, I am eager to apply my skills and contribute to the growth of forward-thinking organizations.

LET'S CONNECT
As I look forward to beginning my international business career, I'm excited to connect with professionals and organizations that share my passion for global growth and collaboration. Feel free to reach out to me here on LinkedIn or via email at [email].

Formula 6: The Passion-Driven Formula

This formula focuses on personal passion and commitment to a specific cause or industry.

Opening: Lead with a statement about your passion or commitment to your industry.

MY PASSION / WHY I DO WHAT I DO:
Describe why you're passionate about your field or what motivates you.

WHAT I BRING TO THE INDUSTRY:
Outline your contributions or unique approach.

HOW I MAKE A DIFFERENCE:
Explain the impact you've made in your field.

CALL TO ACTION:
End with a simple, professional call to action.

Example "Passion-Driven" Profile:

I've always believed that businesses can be a powerful force for good, and that conviction has driven my passion for sustainability and environmental stewardship. With a background in environmental science and consulting, I help organizations not only meet their sustainability goals but exceed them by integrating innovative, eco-friendly practices into their operations.

WHAT DRIVES ME
My passion lies in helping businesses transform their operations to be more sustainable, not just because it's the right thing to do but because it leads to long-term success. I believe that sustainability isn't just a buzzword—it's a strategic advantage that can drive innovation, increase efficiency, and create lasting value for both companies and the communities they serve.

WHAT I DO
I work with companies to develop and implement sustainability strategies that balance environmental responsibility with profitability. My areas of focus include:

• SUSTAINABILITY STRATEGY DEVELOPMENT: Crafting tailored plans that reduce carbon footprints, minimize waste, and improve resource efficiency.

• RENEWABLE ENERGY SOLUTIONS: Helping businesses transition to renewable energy sources, from solar to wind power, to reduce reliance on fossil fuels.

• CIRCULAR ECONOMY MODELS: Designing and implementing circular economy practices, such as recycling, repurposing, and waste-to-energy initiatives.

• ENVIRONMENTAL COMPLIANCE: Ensuring companies meet regulatory standards while adopting best practices that protect the environment and reduce risk.

CAREER HIGHLIGHTS

• Reduced operational waste by 35% for a manufacturing client through the introduction of a circular waste management system, saving the company over $1M annually.

• Guided the transition of a mid-sized corporation to 100% renewable energy, reducing their carbon footprint by 40% in the first year.

• Developed sustainability plans for a Fortune 500 client that resulted in LEED certification for their corporate headquarters.

• Led a cross-functional team to implement energy-saving solutions across five international offices, resulting in a 20% reduction in energy consumption.

MY APPROACH

I am deeply committed to finding solutions that benefit both businesses and the planet. I work closely with teams across departments to foster collaboration and ensure that every sustainability initiative is actionable and scalable. My hands-on approach allows me to guide organizations through the complexities of adopting sustainable practices, while always focusing on measurable, impactful outcomes.

WHY WORK WITH ME?

Sustainability is more than a career for me—it's my calling. I combine my technical expertise with a deep commitment to environmental advocacy, ensuring that every project I work on contributes to a more sustainable and equitable world. If your company is ready to take the next step in its sustainability journey, I'm here to help you achieve real, measurable progress.

LET'S CONNECT

If you're interested in discussing how sustainability can drive both environmental and business success, feel free to connect with me here or reach out via email at [email]. I look forward to collaborating with like-minded professionals who share my passion for making a difference.

Using AI Tools to Enhance Your "About" Section

AI tools like ChatGPT can be powerful allies in crafting your LinkedIn "About" section. These tools can help generate ideas, overcome writer's block, and even provide a starting point for your content. However, it's crucial to use them wisely and maintain your authentic voice. Let's explore how to leverage AI effectively in your "About" section creation process.

AI PROMPTS FOR WRITING YOUR ABOUT SECTION

"I'm a [your profession] with [X] years of experience. I am ready for my next career step and am pursuing [Job Title] opportunities. Here is the text of my résumé: [paste résumé]. I'm working on crafting my LinkedIn profile "About" section and want help with an engaging opening. Here's an example of an opening that I like: [paste example opening]. Can you suggest 5 unique openings written in a similar style for my LinkedIn "About" section that highlight my expertise and grab attention?"

- "Based on my role as a [your job title] in [your industry], I'm aiming to highlight my key skills and achievements in my LinkedIn "About" section. Here's a summary of my major projects and accomplishments: [list 3-5 key achievements]. Can you suggest 10 impactful ways to present these in my "About" section, using specific metrics and action verbs?"

- "I want to incorporate a brief anecdote in my "About" section that demonstrates my problem-solving skills in [your field]. Here are three challenging situations I've faced in my career: [briefly describe 3 situations]. Can you help me craft a concise, engaging story for each that highlights how I overcame the challenge and the results I achieved?"

- "I'm showcasing my leadership style in my "About" section. I would describe my approach as [your leadership style, e.g., 'collaborative and results-driven']. Here are a few examples of how I've applied this style: [provide 2-3 examples]. Can you suggest 5 ways to describe this leadership approach using vivid language and avoiding clichés?"

- "I want to incorporate data about my career achievements in my LinkedIn "About" section. Here are my top 3 accomplishments with their associated metrics: [list achievements with data]. Can you suggest 3 creative ways to present this information that will grab a recruiter's attention and demonstrate my impact?"

AI PROMPTS LEVERAGING THE FORMULAS

Value Proposition Focus Formula: "I'm using the Value Proposition Focus formula [explain formula] for my "About" section. Based on my résumé [paste résumé] and target job of [job title], can you suggest 3-5 bullet points for the 'WHAT I DO / THE VALUE I BRING' section that highlight my unique skills and the problems I solve for employers?"

- **Storyteller Approach Formula:** "I'm applying the Storyteller Approach formula [explain formula] to my "About" section. Here's a brief overview of my career journey: [provide career summary]. Can you help me craft an engaging opening paragraph that tells the story of my professional evolution and sets the stage for why I'm the ideal candidate for [target job]?"

- **Expertise-Driven Formula:** "I'm using the Expertise-Driven formula [explain formula] for my "About" section. Based on my experience in [your field] and these key achievements [list 3-5 achievements], can you suggest a compelling opening statement and 5 areas of expertise that position me as a subject matter expert in my field?"

Inject AI-Generated Content With Personal Touches

Remember, the goal is to use AI as a tool to enhance your creativity and overcome writer's block, but the final product should always sound genuinely like you. Your unique experiences, voice, and perspective are what will truly make your "About" section stand out. Here are some strategies for infusing AI-generated content with personal touches:

- **Personalize with Specific Examples:** After receiving AI-generated content, inject specific examples from your own experience. For instance, if the AI suggests you're "skilled at leading cross-functional teams," add a brief example like, "such as when I led a team of engineers and marketers to launch our flagship product in record time."

- **Incorporate Your Professional Jargon:** Add industry-specific terms or company names that the AI might not know but are relevant to your experience. This adds credibility and shows insider knowledge.

- **Adjust the Tone:** If the AI-generated content doesn't match your personal communication style, adjust the language. If you're known for your direct communication, make sentences more concise. If you have a more collaborative style, soften any overly assertive language.

- **Add Personal Touches:** Include references to your professional philosophy or approaches that are uniquely yours. For example, "I believe in the power of 'learning by doing,' a philosophy I've applied in every role from junior developer to CTO."

- **Fact-Check Achievements:** If the AI suggests impressive achievements, ensure they accurately reflect your experience. Adjust numbers or scope to match your actual accomplishments.

- **Maintain Consistency with Your Brand:** Ensure the language aligns with your personal brand across other platforms. If you're known for your sense of humor, add a touch of wit where appropriate.

- **Seek Feedback:** After refining the AI-generated content, share it with a trusted colleague who knows your work style. Ask if it sounds authentically like you and accurately represents your professional persona.

AI is a tool to assist you, not to define you. The most compelling LinkedIn profiles are those that showcase the unique combination of skills, experiences, and personality that only you possess. By thoughtfully blending AI-generated content with your personal insights and style, you create a profile that is both polished and authentically you. This approach allows you to harness the efficiency of AI while ensuring that your true professional self shines through.

As you refine your profile, always ask yourself: "Does this sound like me at my best?" If the answer is yes, you're on the right track to creating a LinkedIn presence that will resonate with your network and potential employers alike.

Your Action Plan for Crafting Your "About" Section

Your LinkedIn "About" section is the heart of your professional narrative - it's where you transform from a name and a title into a unique, valuable professional with a story to tell. You've learned the key elements of a standout "About" section, from formulas to hooks to value propositions. Now, it's time to weave these elements into a compelling story that captivates your audience and showcases your professional worth.

Don't let your "About" section be an afterthought - it's your chance to make a powerful first impression. Let's turn your professional journey into an engaging narrative that opens doors! Ready to revamp your LinkedIn

"About" section? Here's your action plan:

- Select the "About" section formula that best fits your career stage and goals (e.g., Value Proposition, Storyteller, Expertise-Driven). Outline the key elements you want to include based on your chosen formula.

- Craft your opening. Write 3-5 different attention-grabbing opening sentences, remembering that the first 300 characters are crucial. Ask a trusted colleague for feedback on which is most effective.

- Articulate your unique value proposition and key achievements. Include 2-3 quantifiable accomplishments that demonstrate your impact. Break up your text into short, digestible paragraphs, using bullet points or symbols to highlight key information.

- Incorporate keywords and refine your content. Weave in relevant industry keywords naturally throughout your "About" section. Use AI tools like ChatGPT for alternative phrasings if needed, but always personalize the content. Read your section aloud to check for flow and authenticity.

- Edit and optimize. Ruthlessly edit to stay within the 2600-character limit while maintaining impact. Ensure your "About" section is engaging from start to finish and truly sounds like you.

- Implement, monitor, and refine. After making changes, monitor your profile views and connection requests for a month. Set a reminder to review and refresh your "About" section quarterly. Consider asking for feedback from 2-3 industry professionals to refine your message further.

Remember, your "About" section is not just a summary - it's your professional story, your pitch, and your handshake all rolled into one. It's an ever-evolving piece of content that should grow and change as you do. Each word you choose is an opportunity to connect with potential employers, clients, or collaborators. Your compelling LinkedIn narrative is just a few edits away - let's bring your professional story to life!

Chapter Eight

Crafting Your Professional Narrative

Mastering the "Experience" and "Education" Sections

Your "Experience" and "Education" sections are more than just a list of jobs and degrees—they're the backbone of your professional narrative. These sections weave together the story of your career journey, showcasing your growth, accomplishments, and lasting impact. They form the foundation on which recruiters and hiring managers build their understanding of your skills, potential, and value.

Why are these sections so critical? Simple. They offer tangible proof of your abilities—showing how you've applied your skills, adapted, and grown over time. While your profile photo and headline might capture a viewer's attention, it's in the "Experience" and "Education" sections where they truly engage with your professional journey. Each role, project, and educational milestone tells a chapter in your evolving career, providing insights into your expertise, problem-solving capabilities, and track record of driving results.

Understanding LinkedIn Recruiter: How It Interprets Your Background

Ever wondered how recruiters actually find candidates on LinkedIn? It's not as mysterious as you might think! Understanding how LinkedIn Recruiter interprets your experience and education is key to boosting your visibility with potential employers.

The Anatomy of LinkedIn Recruiter

LinkedIn Recruiter is like a high-tech casting director for the professional world. It uses a complex set of filters and search options to help recruiters find the perfect candidates for their roles. However, unlike a human reader who might skim your profile, LinkedIn Recruiter methodically analyzes every detail you provide.

Date-Driven Decisions

One of the key ways LinkedIn Recruiter interprets your experience is through dates. It's like a time-traveling detective, piecing together your professional timeline based on the start and end dates you provide in your "Experience" section. Here's what it's looking at:

- **Total Years of Experience:** This isn't just a ballpark figure. LinkedIn Recruiter calculates this precisely, starting from the earliest job entry in your profile.

- **Time in Current Role:** It checks how long you've been in your current position, which can be a key factor for recruiters looking for either fresh talent or seasoned professionals.

- **Company Tenure:** The tool also calculates how long you've been with your current company, which can indicate loyalty and career progression.

The Education Equation

Your educational background isn't just a footnote—it's a significant part of the equation for LinkedIn Recruiter. Here's how it factors in:

- **Degree Levels:** Whether you have a Bachelor's, Master's, or Ph.D. can be a crucial filter for many positions.

- **Fields of Study:** Your major or specialization can be a key search criterion for recruiters looking for specific expertise.

- **Graduation Dates:** Recent graduates or those with a certain number of years post-graduation can be filtered based on this information.

Keyword Conundrum

While dates and structured data are important, as we've already discussed in detail, don't underestimate the power of keywords. LinkedIn Recruiter doesn't just look at job titles—it scans your entire profile for relevant terms. Think of it as a linguistic treasure hunt, where the right words can lead recruiters straight to your profile.

The Visibility Verdict

Now, you might be wondering, "What if I leave out some information?" Here's the truth: omissions can make you invisible. If you don't provide dates or key details, you might not show up in filtered searches. It's like trying to win a game of hide-and-seek by hiding too well—you won't be found.

Navigating Age Concerns

There's an elephant in the room we need to address: age discrimination. While it's illegal and unethical, it's a concern for many professionals. Some choose to limit their work history to the last 10-20 years or remove graduation dates. It's a personal decision, but remember that LinkedIn Recruiter needs dates to function effectively. I'll dive deeper into strategies for different career stages later in this chapter.

Balancing Algorithm Appeal and Human Engagement

Think of LinkedIn Recruiter as your profile's first audience. It's a powerful tool that scans countless profiles, analyzing your experience, career timeline, and keywords to identify potential candidates. Understanding how it works lets you craft a profile that's both visible and relevant in search results.

But here's the thing: while LinkedIn Recruiter is your gateway, it's not your final destination. Your ultimate goal? Impressing the human recruiter who'll review your full profile. In the coming sections, we'll show you how to optimize your profile for both the algorithm and the person behind it.

It's like learning to speak two languages fluently – the language of AI and the language of human recruiters. Master this dual approach, and you'll stand out in even the most competitive job markets. Ready to craft a professional narrative that resonates with both tech and people? Let's dive in and set the stage for your career success!

Structuring Your "Experience" Entries

Struggling to decide what to include in your "Experience" section? Let's break it down together. Think of it as creating a reverse-chronological high-light reel of your career.

Double-Duty Résumé?

Here's the million-dollar question that almost everyone asks: Can't you just copy and paste from your résumé to complete the "Experience" section of your LinkedIn profile?

Well, yes and no.

If your résumé is keyword-rich and well-written to tell a compelling story of your contributions, then absolutely use it as a starting point. But remember, LinkedIn is different. You'll want to adapt your content to fit the more conversational, first-person tone that works best on this platform. Think of it as translating your résumé from "formal business speak" to "professional conversation at a networking event."

For example, here is an entry from the résumé of a software engineering director:

DIRECTOR OF SOFTWARE ENGINEERING | Acme Corporation, City, State | May 2022 to Present

Led international expansion and technological transformation, managing a global, cross-functional team of 25+. Provided strategic oversight to develop cloud infrastructure and modernize mobile applications, positioning Acme as a leader in the industry.

Key Contributions:

- **Global Expansion & Cloud Infrastructure:** Directed development of automated cloud infrastructure and supported market expansion into Brazil, Mexico, Canada, Argentina, and England. Redesigned AWS infrastructure for scalable, multi-region deployments and disaster recovery.

- **Mobile Application Development:** Unified Android and iOS tech stacks, streamlining development and enabling global app deployments.

- **Cybersecurity Enhancements:** Strengthened security through Single Sign-On, code scanning, password vaults, and role-based access, enhancing security posture and operational efficiency.

- **Cost Optimization & Funding:** Reduced expenses through AWS optimization and secured $500k in funding through the AWS Migration Acceleration Program, driving financial efficiency.

- **Agile Implementation:** Championed Agile methodologies, improving project visibility, prioritization, and team delivery timelines.

Here is the same entry rewritten for LinkedIn:

Director of Software Engineering | Acme Corporation | May 2022 to Present

At Acme Corporation, I lead a global team of over 25 engineers, driving our international expansion and transforming our technology landscape. My focus has been on building cutting-edge cloud infrastructure, modernizing mobile applications, and boosting operational efficiency across markets.

⬚ Driving Global Expansion & Modernizing Infrastructure: One of my proudest achievements has been spearheading Acme's expansion into five key international markets: Brazil, Mexico, Canada, Argentina, and England. This involved designing a modern, automated cloud infrastructure and completely reworking our AWS setup to ensure scalable, multi-region deployments and robust disaster recovery processes.

⬚ Revolutionizing Mobile App Development: I led the effort to streamline our mobile development by unifying the Android and iOS tech stacks into one code base. This change has made global app deployments faster and more efficient while simplifying our overall development process.

⬚ Enhancing Cybersecurity & Efficiency: Security has been a top priority. I introduced Single Sign-On, automated code scanning, and role-based access controls, replacing outdated manual processes. These improvements have strengthened our security posture and significantly boosted our operational efficiency.

⬚ Optimizing Costs & Securing Funding: By optimizing our AWS infrastructure and storage, we've significantly cut costs. I also secured $500k in funding through the AWS Migration Acceleration Program, which has been instrumental in fueling our growth and technological advancements.

⬚ Championing Agile & Team Empowerment: I'm passionate about building agile teams that deliver. I implemented Agile methodologies across our engineering processes, leading to better project visibility, improved prioritization, and faster delivery times. This has fostered a culture of continuous improvement and innovation.

Why the LinkedIn Version Works:

- **Conversational Tone:** The LinkedIn version is more conversational and approachable, which fits the platform's professional yet informal style.

- **Clear Achievements**: It still conveys the core achievements but in a less formal and more narrative-driven way, making it engaging.

- **Bullet Points for Clarity**: The use of headers and bullet points improves readability, especially for online profiles.

- **Keyword Optimization**: Similar to the résumé, the LinkedIn version seamlessly incorporates relevant keywords such as "global expansion," "cloud infrastructure," "AWS," "mobile application development," "cybersecurity," "Agile methodologies," and "cost optimization," ensuring that the profile remains searchable and optimized for recruiters and industry professionals, while still reading naturally.

Here are a few more considerations to keep in mind when using your résumé as the foundation for your LinkedIn content.

- **Public Visibility:** Unlike your résumé, which is usually tailored for a specific job or company, your LinkedIn profile is publicly available to a wide audience. This broader exposure requires careful consideration:

  ○ **Confidentiality:** Be mindful of any sensitive or proprietary information. Avoid disclosing details that could violate confidentiality agreements or company policies.

  ○ **Legal and Ethical Boundaries:** Carefully review your content to ensure it doesn't cross any legal or ethical lines. This might include removing or rewording statements about former employers or colleagues that could be construed as defamatory or unprofessional.

  ○ **Cultural Sensitivity:** With a global audience, be aware of cultural differences and avoid language or examples that might be misinterpreted or offensive in different cultural contexts.

- **Consistency:** While you can and should adapt your content for LinkedIn, ensure that the core information – job titles, dates, and key responsibilities – remains consistent with your résumé. Discrepancies between the two could raise red flags for potential employers.

By thoughtfully adapting your résumé content for LinkedIn, you can create a profile that not only showcases your professional story effectively but also respects the platform's public nature and diverse audience. This approach allows you to leverage the strengths of both your résumé and LinkedIn, creating a comprehensive and professional online presence.

Chronological Choreography: Setting the Stage

Start with your most recent role and work backward. This isn't just convention; it's what recruiters expect, and it allows them to see your career progression quickly. Each entry should include:

- **Company name:** Make sure this links to the company's LinkedIn page. It's like tagging them in your career story, and it often adds their logo to your profile for a visual boost.

- **Your title:** Remember our keyword chat? This is a great place to expand on your official title. For example, "Marketing Manager | Digital Strategy Lead" gives a clearer picture of your role.

- **Dates of employment:** Be honest here, but if you're concerned about short stints or gaps, using just years rather than months and years can often smooth things out visually.

Company Snapshot: Setting the Scene

If you worked for the next Apple or Google before they were household names, provide a brief description of the company. Think elevator pitch: "An emerging tech startup disrupting the smart home industry." This gives context to your role and achievements.

Your Role in the Spotlight: Crafting Your Performance

Start with a concise summary of your role and key responsibilities. Think of this as the opening scene of your performance in this role. What was your mission? What were you brought in to do?

PRO TIP

Research shows that stories are 22 times more memorable than facts alone. For each role, craft a concise narrative that outlines a challenge you faced, the action you took, and the results you achieved.

Compelling Bullet Points: Your Career Highlight Reel

Now it's time for the main act: your achievements. This is where you really get to shine.

Each bullet point in your "Experience" section is like a scene in your career movie. You want each one to be impactful and memorable and to showcase your best performances.

The Art of Storytelling: The CAR and STAR Methods

Want to know the trick to writing bullet points that grab a recruiter's attention? It's all about telling a mini-story.

Ever watched a great movie where the hero faces a challenge, takes action, and achieves an amazing result? That's precisely what you want your bullet points to do. Think of each achievement as a mini-movie of your professional life. To script these career highlights, you've got two powerful tools at your disposal: the CAR (Challenge-Action-Result) or STAR (Situation-Task-Action-Result) method. These techniques help you structure your achievements into compelling narratives that grab a recruiter's attention.

For example:

> "Faced with declining customer retention rates (Challenge), I
> developed a new loyalty program (Action) that increased cus-

tomer retention by 25% in six months (Result)."

Quantify Your Impact: Numbers Speak Louder Than Words

Whenever possible, use numbers to quantify your achievements. It's the difference between saying, "I improved sales" and "I increased sales by 50% year-over-year, adding $2M to the company's bottom line." Which one makes you sit up and take notice?

Action-Packed Language: Lights, Camera, Action Verbs!

Start each bullet point with a strong action verb. Instead of "Was responsible for managing a team," try "Led a cross-functional team of 10 to deliver project 20% under budget." It's more dynamic and gives a clearer picture of your impact.

Keyword Choreography: Dancing to the Recruiter's Tune

Remember the chapter about keywords? Weave them naturally into your bullet points. If you're targeting roles in digital marketing, make sure terms like "SEO," "content strategy," or "marketing automation" appear in your achievements where relevant.

Transferable Skills: Your Career Superpower

Highlight skills that can transfer across industries or roles. Problem-solving, leadership, communication – these are valuable in almost any position. Show how you've used these skills to drive results.

Relevance is Key: Tailoring Your Highlight Reel

Focus on achievements and responsibilities most relevant to your current career goals. If you're moving from sales to marketing, emphasize the marketing-related aspects of your sales roles.

Navigating Plot Twists: Unconventional Career Paths

Not every career follows a straight line, and that's okay. Here's how to handle some common plot twists in your professional story:

Addressing Gaps: Honesty with a Positive Spin

Got gaps in your employment history? Don't panic! Here's how to address them. Rather than trying to hide them, address them honestly and positively.

LinkedIn now offers a "Career Break" feature – use it! Whether you were caring for family, traveling, or pursuing education, frame it as a period of growth and learning. For example:

> "Career Break: Pursued advanced certification in project management while volunteering as a team leader for Habitat for Humanity, enhancing both technical and leadership skills."

The Art of Minimalism: Sometimes Less is More

If you have several short-term positions or gaps, consider listing just the years of employment rather than months and years. This can create a cleaner, less choppy timeline.

Expanding Your Cast: Including Non-Traditional Experiences

Don't discount freelance work, consulting gigs, or significant volunteer roles. These can fill gaps and demonstrate valuable skills and experiences. List them as you would any other job, focusing on your contributions and achievements.

Partner with AI as Your Co-Writer

Struggling to find the right words to describe your experiences? AI can be your brainstorming buddy.

**AI PROMPTS FOR WRITING EXPERIENCE DESCRIP-
TIONS**

- "I was a [Your Job Title] at [Company Name], a [brief company description], from [Start Date] to [End Date]. My main responsibilities included [List 3-5 Key Responsibilities]. Some of my key achievements were [List 2-3 Major Accomplishments with metrics if possible]. Can you help me write 5 impactful bullet points for my LinkedIn profile that highlight my achievements in this role, using the CAR (Challenge-Action-Result) method and incorporating relevant keywords for [Your Industry/Field]?"

- "I'm transitioning from [Current Industry] to [Target Industry]. My current role is [Current Job Title] at [Company Name], where I've been working since [Start Date]. My key responsibilities include [List 3-4 Main Duties]. I'm targeting positions as a [Target Job Title]. Based on this information, can you suggest 6-8 ways to describe my achievements and responsibilities that would be relevant to my target role? Please include industry-specific keywords and focus on transferable skills."

- "In my role as [Job Title] at [Company Name], I led a project that increased [Specific Metric, e.g., sales, efficiency, customer satisfaction] by [Percentage/Number] over [Time Period]. The challenge we faced was [Describe the Problem]. Can you help me craft 3 different versions of a compelling bullet point that showcases this achievement using the STAR (Situation-Task-Action-Result) method? Please vary the action verbs and incorporate relevant keywords for [Your Industry/Field]."

- "I'm updating my LinkedIn profile for a [Target Job Title] role. Here's a job description for my target position: [Paste Full Job Description]. Based on this, can you: a) Identify 10 relevant keywords or phrases I should try to incorporate into my "Experience" section, b) Suggest 5 skills mentioned in the job description that I should highlight in my current role descriptions, c) Provide 3 examples of how I might reframe my current responsibilities to align with this job's requirements"

- "As a [Your Job Title] at [Company Name], I managed a team of [Number] people across [Number] departments/countries. We successfully [Brief Description of a Major Project or Achievement]. Can you help me write: a) A brief introductory paragraph (2-3 sentences) summarizing my role and its impact on the organization, b) 4-5 bullet points that highlight my leadership skills, the project's impact, and any relevant metrics, c) A closing sentence that summarizes my overall contribution to the company. Please incorporate leadership-focused keywords and phrases that would be relevant for senior roles in [Your Industry]."

Remember, as I have repeatedly stressed, AI is a tool to help you brainstorm and refine your ideas. Always review and personalize the content to ensure it accurately reflects your experiences and voice.

Showcasing Your Educational Journey

Your educational background is more than just a list of degrees—it's a testament to your knowledge, skills, and commitment to learning. In this section, we'll explore how to transform your "Education" section into a powerful tool that enhances your professional narrative and catches the eye of both AI recruitment tools and human recruiters.

Crafting Your Educational Story

Think of your "Education" section as the origin story of your professional journey. It's where you lay the foundation for the skills and knowledge that define your career. Here's how to make it shine:

- **Prioritize Relevance Over Chronology:** Unlike your work experience, your education doesn't need to be in strict chronological order.

- **Showcase Your Crown Jewel:** Place your most relevant or impressive qualification at the top. For instance, if you're a software engineer with a recent Machine Learning certification, that might take precedence over your earlier Computer Science degree.

- **Tailor to Your Audience:** Align your educational highlights with your current career goals. If you're pivoting industries, emphasize the education that supports your new direction.

Details That Dazzle

Don't just list your degree—bring it to life:

- **Full, Formal Titles:** Instead of "BA in English," opt for "Bachelor of Arts in English Literature, concentration in Creative Writing."

- **Honors and Achievements:** "Summa Cum Laude" or "Dean's List" can set you apart.

- **Relevant Coursework:** Highlight courses that align with your target roles. "Advanced Data Structures and Algorithms" speaks directly to a software engineering position.

- **Projects and Research:** Briefly mention significant projects. "Thesis: Artificial Intelligence Applications in Healthcare" can pique a recruiter's interest.

To Date or Not to Date?

The inclusion of dates in your "Education" section is a nuanced decision that can impact how recruiters perceive your profile. Here's a balanced approach:

- **Graduation Dates:** For completed degrees, including the graduation year provides context without being overly specific. For instance, "Bachelor of Science in Computer Science, 2018".

- **Ongoing Education:** If you're currently pursuing a degree, use the format "Expected 2025" or "2022 - Present" to show active engagement in learning.

- **Early Career Professionals:** Including recent graduation dates can highlight your fresh knowledge and skills.

- **Experienced Professionals:** Consider omitting dates for degrees obtained more than 15-20 years ago to mitigate potential age bias. Your work experience will often speak louder than your education timeline.

- **Start Dates:** Generally, start dates for degrees are less crucial. Focus on completion or expected completion dates unless the duration of study is particularly relevant to your field.

Remember, consistency is key. Whatever approach you choose, apply it uniformly across your "Education" section. I'll explore more strategies for navigating age-related concerns later in this chapter, providing guidance for professionals at all career stages.

PRO TIP

By visiting your school's LinkedIn page and clicking on the Alumni tab, you can find and connect with fellow alumni working in your target industry or company. This shared background can be a great icebreaker for networking and can potentially lead to job opportunities. Studies show that referrals from alumni are 2.6 times more likely to be hired than other candidates.

Leveraging Additional Education-Related Sections

LinkedIn offers more than just the standard "Education" section. Let's explore how to use these additional features to create a comprehensive picture of your learning journey.

The Power of "Courses"

The "Courses" section is your opportunity to showcase ongoing learning and specific skills:

- **Relevance is Key:** List courses that directly relate to your current career goals or showcase in-demand skills.

- **Context Matters:** Briefly explain how each course enhanced your professional toolkit. "Advanced Python for Data Science: Deepened expertise in predictive modeling and data visualization."

- **Keep it Current:** Regularly update this section to demonstrate your commitment to continuous learning.

"Licenses & Certifications:" Your Professional Passport

LinkedIn reports that profiles with certifications receive twice as many profile views. This section validates your expertise and shows your dedication to professional growth:

- **Industry Recognition:** Prioritize certifications that are well-regarded in your field.

- **Details Matter:** Include the issuing organization, date obtained, and expiration date (if applicable).

- **Link to Verify:** Many certifications offer a verification link—use it to add credibility to your profile.

Many people mistakenly list courses as certifications on their LinkedIn profiles. Courses, including online ones like LinkedIn Learning, should be placed in the "Courses "section. Certifications, on the other hand, are professional credentials awarded by industry-recognized organizations after passing exams or meeting specific criteria.

Keyword Optimization: The Language of Recruiters and AI

Remember our discussion about LinkedIn Recruiter? Here's where we put that knowledge into action:

- **Industry-Specific Terminology:** Use the language of your industry. For a marketing professional, "Inbound Marketing Certification" resonates more than "Online Marketing Course."

- **Skill-Based Keywords:** Integrate keywords that align with your skills section. If you've listed "Data Analysis" as a skill, mentioning

"Advanced Statistics for Data Science" in your Courses section reinforces this.

- **Avoid Keyword Stuffing:** While it's important to use relevant terms, ensure your descriptions remain natural and readable.

Bringing It All Together: A Holistic View of Your Education

Your formal education, ongoing courses, and professional certifications should tell a cohesive story about your expertise and passion for learning. Here's how to ensure they work in harmony:

- **Consistency is Key:** Ensure the skills highlighted in your "Education" section align with those in your "Experience" and "Skills" sections.

- **Show Progression:** Your educational journey should demonstrate growth. From your degree to your latest certification, show how you've built upon your knowledge base.

- **Quality Over Quantity:** It's not about listing every course you've ever taken. Focus on the most impactful and relevant educational experiences.

The Alumni Advantage: Networking Through Education

Don't overlook the networking potential of your "Education" section:

- **Alumni Connections:** Listing your school opens doors to alumni networks. These connections can be invaluable for mentorship, job opportunities, and industry insights.

- **Conversation Starters:** Shared educational experiences can be great icebreakers when reaching out to new contacts.

Your Education as Part of Your Living Professional Profile

Your educational journey doesn't end with your degree. By strategically using

LinkedIn's "Education," "Courses," and "Licenses & Certifications" sections, you create a dynamic representation of your commitment to learning and professional growth. Remember to regularly review and update these sections, ensuring they always align with your current career goals and industry trends.

By crafting a compelling educational narrative, you're not just listing qualifications—you're telling the story of how you've prepared yourself for success in your chosen field. This approach not only appeals to AI-driven recruitment tools but also resonates with human recruiters looking for candidates who demonstrate a passion for continuous learning and growth.

Tailoring Your Profile for Different Career Stages

Your LinkedIn profile isn't just a digital résumé—it's a dynamic tool that should evolve with your career. In this section, we'll explore strategies for two distinct career stages: seasoned professionals navigating potential age discrimination and recent graduates maximizing limited work experience. By tailoring your profile to your specific career stage, you can showcase your unique value proposition and stand out to recruiters and hiring managers.

Strategies for Combating Age Discrimination

What's the best way to showcase your wealth of experience without dating yourself? As an experienced professional, you bring a wealth of knowledge and skills to the table. Unfortunately, in today's job market, concerns about age bias can be real. Let's explore some savvy strategies.

Curate Your Timeline Thoughtfully

- **Focus on Relevance:** Highlight the most recent 15-20 years of your career, emphasizing roles most relevant to your current goals.

- **Strategically Summarize Earlier Experience:** For your earliest listed position, consider adding a brief paragraph summarizing prior roles without specific dates.

For example: "Prior to this role, I developed my leadership acumen through positions including Senior Project Manager at XYZ Corp and Systems Architect at ABC Inc. These roles contributed significantly to my expertise in agile methodologies and enterprise system design."

This approach has its advantages and disadvantages. Let's break them down:

On the positive side, you're showcasing your skills without explicitly revealing your age. It's like presenting a highlight reel of your career. This strategy can improve your chances of passing initial screenings by emphasizing recent and relevant experience, which is often the primary focus for recruiters and hiring managers. Additionally, a streamlined presentation makes your profile more appealing and easier to digest for professionals who are quickly scanning for suitable candidates.

However, this approach isn't without potential drawbacks. Summarizing your early career might raise questions about employment gaps or create curiosity about the specifics of your unlisted roles. For certain positions—particularly senior leadership roles—long-term industry experience may be highly valued, and not fully detailing your career history could result in missed opportunities.

There's another consideration: potential discrepancies between your LinkedIn profile and your résumé. If a recruiter or hiring manager cross-references both documents and notices inconsistencies, it could lead to concerns or uncomfortable questions during an interview.

So, what's the best approach? Be strategic. Consider your career goals, your industry norms, and the roles you're targeting. Your profile should showcase your current value and future potential. It's about finding the right balance between highlighting your experience and keeping your profile current and relevant.

Remember, your LinkedIn profile is telling your professional story. Make sure it's aligned with your career objectives and presents you in the best light for the opportunities you're seeking.

Education: Wisdom Without Timestamps

- **Omit Graduation Years:** Use LinkedIn's "—" option for start and end dates in the "Education" section.

- **Highlight Recent Learning:** Highlight recent certifications, courses, or workshops to demonstrate your commitment to staying current. This not only shows your adaptability but also your enthusiasm for growth.

Craft a Forward-Looking Narrative

- **Future-Focused Summary:** Emphasize your current passions and future aspirations rather than past years of experience.

- **Value-Driven Language:** Instead of quantifying your experience in years, focus on the depth of your expertise and the tangible value you offer. For instance, "Driving digital transformation with deep expertise in AI integration and change management" is more compelling than "25 years of IT management experience."

Showcase Current Skills and Technologies

- **Emphasize Relevance:** Highlight proficiency in current technologies and industry trends. For instance, IT professionals might focus on cloud computing, AI, or cybersecurity rather than older programming languages or obsolete software.

- **Prune Outdated Skills:** Critically review your skills section. Prioritize modern technologies (e.g., AWS, Azure) over older ones (e.g., Windows Server 2003). Marketers, for example, might emphasize digital marketing tools over traditional print skills.

- **Contextualize Older Skills:** If relevant, frame legacy skills in a modern context. For example, "Legacy system modernization, including COBOL to Java migration" instead of just "COBOL programming."

- **Demonstrate Adaptability:** Regularly update your Skills section with new competencies, certifications, and projects involving cutting-edge technologies. This showcases your commitment to professional growth and adaptability.

Optimize Your Visual Presence

- **Professional, Current Photo:** Use a high-quality, recent headshot that portrays you as approachable and energetic.

- **Modern Contact Information:** Opt for a professional email address that doesn't date you (e.g., Gmail over AOL or Hotmail).

Emphasize Achievements and Impact with a Modern Lens

- **Results-Oriented Language:** Focus on specific accomplishments and the value you've delivered, using quantifiable metrics whenever possible. For instance, "Increased customer retention by 30% through implementation of a new CRM system" speaks volumes about your impact without necessarily dating your experience.

- **Reframe Dated Achievements:** Update older accomplishments to highlight timeless skills. Instead of mentioning specific dated events, focus on the transferable skills you demonstrated. For instance, if you navigated your company through a historic financial crisis 20 years ago, rather than mentioning the actual year, you might frame it this way: "Steered company through major market downturn..." This approach highlights your skills without anchoring them to a specific time period.

- **Highlight Forward-Thinking Achievements:** Emphasize projects that showcase your ability to drive change and anticipate industry trends. For example: "Pioneered company's digital transformation strategy, expanding market reach by 50%."

- **Leadership and Mentorship:** Highlight your role in developing teams and nurturing talent, showcasing your ability to contribute to the company's long-term success. For example: "Mentored and developed a team of 15 junior analysts, with 5 progressing to senior management roles within the organization."

- **Continuous Improvement Focus:** Demonstrate your commitment to ongoing learning and adaptation. For instance: "Spearheaded the adoption of agile methodologies, increasing project delivery speed by 40% and improving team collaboration."

- **Industry Recognition:** Be selective with awards and accolades. Highlight recent, relevant recognitions from well-known institutions in your field.

PRO TIP

Combat age bias by showcasing your adaptability and commitment to ongoing learning. Include recent certifications, courses, or workshops, especially in cutting-edge areas of your field. This demonstrates that you're not just experienced but also continuously evolving with the industry.

Combat Age Bias With AI Support

PROMPT 1: REFRAMING EXPERIENCE FOR RELEVANCE

"I'm a [profession] with [##] years of experience, and I'm concerned about age bias in my LinkedIn profile. My earliest role was as a [job title] in [year], and I've progressed to my current position as a [job title]. Can you help me reframe my experience section to focus on the most relevant aspects without explicitly dating myself? Please provide:
a) A template for summarizing my earlier roles (pre-[year]) in a single paragraph at the end of my most distant listed position. b) Suggestions for describing three key achievements from my career that demonstrate valuable skills without revealing their age. For context, these achievements include [brief description of 3 significant career accomplish-

ments]. c) Tips for highlighting my adaptability and continuous learning throughout my career progression."

PROMPT 2: SKILLS OPTIMIZATION FOR CURRENT RELE-VANCE

"As a [profession] with [#] years of experience, I'm updating my LinkedIn profile to combat potential age bias. My skills range from [traditional skills in your field] to [modern techniques/technologies]. Please help me optimize my skills section by: a) Identifying 10 cutting-edge skills or technologies that are highly sought after in [your field] today. b) Suggesting how to frame 5 traditional [your field] skills in a way that emphasizes their ongoing relevance. c) Providing a strategy for highlighting my adaptability and willingness to embrace new technologies throughout my career. d) Recommending 3-5 recent certifications or courses I could pursue to demonstrate my commitment to staying current in the field."

PROMPT 3: CRAFTING AN AGE-NEUTRAL PROFESSIONAL SUMMARY

"I'm a senior [profession] with over [##] years of experience, looking to create an age-neutral yet impactful LinkedIn summary. My career has spanned from [traditional aspects of your field] to [modern practices in your field]. Please help me craft a summary that: a) Highlights my expertise and value without explicitly mentioning years of experience. b) Focuses on my forward-thinking approach and ability to drive organizational change. c) Showcases my proficiency in current technologies and methodologies in my field. d) Demonstrates my role in mentoring and developing talent. e) Emphasizes my unique selling points as a seasoned professional in a way that appeals to modern organizations. Additionally, please provide 3-4 examples of strong opening lines that grab attention without hinting at my age, and suggest some contemporary buzzwords or concepts in [your field] to incorporate naturally into the summary."

Remember, the goal is to create a profile that speaks to your current value and future potential rather than your years of experience. By focusing on relevance, continuous learning, and tangible achievements, you can craft a compelling narrative that resonates with potential employers and mitigates age-related biases.

New Graduate Tactics: Maximizing Limited Work Experience

As a recent graduate, your challenge is to create a robust profile that show-cases your potential despite limited professional experience. Here's how to make your LinkedIn profile shine:

Leverage Your Education

- **Highlight Relevant Coursework:** List key courses that align with your career goals.

- **Showcase Projects:** Feature academic projects that demonstrate ap-plicable skills or knowledge.

- **Emphasize Achievements:** Mention honors, awards, or scholarships to highlight your academic excellence.

Amplify Internships and Part-Time Work

- **Treat Internships as Jobs:** List internships in your "Experience" section, detailing your responsibilities and achievements.

- **Highlight Transferable Skills:** Even if part-time jobs aren't directly related to your field, emphasize skills like customer service, team-work, or problem-solving.

Volunteer Experience Counts

- **Showcase Leadership:** Highlight any leadership roles in volunteer organizations.

- **Emphasize Relevant Skills:** Focus on volunteer experiences that developed skills relevant to your career goals.

Extracurricular Activities as Professional Development

- **Leadership Roles:** Feature positions held in student organizations or clubs.

- **Competitions and Events:** Mention participation in hackathons, case competitions, or industry events.

Skills and Endorsements

- **Comprehensive Skill Set:** List both hard and soft skills you've developed through your education and experiences.

- **Seek Endorsements:** Ask professors, internship supervisors, or project teammates to endorse your skills.

AI Prompts for New Graduates

PROMPT 1: MAXIMIZING ACADEMIC ACHIEVEMENTS & PROJECTS

- "I'm a recent graduate with a degree in [field of study] from [university name]. While I have limited professional experience, I've completed several significant academic projects and internships. Can you help me optimize my LinkedIn profile to showcase my potential? Please provide: a) A template for a compelling 'About' section that highlights my academic achievements, relevant skills, and career aspirations. b) Suggestions for presenting my top 3 academic projects or research papers in a way that emphasizes their real-world relevance. These projects include [brief description of 3 key projects]. c) Tips for describing my internship experience at [company name] to maximize its impact. d) Ideas for leveraging my extracurricular activities, including [mention 1-2 key activities], to demonstrate leadership and teamwork skills. e) Recommendations for 5-7 key skills I should highlight based on my academic background and the current job market in [your field]."

PROMPT 2: BUILDING A PROFESSIONAL PRESENCE WITH LIMITED EXPERIENCE

- "As a new graduate in [field of study], I'm looking to create a LinkedIn profile that stands out despite my limited work experience. My background includes [brief overview of any internships, part-time jobs, or volunteer work]. Please help me: a) Craft a headline that goes beyond 'Recent Graduate' to showcase my unique value proposition. b) Develop a strategy for the 'Featured' section, including ideas for content I could create or showcase (e.g., blog posts, presentations, or projects) related to [your field]. c) Suggest ways to describe my academic achievements and coursework that would be most appealing to potential employers in [target industry]. d) Provide tips for joining and engaging with LinkedIn groups relevant to [your field] to expand my professional network. e) Recommend 3-5 types of posts or content I could share regularly to demonstrate my knowledge and passion for [your field]."

PROMPT 3: TRANSLATING ACADEMIC EXPERIENCE TO PROFESSIONAL VALUE

- "I've just completed my degree in [field of study] and am preparing to enter the job market in [target industry]. While I don't have extensive work experience, I've gained valuable skills through my coursework, a semester abroad in [country], and involvement in [student organization]. Can you assist me in translating these experiences into professional value on my LinkedIn profile? Specifically, I need help with: a) Writing a powerful summary that positions me as a promising entry-level candidate in [your field], highlighting my fresh perspective and eagerness to learn. b) Identifying and articulating 5-7 transferable skills I've gained through my academic and extracurricular experiences that are highly valued in [target industry]. c) Crafting descriptions for my academic projects and coursework that emphasize practical applications and outcomes relevant to potential employers. d) Suggesting ways to leverage my international experience to demonstrate cultural competence and adaptability. e) Providing ideas for the 'Volunteer Experience' section that showcase my commitment to [cause or organization] and the skills I've developed. f) Recommending strategies for requesting impactful recommendations from professors or supervisors that highlight my potential in a professional setting."

By implementing these strategies, you can create a LinkedIn profile that compensates for limited work experience by showcasing your potential, enthusiasm, and readiness to contribute in your chosen field. Remember, your profile should tell the story of who you are, what you've accomplished so far, and the value you're eager to bring to potential employers.

Adding Visual Effects: Leveraging Multimedia Content

In the age of digital storytelling, why limit yourself to text? LinkedIn allows you to add rich media to your Experience, Education, and other select sections of your profile. Think of it as adding a sizzle reel to your career story.

Add links to projects you've worked on, presentations you've given, or articles you've written.

Include images or videos that showcase your work – a picture of an event you organized, a video of a product you developed, or a graph showing the results of a successful campaign you ran. The following are some more specific suggestions.

"Experience" Section Showcase

- **Project Highlights:** Add links to projects you've spearheaded, along with visual representations of outcomes.

- **Presentation Power:** Upload slideshows or video clips of key presentations you've delivered.

- **Publication Prowess:** Include articles you've written or been featured in, showcasing your industry insights.

- **Visual Victories:** Incorporate images or infographics that illustrate your achievements – perhaps a graph showing sales growth or a photo of an award-winning product you developed.

"Education" Section Enhancement

- **Capstone Projects:** Showcase significant academic projects with images, presentations, or video summaries.

- **Thesis Snapshots:** If applicable, include a visual abstract or key findings from your thesis work.

- **Study Abroad Insights:** For international educational experiences, add photos or videos that highlight cross-cultural learning.

- **Academic Honors:** Display certificates or award images to visually reinforce your academic achievements.

"Licenses & Certifications"

- **Digital Badges:** Many certification programs offer digital badges. Include these eye-catching credentials.

- **Course Completion Visuals:** For online courses or workshops, add completion certificates or course project outcomes.

The "Featured" Section: Your Profile's Highlight Reel

Leverage LinkedIn's "Featured" section to spotlight your most impressive

content right at the top of your profile. This could include:
- A video introduction of yourself and your professional philosophy

- Links to your most impactful projects or publications

- An infographic summarizing your key skills and achievements

Technical Tips for Multimedia Success

- **File Types:** LinkedIn supports various formats, including JPG, PNG, GIF (static), PDF, PPT, DOC, MP4, and MP3.

- **Size Matters:** Be mindful of file size limits (typically 100MB max) and image resolution constraints (120 megapixels max).

- **Quality Counts:** Ensure all visual content is high-quality and professionally presented.

- **Mobile-Friendly:** Remember that many viewers will be on mobile devices, so opt for clear, easily viewable content.

Strategic Considerations

- **Relevance is Key:** Every piece of media should serve a purpose in telling your professional story.

- **Update Regularly:** Keep your multimedia content current to reflect your latest achievements and skills.

- **Balance is Beautiful:** While multimedia can be powerful, don't overwhelm your profile. Use it strategically to complement your written content.

- **Accessibility:** Consider adding alt text to images for accessibility.

Ethical and Professional Boundaries

- **Respect Confidentiality:** Ensure you have permission to share any company-related media.

- **Professional Focus:** This is not the place for personal photos or content unrelated to your professional brand.

By thoughtfully incorporating multimedia elements across your profile, you create a rich, engaging presentation of your professional self. This approach not only catches the eye but also provides tangible evidence of your skills, achievements, and unique value proposition. In a sea of text-heavy profiles, your multimedia-enhanced LinkedIn presence will stand out, offering a more comprehensive and memorable snapshot of your professional journey.

Your Action Plan to Craft Your "Experience" and "Education" Sections

Ready to bring your professional story to life? Here's your action plan:

- Collect and organize all relevant materials, including your résumé, transcripts, performance reviews, project notes, and documentation of awards or certifications.

- Build out the chronology of the "Experience" and "Education" sections of your LinkedIn profile, adding employers, educational institutions, dates, and your job titles or degrees (you'll add descriptions later). Ensure that company names link to their LinkedIn pages and educational institutions are correctly identified.

- Optimize your job titles and degree descriptions with relevant keywords that accurately represent your roles and academic accomplishments while enhancing searchability.

- Write a concise overview of your job scope for each professional role, then craft 3-5 impactful bullet points using the CAR (Challenge-Action-Result) or STAR (Situation-Task-Action-Result) method to highlight key achievements.

- Enhance your "Education" section by adding relevant coursework, academic projects, and extracurricular activities that demonstrate skills applicable to your career goals, emphasizing leadership roles and notable achievements.

- Integrate industry-specific keywords and skills throughout both sections, focusing on terms that align with your target roles or industries.

- Upload multimedia content such as project photos, presentation slides, or links to published work in both your "Experience" and "Education" sections, ensuring each addition enhances your professional story.

- Review and refine each entry in both sections, ensuring clarity, impact, and relevance to your current career objectives. Consider using AI tools like ChatGPT to optimize your content and language.

- Perform a thorough proofread of your entire profile, cross-checking dates, job titles, and degree information for consistency with your résumé.

- Request feedback on your "Experience" and "Education" sections from trusted colleagues, mentors, or industry peers, and implement relevant suggestions to strengthen your professional narrative.

Remember, your LinkedIn "Experience" and "Education" sections are living documents of your career journey. They should evolve and grow as you do, reflecting your latest achievements and skills.

Set a reminder to review and update these sections regularly, especially after completing major projects or reaching significant milestones. By consistently refining your profile, you ensure that it always presents the most current and compelling version of your professional narrative.

Chapter Nine

Beyond the Basics

Unleashing the Power of LinkedIn's Optional Sections

Y ou've got the LinkedIn basics down - a snappy headline, a solid about section, your work history all lined up. But there's still that nagging feeling that you're missing something. Well, guess what? You are.

Think of your LinkedIn profile as a gourmet meal. Sure, the main course (your work experience) is crucial. But what elevates a good meal to an unforgettable experience? It's the appetizers, the side dishes, the unexpected flavor combinations. On LinkedIn, these are the often-overlooked "optional" sections.

Why Optional Sections Matter

Why invest the time and effort in these seemingly supplementary areas? Let's dive into the compelling reasons that make these optional sections not just nice-to-haves but must-haves for a standout profile.

First and foremost, completeness is key. LinkedIn's algorithm favors profiles that utilize a wide range of sections, boosting your visibility in search results. This increased searchability isn't just a vanity metric – as we've explained, it's your ticket to being discovered by recruiters, potential clients, or collaborators who are seeking someone with your unique blend of skills and experiences.

But the benefits go far beyond mere visibility. These optional sections are your opportunity to paint a vivid, multidimensional portrait of your professional self. They allow you to showcase the diverse facets of your expertise that might not fit neatly into traditional résumé categories. Your volunteer work, for instance, might reveal leadership skills that your day job hasn't yet allowed you to demonstrate. Or perhaps your involvement in professional organizations speaks to your commitment to ongoing learning and industry engagement.

These additional sections also serve as powerful credibility boosters. Publications showcase your thought leadership, while certifications and courses demonstrate your commitment to staying current in your field. Awards and honors provide third-party validation of your excellence. Each of these elements adds a layer of depth to your professional story, setting you apart in a sea of similar candidates.

Moreover, these sections can be invaluable conversation starters. When a potential connection or employer visits your profile, details about your volunteer work, causes you support, or unique projects you've undertaken can provide common ground, sparking meaningful interactions that go beyond surface-level shop talk.

Perhaps most importantly, these optional sections allow you to control the narrative of your professional journey. They give you the space to highlight experiences and achievements that truly define you as a professional, even if they don't fit the traditional mold of work history or education.

In essence, by fully utilizing these optional sections, you're not just completing a profile – you're crafting a compelling professional narrative. You're providing a 360-degree view of your skills, experiences, and values that can resonate deeply with the right opportunities and connections.

So, as you consider whether to invest time in these "optional" sections, remember: in the competitive landscape of professional networking, it's often these extras that make the difference between blending in and standing out. Your unique experiences and achievements deserve to be showcased. By going the extra mile to complete these sections, you're not just filling out a profile – you're opening doors to new opportunities, meaningful connections, and professional growth.

PRO TIP

Boost your visibility with a complete profile. LinkedIn's algorithm favors complete profiles, giving them higher visibility in search results. Past studies by LinkedIn have indicated that a 100% complete profile is up to 40 times more likely to receive opportunities. To maximize your profile's potential, fill out every relevant section. Each completed section not only improves your visibility but also provides more opportunities to showcase your expertise and incorporate relevant keywords.

Volunteer Experience: Your Heart on Your Digital Sleeve

Ever thought volunteering was just for padding out a sparse résumé? Think again. This section is your chance to show you're not just about the paycheck – you're about making a difference.

Volunteer experience demonstrates your commitment to causes beyond your professional life. It highlights valuable soft skills, showcases leadership abilities, and reveals aspects of your character that resonate with potential employers.

For students or those changing careers, volunteer work can fill experience gaps and demonstrate relevant skills. Moreover, including volunteer work can boost your profile's keyword richness, enhancing your visibility in LinkedIn searches.

When to list volunteer work in the "Experience" section vs. the "Volunteer" experience section:

- **"Experience" section:** Consider including volunteer work here if:

    ○ It directly relates to your career goals or target industry

- You have limited paid work experience (e.g., recent graduates)

- The role involved significant responsibility or leadership

- It fills a gap in your employment history

- **Volunteer "Experience" section:** Use this section when:

  - The volunteer work is ongoing but not your primary focus

  - You have a robust work history and want to highlight additional community involvement

  - The experience is valuable but not directly related to your professional goals

  - You want to showcase a variety of community engagements without cluttering your main experience section

 **PRO TIP**

LinkedIn's research shows that 41% of hiring managers consider volunteer experience equally as valuable as paid work experience when evaluating candidates. Including relevant volunteer work can set you apart, especially if you're early in your career or transitioning to a new field.

Types of volunteer experiences to include:

- Ongoing commitments to organizations

- One-time or short-term project work

- Pro-bono professional services

- Community leadership roles

• Virtual or remote volunteering initiatives

Structuring your volunteer entries:

While you can always list your volunteer work without a description, doing so misses the opportunity to not only highlight your community impact but also significantly enhance your profile's searchability (make sure to use important keywords in the description) and appeal to potential employers or connections.

Example volunteer work description:

"Led a cross-functional team of 10 volunteers in implementing an AI-powered digital tracking system for a local animal shelter, resulting in a 30% increase in adoption rates and 25% reduction in administrative workload. Leveraged data analytics to optimize animal care schedules and streamline volunteer management, enhancing overall operational efficiency."

Projects: Bringing Your Achievements to Life

Do you feel like your résumé doesn't quite capture all the cool stuff you've actually done? The "Projects" section of LinkedIn is your chance to shine a spotlight on those standout achievements that might not fit neatly into your work history.

This section allows you to showcase specific projects and accomplishments, demonstrating your ability to see initiatives through from concept to completion. It's an opportunity to highlight your problem-solving skills, creativity, and the tangible impact of your work. For job seekers, students, or career changers, it can be a powerful way to demonstrate relevant skills and experience.

PRO TIP

Consider leveraging LinkedIn's "Projects" section to highlight relevant skills and experiences gained outside traditional employment. This "shadow experience" can include self-directed learning, volunteer work, or personal initiatives that demonstrate key competencies for your target role. Frame these projects professionally to bridge gaps in your formal work history and showcase your initiative and passion.

Types of projects to include:

- Professional projects outside your primary job responsibilities

- Academic research or capstone projects

- Personal initiatives (including projects related to hobbies) relevant to your field

- Open-source contributions

- Projects related to side hustles

- Hackathon or competition entries

- Multimedia productions (podcasts, videos, art installations)

Enhancing your projects with multimedia:

LinkedIn allows you to add rich media to your project entries, which can significantly boost engagement and provide tangible evidence of your work. Consider including:

- **Images:** Before-and-after shots, infographics, or project visuals

- **Videos:** Project demos, presentations, or explainer videos

- **Documents:** White papers, reports, or slide decks

- **Links:** GitHub repositories, live websites, or articles about your project

To add media, click the "Upload" or "Link" option when editing your project entry. Remember, any media you include should be professional and directly related to the project.

Example project description:

"Spearheaded 'Project Green Stride,' an innovative sustainability initiative aimed at reducing our company's carbon footprint. Led a cross-functional team of 8 members in developing and implementing an AI-powered energy management system. Leveraged IoT sensors and machine learning algorithms to optimize HVAC and lighting systems across 5 office locations. Resulted in a 40% reduction in energy consumption and $500,000 annual cost savings. Created an interactive dashboard for real-time monitoring and presented findings at the Global Sustainability Summit 2023."

By thoughtfully crafting your project descriptions and incorporating relevant media, you can create a compelling showcase of your abilities that goes beyond what a traditional résumé or job history can convey. This section is your opportunity to bring your achievements to life, making them more tangible and impactful for potential employers or connections.

PRO TIP

Leverage LinkedIn's "Featured" section to showcase projects, articles, or media that support your UVP. This visual element can quickly demonstrate your expertise to profile visitors.

Honors & Awards: Your Professional Trophy Case

Accolades aren't just for athletes and academics. Your "Honors & Awards" section is where you get to humblebrag about the times you've knocked it out of the park professionally.

This section provides third-party validation of your skills and accomplishments. It sets you apart from other candidates and demonstrates a track record of excellence in your field. For recent graduates or those early in their careers, it can be particularly impactful in establishing credibility.

Types of honors and awards to include:

- Industry-specific recognitions

- Company or departmental awards

- Professional association honors

- Academic achievements

- Community service awards

- Patents or intellectual property rights

- Scholarships or fellowships

- Speaking engagements or keynote invitations

When to include an award:

Not all awards are created equal. Consider including an award if...

- It's relevant to your current career goals or industry

- It's from a recognized organization in your field

- It demonstrates a unique skill or achievement

- It's recent (within the last 5-10 years, unless exceptionally prestigious)

Example award description:

"Recipient of the 'Innovator of the Year 2023' award from the National Association of Software Engineers (NASE). Recognized for developing a groundbreaking machine learning algorithm that reduced data processing time by 75% in cloud-based applications. This innovation has been adopted by three Fortune 500 companies, resulting in an estimated $10 million in annual efficiency savings across the industry. Presented findings at the International Conference on Machine Learning (ICML) and published in the Journal of Artificial Intelligence Research."

Tips for maximizing your "Honors & Awards" section:

- **Be selective:** *Quality* trumps *quantity*. Focus on your most impressive and relevant awards.

- **Keep it current:** Unless it's a major, career-defining award, focus on recent achievements.

- **Provide context:** Briefly explain why the award is significant in your field.

- **Link to more info**: If possible, include a URL where viewers can learn more about the award or your winning work.

- **Update regularly:** As you receive new accolades, make sure to add them promptly to keep your profile current.

The "Honors & Awards" section isn't about showing off—it's about providing concrete evidence of your expertise and the value you bring to your field. By listing your accolades, you're giving potential employers or connections a clear picture of your professional excellence.

Publications: Your Professional Voice, Amplified

Do your career goals include being a thought leader in your field? Your "Publications" section is where you prove you're not just along for the ride—you're driving the conversation.

This section establishes you as an expert in your domain. It demonstrates your ability to articulate complex ideas, shows ongoing engagement with industry trends, and proves you're committed to contributing to your field's body of knowledge. Even if you're not in a traditionally publication-heavy field, sharing your insights can set you apart.

Types of publications to include:

- Academic journal articles

- Industry white papers

- Books or book chapters

- Blog posts or articles on professional platforms

- Podcasts or video content

- Conference presentations or proceedings

- Case studies

- Research reports

- Trade magazine articles

Example publication description:

"Authored 'Revolutionizing Customer Experience: AI-Driven Personalization in E-Commerce,' published in the Harvard Business Review (June 2024). This data-driven article explores how machine learning algorithms and predictive analytics are reshaping online retail. Analyzed case studies from leading e-commerce platforms, demonstrating a 35% increase in customer retention and a 28% boost in average order value through AI-powered personalization strategies. Featured expert insights on ethical considerations and future trends in AI adoption for enhancing customer experiences."

Tips for maximizing your "Publications" section:

- **Prioritize quality over quantity:** Feature your most impactful and relevant publications.

- **Keep it current:** While seminal works can be timeless, aim to showcase recent publications to demonstrate ongoing engagement in your field.

- **Vary your media:** Don't limit yourself to traditional written publications. Include podcasts, videos, or interactive content if relevant.

- **Highlight collaborations:** If you've co-authored with notable figures in your industry, make sure to mention them.

- **Showcase the impact:** If your publication has been widely cited, received awards, or led to speaking engagements, briefly mention this.

- **Tailor to your audience:** If you're targeting a specific role or industry, prioritize publications most relevant to that field.

Your "Publications" section is a showcase of your professional thoughts and contributions. Each entry is an opportunity to demonstrate your expertise, insight, and ability to contribute meaningfully to your field's discourse. You're not just filling out a profile section—you're positioning yourself as a valuable voice in your industry, not just keeping up with your field—but helping to shape its future!

Organizations: Your Professional Tribes

The "Organizations" section is where you showcase the communities that shape your career beyond your 9-to-5. Think of this section as your professional extracurricular activity list. It's your chance to demonstrate that you're not just punching a clock but actively engaging with your industry. By listing your affiliations with professional organizations, you're telling potential employers and connections that you're committed to ongoing learning and networking.

But why does this matter? For starters, it shows you're plugged into your industry. You're not just sitting on the sidelines; you're in the game, staying current with trends and best practices. It's like having a flashing neon sign that says, "I'm serious about my career!"

Moreover, these affiliations can highlight leadership roles you've taken on. Maybe you've organized events or led committees within these organizations. That's gold for your professional profile, demonstrating initiative and leadership skills that might not be apparent from your work history alone.

Lastly, shared organizational memberships can be great conversation starters. They provide common ground for connections, potentially opening doors to new opportunities. It's networking made easy!

Types of organizations to include:

- Professional associations

- Industry-specific groups

- Alumni organizations

- Networking groups

- Charitable organizations related to your field

- Think tanks or research groups

- Professional development communities

- Trade unions or guilds

Example organization description:

"Active member of the Artificial Intelligence Society (AIS) since 2019. Served as Chair of the Ethics in AI committee (2021-2023), where I led the development of industry guidelines for responsible AI implementation, now adopted by over 100 tech companies. Regular speaker at AIS annual conferences, presenting on topics such as 'Machine Learning in Healthcare' and 'Bias Mitigation in AI Systems'. Mentor in the AIS Young Professionals Program, guiding 5 early-career AI specialists annually."

Tips for maximizing your "Organizations" section:

- **Be selective:** Focus on organizations most relevant to your current career goals.

- **Highlight active involvement:** Don't just list memberships; showcase your contributions.

- **Update regularly:** Add new organizations or roles as you join them.

- **Align with your brand:** Choose organizations that reinforce your professional identity.

- **Show progression:** If you've held different roles within an organization, list them to show growth.

- **Link to profiles:** If the organization has a LinkedIn page, link to it for added context.

- **Explain niche groups:** For lesser-known organizations, briefly describe their purpose or significance in your field.

Your "Organizations" section isn't just a list of memberships—it's a reflection of your professional community and values. It shows potential employers or connections that you're not just doing a job but actively engaging with and contributing to your field. Your organizational involvement paints a picture of a well-rounded professional who's connected, engaged, and committed to growth.

Patents: Your Eureka Moments, Documented

Think of patents as your professional bragging rights. They're concrete proof that you're not just following the playbook – you're writing new chapters. Whether you're in tech, engineering, or any field where innovation is key, showcasing your patents can set you apart from the crowd.

But why should you care about flaunting your patents? Well, for starters, it's like having a neon sign that screams "innovator" to anyone who visits your profile. It shows you're not just solving problems; you're creating solutions that are unique enough to be legally protected. That's pretty impressive stuff!

Moreover, patents demonstrate your deep technical expertise. They're evidence that you're not just skimming the surface of your field – you're diving deep and emerging with pearls of innovation. It's a clear sign that you're a valuable asset in your industry.

And let's not forget the problem-solving angle. Each patent represents a challenge you've tackled head-on and conquered. It's like having a trophy case of your professional victories, showing potential employers or clients that you're equipped to handle complex issues.

Types of patents to include:

- Utility patents (for new processes, machines, manufactures, or compositions of matter)

- Design patents (for new, original, and ornamental designs for an article of manufacture)

- Plant patents (for distinct and new varieties of plants)

- Provisional patent applications (if full patent is pending)

Example patent description:

"Lead inventor on US Patent 10,789,456: 'AI-Driven Predictive Maintenance System for Manufacturing Equipment' (issued September 2024). Developed a novel machine learning algorithm that analyzes real-time sensor data to predict equipment failures with 95% accuracy, reducing unplanned downtime by up to 40%. This innovation has potential applications across various manufacturing sectors, estimated to save the industry over $1 billion annually in maintenance costs. Currently in talks with three Fortune 500 companies for implementation."

Tips for maximizing your "Patents" section:

- **Focus on relevance:** Highlight patents most closely related to your current career goals.

- **Explain in layman's terms:** Make the innovation understandable to non-experts.

- **Highlight collaboration:** If you're a co-inventor, mention the collaborative nature of the work.

- **Show the journey:** If comfortable, briefly mention the problem that led to the invention.

- **Update status:** If a patent is pending, note this and update when it's granted.

- **Link to patent:** Include a link to the patent on the USPTO website or Google Patents for easy verification.

- **Mention related achievements:** If the patent led to awards, publications, or speaking engagements, briefly note these.

Your "Patents" section isn't just a list of legal documents—it's a showcase of your innovative thinking and problem-solving skills. Each patent tells a story of how you've pushed the boundaries in your field. By describing your patents, you're not just listing accomplishments—you're demonstrating your capacity to create real, impactful solutions.

Rounding Out Your Profile: The Final Touches

Your LinkedIn profile is nearly complete, but these last few sections can add that extra polish to truly make it shine. Let's briefly explore how Test Scores," "Languages," and "Causes" can enhance your professional story.

"Test Scores" offer a way to quantify your expertise, providing objective validation of your skills and knowledge. This section can be especially useful for recent graduates or those in fields where standardized tests are highly relevant. Consider including standardized test scores like GRE or GMAT, professional certification exam results, or language proficiency test scores. However, be selective - only showcase scores that are impressive and relevant to your career goals. A mediocre score might do more harm than good.

The "Languages" section can be your passport to global opportunities. This section allows you to showcase your linguistic abilities, demonstrating not just communication skills but also cultural competence. When listing languages, be sure to accurately represent your proficiency level, using terms like Native, Fluent, Professional working proficiency, Limited working proficiency, or Elementary proficiency. Remember, it's better to slightly undersell your abilities than to claim a fluency you don't possess.

The "Causes" section offers a unique opportunity to align your values with potential employers. This area provides insight into your passions and commitments outside of work, helping you connect with like-minded professionals and organizations. You might include social issues you're passionate about, environmental concerns, economic or political causes, or health and wellness initiatives. Choose causes that genuinely resonate with you and, if possible, align with your professional field or target industry. This section allows others to see you as a well-rounded individual who's engaged with the world beyond your professional sphere.

For each of these sections, remember that relevance is key. Only include information that adds value to your professional narrative. Keep these sections current, updating them as your skills and interests evolve. Above all, be authentic. These sections offer a glimpse into who you are beyond your job title – let your true self shine through. By thoughtfully completing these final sections, you're adding depth to your profile and giving potential connections or employers a more holistic view of who you are as a professional and as a person.

Note: For detailed information about enhancing your profile with a listing of your "Courses" and "Certifications & Licenses," please refer back to Chapter 8, where these important sections are covered in depth.

Your Action Plan to Maximize Optional Sections

Ready to take your LinkedIn profile from good to great? Here's your action plan to make those optional sections shine:

- Review your current LinkedIn profile and prioritize the optional sections most relevant to your industry and career goals. Not all sections may be necessary for your unique professional story.

- Focus on high-impact sections like "Volunteer" experience and "Projects." Use the CAR or STAR method to craft compelling descriptions that highlight transferable skills and measurable results.

- Showcase your achievements through the "Honors & Awards" and "Publications" sections. Provide context for each accolade and emphasize the impact of your published works.

- Enhance your professional identity with "Organizations," "Languages," and "Causes" that align with your values and industry. Be selective and highlight active involvement or leadership roles.

- Throughout all sections, integrate industry-specific keywords and add rich media like images or documents where possible to bring your achievements to life.

- Perform a thorough proofread of your entire profile, ensuring consistency in tone and format across all sections. Consider using AI tools like ChatGPT to refine your language and optimize content.

- Set a reminder to review and update these optional sections quarterly or after any significant professional developments.

Remember, these optional sections are your opportunity to paint a fuller picture of your professional self. They tell the story that your work history alone can't capture. So take the time to craft them thoughtfully, and watch as your LinkedIn profile transforms from a simple résumé into a compelling professional narrative.

Chapter Ten

Picture-Perfect Multimedia Strategies

Crafting a LinkedIn Profile That Stops the Scroll

E ver heard the saying, "A picture is worth a thousand words"? Well, on LinkedIn, it might be worth a thousand connections. In the bustling digital marketplace of professionals, your visual brand is the neon sign that catches the eye of recruiters and potential collaborators. It's the handshake before the conversation, the smile before the pitch.

But let's be real – how many of us have slapped up a hastily cropped photo from a wedding or used the default blue banner? If that's you, don't worry. But it's time to level up.

Think of your LinkedIn profile as your personal billboard. Would you paste up a blurry selfie on a 50-foot screen? Probably not. So why settle for less on the platform where your next big break could be just a scroll away?

From Overlooked to Can't-Look-Away

Here's a little secret: Our brains are wired for visual stimuli. Studies suggest we process images up to 600 times faster than text. That's right – while someone's still reading your job title, they've already made a dozen micro-judgments based on your profile picture and banner.

And get this – it happens in the blink of an eye. Research shows it takes about 1/10th of a second to form a first impression from a photo. That's faster than you can say "LinkedIn"! In this split second, before they've read a single word of your carefully crafted summary, visitors have already subconsciously decided whether they want to connect with you or keep scrolling.

Need more proof of the power of visuals? Consider this: 59% of consumers believe visual information is more important than textual information when shopping online. Your LinkedIn profile is no different – it's where you're selling your professional brand.

But don't panic! This isn't about being the next cover model. It's about authenticity with a professional polish. It's about telling your career story in pixels and colors.

Imagine scrolling through LinkedIn and suddenly stopping, your finger hovering over a profile that just... pops. The photo strikes that perfect balance of confidence and approachability. The banner cleverly hints at the individual's passion and expertise. That could be you.

How Visuals Boost Your Entire Profile

A strong visual presence doesn't just make you look good – it makes everything you do on LinkedIn more impactful. It's like a megaphone for your personal brand.

- **Profile views skyrocket:** LinkedIn reports that profiles with photos receive up to 21 times more views and 9 times more connection requests.

- **Engagement amplifies:** Your posts and comments stand out in the feed, garnering more likes, shares, and meaningful interactions. Posts with images receive 2X the engagement of those without, and video posts get 5X more engagement.

- **Credibility climbs:** A polished visual brand subconsciously signals professionalism and attention to detail.

- **Memorability multiplies:** In a sea of blue suits and white backgrounds, a thoughtfully crafted visual identity helps you stick in people's minds.

In short, your visual brand sets the tone for everything else on your profile. A vibrant, industry-appropriate image primes visitors to view your experience and skills in a more positive light. It's the LinkedIn equivalent of walking into an interview with a confident stride and a winning smile.

Crafting Your Visual Masterpiece

Now, you might be thinking, "Great, but I'm not a graphic designer or a photographer." Don't worry – in the following sections, we'll break down exactly how to:

- Choose and optimize a profile picture that makes people want to connect

- Design a banner that reinforces your personal brand (no Photoshop degree required)

- Sprinkle in multimedia elements that showcase your expertise

We'll explore AI-powered tools that take the guesswork out of image selection, and we'll look at industry-specific tips to ensure your visual brand resonates in your professional niche.

Remember, this isn't about creating a false image. It's about letting the best, most authentic version of your professional self shine through. It's about opening doors and creating opportunities through the power of visual storytelling.

So, are you ready to transform your LinkedIn profile from wallflower to show-stopper? Let's dive in and create a visual brand that demands attention, exudes professionalism, and leaves a lasting impression. Your career glow-up starts now!

Mastering Your LinkedIn Profile Photo

Let's face it – your profile picture is your digital handshake. It's the first thing people see, and it can make or break that crucial first impression. But why is it so important? Well, as already noted, profiles with photos get up to 21 times more views and 9 times more connection requests. That's like having a superpower in the LinkedIn universe!

But don't just take my word for it. Think about your personal browsing habits. When you're scrolling through LinkedIn, which profiles catch your eye? The ones with clear, professional photos, right? It's not vanity – it's human nature. We're drawn to faces, to the human element in a sea of digital information.

The Science of Snap Judgments

Now, let's get a bit nerdy (in a cool way, of course). There's actual science behind what makes a profile picture effective. It's not just about looking good – it's about psychology.

Eye Contact: The Window to Your Professional Soul

Ever felt like a photo was looking right at you? That's the power of eye contact. In the digital world, eye contact through your profile picture creates an instant connection. It says, "Hey, I'm here, I'm engaged, and I'm ready to connect." Studies show that photos with direct eye contact are perceived as more trustworthy and competent. So, look straight into that camera lens like you're making eye contact with your next big opportunity!

Smile Like You Mean It

Your facial expression sets the tone for your entire profile. A genuine smile (yes, we can tell when it's forced!) makes you appear approachable and confident. It's the difference between "I'm here because I have to be" and "I'm excited about what I do!" But here's a pro tip: a slight smile often works better than a full grin. It strikes that perfect balance between approachable and professional.

Frame it Right: The Art of Composition

Think of your profile picture as a tiny billboard for your personal brand. The framing can make or break the impact. Here's the golden rule: your face should occupy about 60% of the frame. Too close, and you're invading personal space. Too far, and you lose that crucial connection.

Also, stick to a straight-on or slightly angled pose. Extreme angles might work for Instagram, but on LinkedIn, they can come off as unprofessional or trying too hard. Remember, we're going for "trustworthy professional," not "aspiring influencer."

Dress for Success (Even If It's Just from the Waist Up)

You've heard "dress for the job you want, not the job you have," right? Well, that applies to your profile picture too. Your clothing should reflect your industry and the image you want to project. Working in finance? A suit might be your best bet. Tech startup? Maybe a nice button-down or blouse will do the trick.

But here's a tip: solid colors tend to work best. They're less distracting and keep the focus where it should be – on your face. And please, whatever you do, iron that shirt. Nothing says "I don't care about details," like wrinkled clothing in a professional photo.

Background Check: Keep It Clean

Your background should be like a good assistant – helpful but not stealing the show. A plain, light-colored background often works best. It keeps the focus on you and looks clean and professional. If you opt for an outdoor shot or office background, make sure it's not cluttered or distracting.

AI to the Rescue: Analyze Your Headshot

Feeling overwhelmed? Don't worry – AI is here to help! Tools like Snappr Photo Analyzer (Google it) can give you instant feedback on your profile picture. It's like having a professional photographer and a team of psychologists in your pocket.

Here's how it works:

1. Upload your photo to Snappr Photo Analyzer.

2. The AI analyzes everything from your smile and eye contact to the composition and background.

3. You get a detailed report with suggestions for improvement.

But remember, AI is a tool, not a rulebook. Use its suggestions as guidelines, not gospel. After all, you're unique, and your photo should reflect that!

Interpreting the Robot's Advice

When you get your Snappr report, don't panic if you don't score 100%. Focus on the big stuff:

- Is your face clearly visible?

- Are you making eye contact with the camera?

- Does your expression look natural and approachable?

- Is the background clean and non-distracting?

If you've nailed these, you're on the right track. The rest is fine-tuning.

The Balancing Act: Professional Yet Approachable

Here's the million-dollar question: How do you look professional without seeming stuffy? The answer: It's all about balance.

- Dress one notch above your daily work attire.

- Aim for a natural, slight smile rather than a forced grin or a super-serious expression.

- Choose a background that's clean but not sterile – a hint of your workspace can add personality.

- Let a bit of your personality shine through – if you always wear quirky glasses, don't ditch them for the photo.

Remember, you're not trying to be someone else. You're trying to be the best professional version of yourself.

The Photo Finish

Your profile picture is more than just a photo – it's the cornerstone of your personal brand on LinkedIn. It's your chance to make a powerful first impression in less than a second. So take the time to get it right. Invest in a professional photo if you can, or enlist a friend with a good camera and an eye for composition.

Remember, this photo will be seen by recruiters, potential clients, and future colleagues. Make it count. With the right profile picture, you're not just another face in the LinkedIn crowd – you're a standout professional ready to make your mark.

Banner Brilliance: Your Visual Headline

So now you've nailed your profile photo. You're looking sharp, approachable, and ready to conquer the world. But there's one more visual element to consider: your LinkedIn banner - the unsung hero of your visual branding.

Think of your banner as the establishing shot in the movie of your career. It sets the scene, creates the mood, and gives visitors a glimpse into your professional world before they've read a single word. It's your chance to make a statement, showcase your personality, and reinforce your personal brand - all in one 1584x396 pixel space.

Too many people overlook this valuable space or stick with LinkedIn's default. If that is you, it's time to change that. Let's turn your banner into a powerful branding tool that makes recruiters and connections take notice.

Elements of an Eye-Catching LinkedIn Banner

So, what goes into a banner that wows? Let's break it down:

Your Value Proposition in Visual Form

Your banner should be a visual representation of what you bring to the table.

Are you a data wizard? Consider incorporating sleek graphs or circuit-board patterns. A creative professional? This is your chance to showcase your design skills or feature examples of your work.

Remember, subtlety is key. You're not creating a billboard ad - you're setting a professional tone. Think less "Used Car Salesman" and more "TED Talk Presenter."

Industry-Relevant Imagery

Choose images or graphics that resonate with your field. A software developer might opt for clean lines and code snippets, while an environmental scientist could use nature imagery. The goal is to create an immediate visual connection to your professional identity.

Color Psychology at Play

Colors aren't just pretty - they're powerful communicators. Blue evokes trust and professionalism (there's a reason it's LinkedIn's default). Green suggests growth and balance. Orange radiates enthusiasm and creativity. Choose colors that not only look good but also align with your personal brand and industry.

The Power of White Space

Don't feel pressured to fill every pixel. Sometimes, less is more. Strategic use of white space can make your banner look clean, modern, and sophisticated. It also ensures that any text or focal points stand out clearly.

Text: Handle with Care

While it's tempting to plaster your banner with your job title and achievements, resist the urge. If you do include text, keep it minimal. A short tagline representing your UVP or a few words speaking to your expertise can be effective. Remember, your banner complements your profile - it doesn't replace it.

Common Mistakes: Banner Blunders to Avoid

Even with the best intentions, it's easy to stumble when creating your LinkedIn banner. Let's shine a spotlight on some of the most common faux pas:

- **The Default Dilemma:** Leaving the default LinkedIn banner is like showing up to a job interview in your pajamas. It screams, "I couldn't be bothered." Your banner is prime real estate for personal branding - don't let it go to waste with a generic blue gradient.

- **The Résumé Regurgitation:** Imagine walking into a networking event with your entire résumé plastered on your shirt. Overwhelming, right? That's exactly what happens when you try to cram too much text into your banner. Your banner is a teaser, not your life story. Save the details for your profile sections.

- **The Irrelevant Image Issue:** Using an image that has nothing to do with your professional brand is like wearing beachwear to a board meeting. Sure, it might get attention, but for all the wrong reasons. Your vacation photos or your pet, no matter how cute, probably don't belong in your professional banner.

- **The Resolution Revolution:** Nothing screams "I don't pay attention to detail" like a pixelated, blurry banner. Using low-resolution images or stretching small images to fit can make your profile look unprofessional. Always use high-quality images that look crisp and clear on all devices.

- **The Invisible Ink Syndrome:** Dark text on dark backgrounds, light text on white clouds - it's a recipe for illegibility. If you're including text in your banner, make sure it's easily readable. Contrast is your friend here. Your message should pop, not disappear.

- **The Misaligned Mishap:** Ever seen a banner where half the text is cut off, or the main image is awkwardly cropped? That's what happens when you forget about how LinkedIn displays banners on different devices. Always check how your banner looks on desktop, mobile, and tablet views before finalizing.

Remember, your banner is often the first impression you make on LinkedIn. By avoiding these common mistakes, you're already ahead of the game. Now, let's move on to creating a banner that not only avoids these pitfalls but truly shines!

AI to the Rescue: Designing Like a Pro

Now, I know what you're thinking. "This all sounds great, but I'm not a graphic designer!" Fear not, because this is where AI-powered tools come to the rescue. Enter Canva, the Swiss Army knife of design tools for non-designers.

Here's a step-by-step guide to get you started:

1. Go to Canva.com and create an account if you haven't already.

2. On the Canva homepage, click the purple "Create a design" button in the top right corner.

3. In the search bar that appears, type "LinkedIn Banner" or "LinkedIn Background Image."

4. Canva will open a new design that is perfectly sized for LinkedIn and has a variety of templates to choose from.

5. Browse the templates and select one that resonates with your professional brand. Don't worry if it's not perfect - you'll customize it!

Now, here's where Canva's AI magic comes into play. The platform offers AI-powered design suggestions to help you customize colors, fonts, and layouts with ease. You'll have access to millions of stock photos and graphics, or you can upload your own images for a personal touch. Canva's AI doesn't stop there – it can generate unique backgrounds and patterns, ensuring your banner stands out with a professional look.

What's more, the tool provides instant feedback on crucial design principles such as balance, contrast, and alignment, guiding you toward a polished final product. The best part? Canva's intuitive interface allows you to drag, drop, and design your way to a stellar banner without ever needing to open complex software like Photoshop. With these AI-powered features at your fingertips, creating a professional-looking LinkedIn banner becomes a breeze, even for those with little to no design experience.

Here are a few examples of LinkedIn profile banners that I was able to create in Canva in just 15 minutes. Although these are displayed in monochromatic colors in this book, the originals were designed with brand-appropriate colors.

Revolutionizing Finance FOR THE DIGITAL AGE
- Blockchain Solutions
- AI-Driven Risk Assessment
- Digital Payment Systems

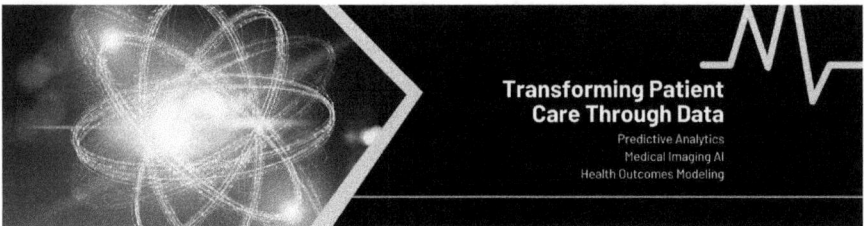
Transforming Patient Care Through Data
Predictive Analytics
Medical Imaging AI
Health Outcomes Modeling

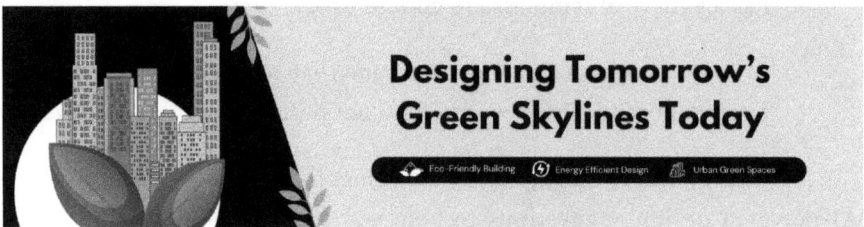
Designing Tomorrow's Green Skylines Today
Eco-Friendly Building   Energy Efficient Design   Urban Green Spaces

Making Your Banner Uniquely You

While templates are a great starting point, the key to a truly effective banner is personalization. Here are some ideas on how to make your banner stand out:

- **Showcase Your Unique Value Proposition (UVP):** Include a short, impactful tagline that encapsulates your professional value. For example, "Transforming Data into Business Insights" for a data analyst or "Crafting Digital Experiences That Inspire" for a UX designer.

- **Align with Your Brand Colors:** If you have a personal brand color scheme, incorporate it into your banner. This could be as simple as changing the background color or adjusting graphic elements to match your palette.

- **Choose Fonts That Reflect Your Style:** Select typography that aligns with your professional image. A sleek, modern sans-serif might work well for a tech professional, while a more traditional serif font could suit a lawyer or academic.

- **Incorporate Relevant Imagery:** Use icons or simple graphics that represent your field. For instance, a marketing professional might include subtle social media icons, while an architect could use a stylized blueprint or skyline.

- **Highlight Key Achievements:** If you've won a major award or reached a significant milestone, consider incorporating a small icon or subtle graphic representing this achievement. Just remember - less is more!

- **Include Your Contact Information:** If appropriate for your situation, consider adding your professional email or website URL. This can be particularly useful for freelancers or consultants.

- **Use Industry-Specific Elements:** Depending on your field, you might include elements such as a stylized code snippet for developers, a stock chart or graph for finance professionals, a paintbrush or color palette for creatives, and medical symbols for healthcare workers.

Remember, the goal is to create a banner that's professional, visually appealing, and reflective of your personal brand. Don't try to include everything - choose 2-3 key elements that best represent you and your professional identity.

PRO TIP

Always ensure you have the proper permissions to use any imagery on your profile. Unauthorized use of images can lead to serious copyright issues. To simplify the process, consider using Canva to create your banner; it provides a wealth of templates and stock images that are free to use, ensuring you stay compliant while enhancing your profile's visual appeal.

The Final Touch: Ensuring Clarity Across Devices

Before you hit that "Save" button, there's one crucial step left. Your beautifully crafted banner needs to look good on all devices - desktop, tablet, and mobile. Here's a tip: Design with mobile in mind first. If it looks good on a small screen, it'll look great on larger ones.

Test your banner on different devices and browsers. Ensure that any text is legible and key visual elements aren't cut off. Remember, LinkedIn crops banners differently on mobile, so what looks perfect on a desktop might lose important elements on your phone.

Your Banner, Your Brand

Your LinkedIn banner is more than just a pretty picture - it's a powerful branding tool. It's your chance to make a visual statement about who you are as a professional. With the right design, your banner can set you apart in a sea of blue gradients and stock photos. Remember, in the world of LinkedIn, your banner is your billboard. Make it count!

Multimedia Magic for Your LinkedIn Profile

With your professional headshot and carefully crafted banner in place, you're ready for the next step: bringing your LinkedIn profile to life. While many profiles remain text-only documents, yours can become an engaging showcase of your professional journey through the strategic use of multimedia elements. Let's explore how to transform your profile from a static presentation into a compelling digital portfolio.

The Power of Show, Don't Just Tell

In a world where attention spans are shorter than a TikTok video, multimedia elements can be your saving grace. They break up text, engage visitors, and provide tangible proof of your skills and accomplishments. It's one thing to say you're a "dynamic public speaker," but it's another to show a video clip of you commanding the stage at a conference.

Types of Multimedia Content: Your Career Highlight Reel

Let's explore the different types of multimedia content you can add to your LinkedIn profile:

Images and Infographics

Perfect for: Showcasing visual work, summarizing data, or illustrating concepts.

- A graphic designer could share a portfolio of logos they've created.

- A data analyst might include an infographic summarizing a successful project.

- A marketer could showcase before-and-after visuals of a rebranding project.

Videos and Animations

Ideal for: Demonstrating skills, sharing presentations, or adding a personal touch.

- A software developer could share a short demo of an app they've built.

- A public speaker might include a clip from a recent presentation.

- A teacher could share an animated explainer video they created for students.

Presentations and Documents

Great for: Sharing in-depth knowledge, case studies, or research.

- A consultant could upload a slide deck from a recent client presentation.

- A researcher might share a published paper or poster.

- A project manager could include a case study of a successful project.

Audio Recordings

Perfect for: Podcasters, musicians, or language professionals.

- A voice actor could share samples of their work.

- A language teacher might include pronunciation guides.

- A musician could showcase original compositions.

Your Expertise Showcase

While images and documents can undoubtedly spice up your profile, creating a dynamic presentation or video takes your LinkedIn game to a whole new level. Think of it as your own personal TED Talk, minus the nerve-wracking live audience. While videos can be incredibly powerful, let's face it - not everyone is ready for their close-up. That's where PowerPoint presentations come in handy. They're the perfect middle ground between a static document and a full-blown video production.

Crafting a killer presentation isn't just about flexing your design muscles (though that doesn't hurt). It's about packaging your professional insights in a way that's digestible, engaging, and, dare we say, scroll-stopping. When done right, these presentations can turn your profile from a yawn-inducing list of job titles into a treasure trove of industry wisdom.

So, why bother with all this extra effort? Well, for starters, it's a surefire way to grab attention in a sea of text-heavy profiles. It's also a fantastic opportunity to showcase your communication skills and prove you can break down complex ideas into bite-sized, visually appealing chunks. Plus, it's versatile - your presentation can be viewed on anything from a smartphone to a desktop, making it accessible to recruiters and connections on the go.

Now, let's talk content. Your presentation should be more than just a rehash of your résumé. Instead, think of topics that position you as a thought leader in your field. Here are some ideas to get your creative juices flowing:

- "Why You Should Hire Me" (showcase your unique skills, experiences, and value proposition)

- "The Future of [Your Industry]: Trends and Predictions"

- "How I Tackled [Specific Challenge] and Came Out on Top"

- "My Secret Sauce: Unique Strategies for [Your Area of Expertise]"

- "[Your Industry] Myths Debunked: What Really Works"

- "The Evolution of [Your Field]: A Decade in Review"

- "My Leadership Philosophy in 10 Slides"

 **PRO TIP**

Want to really turn heads? Try the contrarian approach. Take a popular industry belief and flip it on its head. For example, "Why [Trendy Industry Practice] Might Be Holding You Back" or "The Unpopular Truth About [Common Industry Belief]." This approach not only showcases your critical thinking skills but also sparks engaging discussions, positioning you as a bold, independent thinker in your field.

When crafting your presentation, remember that less is more. Aim for 10-15 slides that pack a punch. Use eye-catching visuals, but keep the design consistent. And don't forget to optimize for mobile - your masterpiece should look just as good on a tiny screen as it does on a desktop.

Finally, end with a bang. Include a call-to-action that encourages viewers to connect, comment, or reach out for more insights. After all, the goal isn't just to impress - it's to start meaningful professional conversations.

By showcasing your expertise through these dynamic presentations, you're not just filling out your profile - you're positioning yourself as a valuable contributor to your professional community. It's your chance to prove that you're not just another cog in the corporate machine but a thought leader with unique insights to share. So go ahead and give your LinkedIn profile the multimedia makeover it deserves!

Where to Showcase Your Multimedia Masterpieces

Now that you're buzzing with multimedia ideas, where should you put them? LinkedIn offers several prime spots for your content. We've covered these in detail in earlier chapters, but here's a quick refresher on where you can add multimedia elements:

- **"Featured" Section:** This is your highlight reel, front and center on your profile. Use it for your absolute best, most impressive content.

- **"Experience" Section:** Add media to specific job entries to provide evidence of your accomplishments in each role.

- **"Education" Section:** Showcase projects, presentations, or publications from your academic career.

- **"About" Section:** While you can't directly embed media here, you can include links to external content.

- **Additional Sections:** Include scans of awards, certifications, or other achievements that have a visual component in the optional sections, such as "Licenses & Certifications," "Projects," or "Publications."

Each of these sections offers unique opportunities to showcase different aspects of your professional journey. Remember, the key is to strategically place your multimedia content where it will have the most impact. Use this quick reference to remind yourself of the available options, but don't forget to dive back into those earlier chapters for the nitty-gritty details on making each section shine with well-chosen multimedia elements.

Choosing Your Multimedia MVPs

With all these options, it's tempting to go overboard. But remember, quality trumps quantity. Here's how to select the most impactful multimedia elements:

- **Align with Your Personal Brand:** Choose content that reinforces your professional identity and supports your career goals.

- **Showcase Diverse Skills:** Use different types of media to highlight various aspects of your expertise.

- **Keep it Current:** Regularly update your multimedia content to reflect your most recent and relevant work.

- **Consider Your Audience:** Think about what would impress potential employers or clients in your field.

- **Maintain Professionalism:** Ensure all content is high-quality, work-appropriate, and free from errors.

PRO TIP

Before adding any multimedia, ask yourself, "Does this add value to my profile?" If the answer isn't a resounding "Yes!" keep looking for something better.

Making Your Multimedia Shine

Now that you've chosen your star content let's make sure it sparkles:
- **Use Descriptive Titles:** Don't just upload "Presentation.pdf." Use titles that grab attention and explain the content, like "Award-Winning Marketing Strategy Presentation."

- **Add Context:** Use the description field to explain why this piece is important. What impact did it have? What does it demonstrate about your skills?

- **Ensure Accessibility:** If you're uploading videos, consider adding captions. For images, include alt text describing the content.

- **Check for Mobile-Friendliness:** View your profile on different devices to ensure your multimedia elements display correctly on all screens.

The Multimedia Mindset: Always Be Capturing

Adopting a "multimedia mindset" can help you continuously improve your profile:

- At your next presentation, ask a colleague to snap a high-quality photo or record a short video clip.

- After completing a successful project, create a visual summary of the results.

- When you learn a new skill, record a short demo to showcase your new expertise.

By always being on the lookout for profile-worthy moments, you'll build a library of compelling content to keep your LinkedIn presence fresh and engaging.

By now, you should be brimming with ideas to transform your LinkedIn profile into a multimedia masterpiece. Remember, the goal isn't to create a digital scrapbook - it's to craft a compelling narrative of your professional journey and capabilities.

So, are you ready to step into the spotlight? With these multimedia strategies, you're not just telling potential employers or clients about your skills - you're showing them.

Your Action Plan to Elevate Your Visual Brand

Ready to transform your LinkedIn profile into a visual masterpiece? Here's your action plan:

- Audit your current profile picture and banner. Assess if they're professional, high-quality, and reflective of your personal brand. If not, schedule a professional headshot session or arrange for high-quality photos in various professional outfits.

- Use tools like Snappr Photo Analyzer to evaluate potential profile pictures. Choose the one that scores highest and best represents your professional image.

- Design your LinkedIn banner using a platform like Canva. Create a mood board of colors, fonts, and imagery that align with your personal brand. Incorporate your unique value proposition and design 2-3 variations to choose from.

- Test your new profile picture and banner options on different devices (desktop, tablet, mobile) to ensure they look good across all platforms. Ask for feedback from trusted colleagues before finalizing.

- Update your LinkedIn profile with your new picture and banner. Review your profile sections ("Featured," "Experience," "Education," and others) and add 3-5 pieces of relevant multimedia content that showcase your skills and achievements.

- Monitor the impact of your visual updates on your profile views and engagement over the next few weeks.

- Set a reminder to review and refresh your visual branding elements every 6-12 months to keep your profile current and engaging.

Remember, your visual brand is an evolving aspect of your professional identity. Regularly refine and update it to ensure it always represents the best version of your professional self!

Chapter Eleven

Igniting Your LinkedIn Presence

From Static to Sensational

Y ou've put in the effort to create an impressive LinkedIn profile. Now, it's time to ensure it gets seen by the right people at the right time.

Visibility on LinkedIn isn't just about being seen—it's about being discovered for the right opportunities. Think of your LinkedIn profile as a lighthouse in the vast ocean of professional networking. Without proper visibility settings and strategic positioning, even the most brilliantly crafted profile might remain hidden in the shadows, never reaching its full potential.

Your visibility strategy affects everything from your job search success to your networking opportunities:

- For job seekers, enhanced visibility can mean the difference between missing and landing dream opportunities

- For networkers, it determines whether potential collaborators and industry peers can find and connect with you

- For thought leaders, it impacts how widely your insights and contributions reach your professional community

The good news? LinkedIn provides powerful tools to control and amplify your visibility. This chapter will show you how to:

- Fine-tune your profile's visibility settings for maximum impact

- Leverage LinkedIn's job search features to connect with opportunities

- Use strategic tools like "Easy Apply" and résumé uploads to stand out

- Balance professional exposure with privacy when needed

It's time to transform your LinkedIn profile from a static résumé into a dynamic career catalyst. Here are the specific strategies that will help you get noticed by the right people while attracting meaningful professional opportunities.

Optimizing Your Profile's Visibility

First, let's focus on boosting your LinkedIn visibility. Whether you're actively job hunting or simply building your professional network, getting your profile in front of the right audience is crucial.

Turning Up the Visibility Dial

First things first, let's make sure your profile isn't hiding in the shadows. Here's how:

1. Click the "Me" icon at the top of your LinkedIn homepage.

2. Select "View profile."

3. On your profile page, look for the "Edit public profile & URL" button on the right side.

4. In the right column of your public profile page, you'll see "Your profile's public visibility." This is where the magic happens!

Now, here's the golden rule for job seekers: Turn that visibility ON! You want to allow as many sections as you're comfortable with to be visible to the public (ideally all of them). Remember, you're building your brand here. You can't become a LinkedIn superstar if you're hiding behind a digital curtain.

PRO TIP

At a minimum, make sure your profile photo, headline, and summary are visible to the public. These are your virtual handshake, elevator pitch, and conversation starter all rolled into one!

Customizing Your URL: Your Digital Business Card

While you're in the public profile settings, let's give your LinkedIn URL a makeover. By default, LinkedIn assigns you a URL with a bunch of random numbers. But you're not random, so why should your URL be?

PRO TIP

If your name is taken when customizing your profile URL, try adding your middle name, dashes, or your profession (e.g., linkedin.com/in/john-smith, johnsmithmarketing, john-m-smith, or johnmichael-smith). Keep it professional and easy to remember!

Here's how to claim your digital real estate:
1. In the right column of your public profile page, look for "Edit your custom URL."

2. Click the pencil icon next to your current URL

3. Type in your desired URL. Ideally, this should be your name (e.g., linkedin.com/in/johnsmith)

4. Click Save

Expanding Your Reach: Your LinkedIn Profile Everywhere

Now that you've optimized your profile and customized your URL, it's time to maximize its visibility. Think of your LinkedIn profile as a digital extension of your professional identity - one that should be easily accessible across various platforms. Here's where you should consider including your LinkedIn URL:

- **Your résumé:** Include it prominently alongside your contact information.

- **Business cards:** Add the URL to your professional cards for easy reference.

- **Email signature:** Incorporate it into your signature for increased visibility.

- **Other social media profiles:** Link it on your other professional online platforms.

- **Personal website or blog:** If you have one, ensure your LinkedIn profile is easily accessible.

By promoting your LinkedIn URL across these platforms, you increase your chances of being discovered by potential employers, clients, or collaborators. It's an effective way to create multiple touchpoints that lead directly to your professional profile.

Streamlining Profile Access With a QR Code

To further streamline access to your profile, consider utilizing a QR code. This technology can be particularly useful in networking situations, allowing others to access your LinkedIn profile with a simple scan.

Here's how to create and implement a QR code for your profile:

- Visit Canva's free QR code generator (https://www.canva.com/qr-code-generator/).

- Input your custom LinkedIn URL.

- Download the QR code and keep it readily available on your phone.

- Consider printing it on your business cards for an additional access point.

PRO TIP

For networking events, you might find it helpful to temporarily set the QR code as your phone's lock screen. This allows for quick and easy sharing of your profile information.

I encourage you to put these strategies into practice. To see how this works, scan the QR code below to visit my LinkedIn profile. And while you are there, please send a connection request with a note that you have read this book. I'd love to connect with all my readers!

Remember, in the professional world of LinkedIn, visibility is crucial. By implementing these strategies, you're taking proactive steps to enhance your professional presence and open doors to new opportunities.

A Deep Dive into Privacy Settings

Now that we've got your profile shining bright, let's make sure you're in control of who sees what.

Head over to your Settings & Privacy page. You can find this by clicking on "Me" > "Settings & Privacy."

Here are some key settings to review:

- **Profile viewing options:** Choose how you appear to other members when you view their profile. As a job seeker, consider using your full name and headline to maximize networking opportunities.

- **Share job changes, education changes, and work anniversaries:** Keep this turned on to help you stay on your network's radar. (but turn it off temporarily when you are making major edits and changes to your profile to avoid notifying your network of every change)

- **Manage active status:** Being shown as active can increase your chances of being messaged by recruiters. Consider turning this on.

- **Profile visibility off LinkedIn:** Allow search engines such as Google to show your profile. This increases your discoverability beyond just LinkedIn.

- **Manage who can discover your profile from your email address or phone number:** If you're actively job-seeking, consider making this visible to everyone to make it easier for recruiters to find you.

Remember, LinkedIn often updates its privacy settings. Make it a habit to review these settings regularly - think of it as a quarterly check-up for your digital professional health.

The Visibility Balancing Act

I know what some of you might be thinking: "But wait, I'm currently employed. I don't want my boss to know I'm job hunting!" Don't worry—LinkedIn has a feature that allows you to discreetly signal to recruiters that you're open to opportunities without broadcasting it to your entire network. I'll explain how to use that feature in more detail later in this chapter.

Optimizing your visibility isn't about revealing every detail of your professional life to the world. It's about strategically highlighting your skills and experience to the right audience. Think of it like curating your professional art gallery—you choose which pieces to showcase and how to present them for the most significant impact.

Unlocking LinkedIn's Job Search Toolkit

With your privacy and visibility settings in place, it's time to dive into LinkedIn's treasure trove of job-hunting tools. Imagine having a personal career concierge quietly working behind the scenes to connect you with your ideal job. Well, that's exactly what LinkedIn offers—if you know how to make the most of it.

Think of this section as your all-access pass to LinkedIn's job search features. And we're not just talking about scrolling through job listings (though that's part of it). LinkedIn offers a full suite of powerful tools designed to turbocharge your job hunt. From customizing your preferences to highlighting your skills, LinkedIn has packed its platform with features like a Swiss Army knife. We're about to explore them all.

Dialing In Your Job Preferences

First things first - let's tell LinkedIn exactly what you're looking for. It's like programming your GPS before a road trip. The more specific you are, the more likely you are to reach your desired destination.

- **Finding Your Way to the "Jobs" Tab:** It's right there at the top of your LinkedIn homepage, nestled between "My Network" and "Messaging." Click on it, and voila - you've entered job search central!

- **Painting the Picture of Your Ideal Job:** Think of this as creating your professional wish list. LinkedIn acts as your career matchmaker, using your preferences to find fitting opportunities. You'll specify job titles you are interested in (make sure to list variations!), locations you are considering (including remote opportunities), and industries that align with your career goals.

- **Show Me the Money: Salary Expectations:** Yes, you can (and should) tell LinkedIn what you're worth. Don't worry; this info will be kept confidential. It helps filter out jobs that might not meet your financial needs. No more wasting time on roles that can't foot the bill!

- **Work Type:** Your Office, Their Office, or Somewhere in Between? In this post-pandemic world, work arrangements are more varied than ever. LinkedIn lets you specify if you're looking for remote, hybrid, or on-site positions. It's like choosing your own adventure but for your career!

Remember, these preferences aren't set in stone. As your job search evolves, come back and tweak these settings. It's all about refining your search to find that perfect professional fit.

The Green Light: Leveraging the "Open to Work" Feature

Now it's time to talk about LinkedIn's not-so-secret weapon: the "Open to Work" feature. This tool signals to recruiters and hiring managers that you're actively seeking new opportunities. But like any powerful tool, it needs to be wielded wisely.

Understanding and Customizing "Open to Work"

Imagine you're at a networking event, and everyone who's job hunting is wearing a bright green hat. That's essentially what the "Open to Work" feature does on LinkedIn - it's your virtual "Hey, I'm available!" sign.

Here's how to light up your green beacon:

1. Go to your LinkedIn homepage and click the "Me" icon.

2. Select "View Profile."

3. Scroll down to your intro section and click the "Open to" button.

4. Select "Finding a new job."

Now that it's activated, LinkedIn lets you customize this feature to fit your specific job-seeking needs:

- **Job titles:** Be specific but not too limiting. Include related roles you would consider.

- **Job locations:** Cast a wide net if you're flexible, or be specific if you're location-bound.

- **Start date:** Be realistic about when you can start a new role.

- **Job types:** Full-time, part-time, contract, internship - choose what works for you.

- **Visibility:** Choose between "All LinkedIn members" or "Recruiters only" based on your situation.

PRO TIP

If you're currently between jobs or taking a career break, consider using LinkedIn's "Career Break" feature in conjunction with the Open to Work settings. This allows you to explain any gaps in your employment history while signaling your availability for new opportunities.

Addressing the Employed Job Seeker's Dilemma

If you're currently employed and job hunting, you might be feeling a bit like a secret agent. You want opportunities, but you don't want to tip off your current employer. Don't worry - LinkedIn has thought of that.

The "Open to Work" feature allows you to signal your availability to recruiters without broadcasting it to the whole world. You can choose to share your status only with recruiters outside your current company. It's like having an invisibility cloak for your job search!

But remember, while LinkedIn takes steps to hide this information from your current company, they can't guarantee complete privacy. Use this feature wisely and complement it with discreet networking and job search activities.

Debunking the Desperation Myth

Let's bust a myth that's been lingering in the job search world. In the past, some career coaches (including me) advised against using the "Open to Work" feature publicly, fearing it might make candidates appear desperate.

But times have changed, and so has this perception.

The professional landscape has evolved, and with it, the view of the "Open to Work" banner. Many recruiters now see it not as a sign of desperation but as a beacon of clarity and proactiveness. They appreciate the straightforward nature of the feature, as it allows them to quickly identify candidates who are actively seeking new opportunities.

From a recruiter's perspective, the "Open to Work" banner is a time-saving tool. It helps them focus their efforts on candidates who are genuinely interested in new roles, streamlining the recruitment process for everyone involved. They understand that being in the job market is a normal part of professional life, and showcasing this on your LinkedIn profile is not only acceptable but can be advantageous.

The stigma of desperation is gone. In fact, using this feature can signal confidence and readiness for new challenges. It tells recruiters you're proactive about your career development and aren't afraid to put yourself out there. In today's fast-paced job market, this kind of clarity and initiative can set you apart from the crowd.

So, my advice in the current job market is: as long as your job search isn't a secret, embrace the green banner with confidence. It's not a mark of desperation - it's a signal that you're ready for your next big career move.

Strategies for Various Career Situations

The "Open to Work" feature is versatile, but its effectiveness depends on how well you tailor it to your specific career situation. Different job seekers have different needs and constraints. Let's look at how to best use this tool in different career situations, helping you maximize your job search while keeping things appropriately low-key when needed.

- **The Stealth Job Seeker:** Currently employed but looking? LinkedIn's got your back. You can choose to share your "Open to Work" status only with recruiters outside your current company. It's like having an invisibility cloak for your job search!

- **The Career Changer:** Switching industries? Use the "Open to Work" feature to signal your interest in new fields. In the job titles section, include roles from your target profession.

- **The Returning Professional:** Coming back after a break? The "Open to Work" feature can help you announce your return. Use the "About" section to briefly explain your career break and highlight any relevant skills or experiences you gained during that time.

- **The New Graduate:** Just starting out? "Open to Work" can help you get noticed. Be sure to include entry-level positions in your desired field, and don't be afraid to cast a wide net with locations if you're flexible.

- **The Freelancer or Contractor:** Looking for your next gig? Use "Open to Work" to specify you're open to contract or freelance work.

Understanding How Recruiters See "Open to Work"

You might wonder how your "Open to Work" status appears on the other side. Let's take a moment to understand how recruiters view and interact with this feature.

- **LinkedIn Recruiter Interface:** There's a specific "Open to Work" filter in the Spotlights section of LinkedIn Recruiter. This means recruiters can easily find candidates who've enabled this feature.

- **Workplace Preferences:** Recruiters can filter candidates by workplace type (on-site, hybrid, remote) when using the Open to Work filter. Your preferences matter!

- **Location and Job Type:** When recruiters hover over the "Open to work" spotlight in search results or view your profile, they can see your preferred job locations and types.

- **'Recruiters Only' Visibility:** If you choose this option, your "Open to Work" status is only visible to recruiters using LinkedIn Recruiter. It won't appear on your public profile, providing discretion, especially if you're currently employed.

- **'All LinkedIn Members' Visibility:** If you select this option, a green #OpenToWork banner will appear on your profile photo, and your job-seeking status will be visible to all LinkedIn users. This maximizes your visibility but offers less privacy.

Making "Open to Work" Work for You

Now that you know how to activate the "Open to Work" feature, let's explore how to maximize its effectiveness. This tool is more than just a status update—it's a powerful signal to your professional network and potential employers. Here are some tips:

- **Pair it with an updated profile:** Before turning on "Open to Work," make sure your profile is up-to-date and showcases your best professional self. It's like making sure your house is clean before inviting guests over.

- **Be active on LinkedIn:** The "Open to Work" feature works best when combined with regular LinkedIn activity. Comment on posts, share articles, and engage with your network.

- **Use it in conjunction with other strategies:** "Open to Work" is a powerful job search tool, but it shouldn't be your only one. Use it alongside targeted job applications, networking, and other job-seeking activities.

- **Create an announcement post:** Let your network know you're open to opportunities. This can lead to valuable career conversations.

- **Don't forget to turn it off:** Once you've landed that dream job, remember to switch off the "Open to Work" feature. It's like remembering to take off that "Happy Birthday" hat after your party's over.

Remember, the "Open to Work" feature is more than just a button - it's a statement. You're telling the professional world that you're ready for new challenges and opportunities. Use it wisely,

Your Résumé: The Hidden Powerhouse of LinkedIn

Here's a little-known LinkedIn secret that could be a game-changer for your job search: When you upload your résumé and share it with recruiters, you're unlocking a treasure trove of searchable content that goes beyond your visible profile. That's right - recruiters can find you based on skills and experiences mentioned in your résumé, even if they're not listed on your LinkedIn profile. It's like having a secret language that only you and recruiters understand!

Why is this such a big deal? Let's break it down:

- **Additional Keyword Opportunities:** Your résumé provides another layer of content for LinkedIn's search algorithms. This means more chances for your key skills and experiences to be recognized.

- **Increased Keyword Density:** Even if a skill or tool is mentioned on your profile, having it in your résumé also increases its prominence. It's like turning up the volume on your most important qualifications.

- **Niche Skills Spotlight:** Your résumé might include specific tools, technologies, or niche skills that don't fit neatly into your profile sections. Now, recruiters searching for these exact terms can find you.

- **Varied Phrasing:** Your résumé might describe your skills and experiences using words or phrases different from your profile. This variety increases your chances of matching a recruiter's search terms.

- **Up-to-Date Information:** Recently gained a new certification or completed a project? If it's on your résumé but not yet on your profile, recruiters can still discover you for these latest achievements.

- **Passive Job Seeking Superpower:** Even if you're not actively updating your profile, your uploaded résumé keeps working behind the scenes, potentially connecting you with exciting opportunities.

This dual-layer approach - profile plus résumé - essentially doubles your keyword real estate. It's not just about having more keywords; it's about strengthening your overall searchability on LinkedIn. By leveraging both your profile and your uploaded résumé, you're creating a robust, multi-faceted digital presence that's more likely to catch a recruiter's eye, no matter how they phrase their search.

Uploading Your Résumé: More Than Just a File

Uploading your résumé to LinkedIn is a strategic move that can significantly boost your discoverability. This simple action can expand your digital footprint and increase your chances of being found by recruiters. Here's how to do it:

1. Navigate to the "Jobs" section (it's like your career control room)

2. Click on "Preferences" in the left sidebar (your personal job search settings)

3. Scroll down to "My Qualifications" (this is where the magic happens)

4. Under "Résumés and application data," click the "Upload résumé" button and select your file

PRO TIP

LinkedIn keeps your four most recent résumé uploads. It's like having multiple outfits ready for different job interview occasions!

Sharing Your Résumé: Unlocking Your LinkedIn Superpower

Now that you've uploaded your résumé, it's time to make it work for you behind the scenes. Let's explore how to effectively share your résumé with recruiters, leveraging LinkedIn's features to maximize your job search potential.

1. Navigate to the "Jobs" section.

2. Click on "Preferences" in the left sidebar.

3. Scroll down to "My Qualifications."

4. Under "Résumés and application data, find the option that says "Share your résumé data with recruiters" and toggle it on.

5. If prompted, review and accept the terms of service.

By enabling this feature, you're allowing recruiters using LinkedIn's premium tools to see the skills and experiences from your uploaded résumés when they're searching for candidates. But don't worry. This feature doesn't share your entire résumé publicly. It only surfaces matches when there are specific skill or keyword alignments with a recruiter's search. Your privacy is still protected!

PRO TIP

When you upload your resume to LinkedIn, you're essentially creating a shadow profile that works tirelessly to connect you with relevant opportunities. It's one of the most underutilized yet potent tools in your LinkedIn arsenal - so don't let this secret weapon go to waste!

Résumé Best Practices for LinkedIn Success

The following tips reflect tried-and-true résumé strategies that are particularly effective in the context of LinkedIn's search algorithms and recruiter behavior. By implementing these practices, you'll maximize the impact of your résumé, whether it's viewed directly or whether it works behind the scenes, influencing your discoverability through LinkedIn's search function.

- **Keep it Current:** Regularly update your uploaded résumé to reflect your latest experiences, skills, and achievements.

- **Keyword Optimization:** Pack your résumé with industry-specific keywords and phrases. Think about the terms recruiters in your field might be searching for.

- **Multiple Versions:** Take advantage of LinkedIn's four-résumé storage by uploading different versions tailored to various job types or industries you're targeting.

- **Consistency is Key:** Ensure the information on your résumé aligns with your profile. Discrepancies can raise red flags for recruiters.

- **Quantify Achievements:** Use numbers and percentages to highlight your accomplishments.

- **Use Action Verbs:** Start bullet points with strong action verbs to make your experiences more dynamic and impactful.

- **Tailor for ATS:** Keep your résumé format ATS-friendly. Avoid complex layouts that might not parse well in applicant tracking systems. You can download professionally designed, ATS-friendly résumé templates from Distinctive Resume Templates (https://www.distin ctiveresumetemplates.com)

- **Proofread Carefully:** A typo-free résumé demonstrates attention to detail. Proofread multiple times and consider using AI-powered tools like Grammarly for an extra check.

- **Include Relevant Certifications:** Make sure any important certifications or courses are listed, especially if they're recent or highly relevant to your target roles.

- **Refresh Regularly:** Even if your experiences haven't changed, periodically re-upload your résumé. This can give you a boost in LinkedIn's recency-based algorithms.

By following these practices and leveraging LinkedIn's résumé sharing feature, you're not just passively waiting for opportunities – you're actively positioning yourself to be discovered by the right recruiters at the right time. Your résumé becomes a powerful tool working 24/7 to advance your career, even when you're not actively job searching.

Supercharging With AI-Powered Job Alerts

Imagine that you're comfortably sipping your morning coffee when your phone buzzes. It's not another social media notification - it's LinkedIn, telling you about a job that seems tailor-made for you. Sounds like a dream? Well, welcome to the world of AI-powered job alerts!

Gone are the days of endlessly scrolling through job postings, feeling like you're searching for a four-leaf clover on a football field. LinkedIn's job alert system, supercharged with artificial intelligence, is about to become your tireless, 24/7 job-hunting sidekick. It's like having a personal recruiter who never sleeps and is always on the lookout for your perfect role.

Cracking the Code of LinkedIn's Job Alert System

LinkedIn's job alert system is like your personal job-hunting assistant. It scans new job postings and notifies you when positions matching your criteria pop up. But here's the kicker - its effectiveness depends on how well you set it up. Here's how to make it work for you:

1. **Setting Up Basic Job Alerts:**

   ○ Go to the LinkedIn Jobs page.

   ○ Perform a search using your target job title, location, and any other relevant filters.

   ○ Click on the "Create job alert" button at the top of the search results.

   ○ Choose your alert frequency (daily or weekly).

2. **Refining Your Alerts:** While job alerts are primarily based on job titles and locations, you can refine them to be more effective.

   ○ Use variations of job titles (e.g., "Marketing Manager," "Brand Manager," "Digital Marketing Lead").

   ○ Include industry-specific terms if relevant (e.g., "Tech Marketing Manager," "Fintech Marketing Lead").

   ○ Experiment with different location settings, including "Remote" if applicable.

Leveraging AI for Smarter Searches

Here's where AI can give your job alerts a boost:
- **Identifying Relevant Job Titles:** Use AI chatbots to brainstorm

related job titles you might not have considered. Try prompts like "List 10 alternative job titles for a Marketing Manager in the tech industry" and "What are emerging job titles in [your field] for [year]?"

- **Finding Industry-Specific Terms:** AI can help you identify industry-specific terms to include in your searches. For example: "What are the top 5 industry-specific terms I should know for marketing roles in fintech?"

- **Skills-Based Searching:** While job alerts are title-based, you can use AI-suggested skills to perform manual searches and create alerts from those.

- **Optimizing Your Profile for Alerts:** LinkedIn also sends job recommendations based on your profile. Enhance these by:

  - Ensuring your profile is complete and up-to-date.

  - Using AI-suggested keywords in your profile summary and experience sections.

  - Regularly updating your skills section with AI-recommended relevant skills.

- **Staying Ahead of Trends:** Use AI to stay informed about industry trends that might affect job titles and skills:

  - Regularly ask AI chatbots about emerging trends in your field.

  - Use these insights to adjust your job alerts and profile keywords.

By combining LinkedIn's job alert system with AI-powered insights, you're not just passively waiting for job notifications – you're strategically positioning yourself to catch the most relevant opportunities as soon as they appear. It's like having a smart radar system for your dream job!

The Power of Following Company Pages

Think of following a company on LinkedIn as planting a seed in the garden of your career. It might seem like a small action, but it can grow into something much bigger. Let's explore why hitting that "Follow" button is more than just a casual click:

- **Your Personal Industry Newsfeed:** Imagine having a curated news channel just for your professional interests. That's what following company pages on LinkedIn does. You'll get the latest scoop on company news, events, and product launches, all served up in your LinkedIn feed.

- **The Hidden Recruiter Magnet:** Here's another little-known LinkedIn superpower: When you follow a company, you're putting yourself on their recruiters' radar. That's right - recruiters can specifically search for candidates who follow their company. It's like raising your hand in a crowded room and saying, "Hey, I'm interested in what you're doing!" This simple act could be your ticket to getting noticed by your dream company.

- **Your Interview Prep Cheat Sheet:** Following a company is like getting a backstage pass to their world. You'll gain insights into their culture, values, and recent developments. When interview time comes, you'll be armed with talking points that'll make you sound like an insider.

- **Networking on Easy Mode:** Want to connect with people at your target company? Following their page makes it easier to identify and reach out to current employees. It's networking with a purpose, potentially leading to informational interviews or even referrals.

- **First Dibs on Job Openings:** Many companies post job openings on their LinkedIn pages before they hit the big job boards. By following, you're positioning yourself to be among the first to know - and apply.

- **Your Industry Crystal Ball:** Company updates often include insights about industry trends and challenges. It's like having a crystal ball for your professional field, helping you stay ahead of the curve.

- **Engagement Opportunities Galore:** Liking, commenting, and sharing company posts isn't just idle scrolling - it's strategic visibility. Each interaction is a chance to demonstrate your interest and expertise to the company and your network.

- **LinkedIn's AI Working for You:** The more companies you follow, the smarter LinkedIn's algorithm gets at showing you relevant content. It's like having a personal AI assistant curating your professional knowledge.

- **Interview Confidence Booster:** Walking into an interview armed with the latest company news? That's the kind of confidence that impresses interviewers and sets you apart from the competition.

- **Your Career GPS:** Following multiple companies in your industry gives you a bird's-eye view of the professional landscape. It's like having a GPS for your career, showing you different paths and opportunities you might not have considered.

Maximizing Your Company Following Strategy

To really leverage these benefits, especially the recruiter visibility bonus, be strategic about which companies you follow and how you interact with their content. Here are some AI-powered prompts to help you identify the right companies to follow:

AI PROMPTS TO IDENTIFY EMPLOYERS TO FOLLOW

"I'm a [your profession] interested in [specific industry/field]. Can you list 10 innovative companies in this space that I should consider following on LinkedIn?"

- "Based on my background in [your skills/experience], what are 5 companies that might be good fits for my career goals? Please include a mix of well-known and up-and-coming organizations."

- "I'm interested in companies known for [specific aspect, e.g., work-life balance]. Can you suggest 7 companies that excel in this area and explain why they stand out?"

- "What are the top 3 fastest-growing companies in [your industry] that I should be paying attention to? Please provide a brief overview of each."

- "I want to diversify the companies I follow on LinkedIn. Can you recommend 5 companies each in [Industry 1], [Industry 2], and [Industry 3] that are leaders in their respective fields?"

- "Can you list 10 companies in [specific city or region, e.g., Seattle area] that are known for their excellent work culture and career growth opportunities? Please include a mix of large corporations and promising startups."

- "I'm interested in companies that are making significant advancements in [specific technology or field, e.g., artificial intelligence, renewable energy]. Can you suggest 7 companies to follow on LinkedIn that are at the forefront of this innovation?"

- "What are 5 companies that have recently (in the past year) expanded their operations or opened new offices? Please provide a brief overview of their growth and what it might mean for job seekers."

- "I'm looking to transition into a new industry. Can you recommend 8 companies that have strong training or mentorship programs for career changers? Please include companies from various sectors."

- "Who are the top 6 thought leaders or influential CEOs in [your industry] right now? Can you list their companies and explain why following these organizations on LinkedIn could be beneficial for staying ahead in the industry?"

Remember, following companies on LinkedIn isn't just about passive observation. Engage with their content, participate in discussions, and use the insights gained to inform your job search and professional development strategies. By doing so, you're not just following companies - you're actively shaping your professional narrative and increasing your chances of landing that dream role.

Leveraging LinkedIn's "Easy Apply" Feature

In the fast-paced world of job hunting, every second counts. That's where LinkedIn's "Easy Apply" feature comes in - it's the turbo boost for your job application process. But what exactly is Easy Apply? Simply put, it's a streamlined application system that allows you to submit your candidacy for a job with just a few clicks directly through LinkedIn.

Gone are the days of lengthy form-filling and creating new accounts on various company websites. "Easy Apply"leverages your LinkedIn profile to send your information to employers quickly and efficiently. It's like having a personal assistant who knows your professional history by heart and can whip up a job application in seconds. And the impact of this efficiency is staggering: according to LinkedIn, a whopping 9,000 job applications are submitted every minute on LinkedIn, amounting to more than 12 million applications daily. These numbers underscore not only the platform's popularity but also the fierce competition.

However, like any powerful tool, "Easy Apply" comes with its own set of pros and cons. Understanding when and how to use this feature can make the difference between being lost in a sea of applicants and landing an interview for your dream job. With millions of applications flowing through the system each day, it's crucial to make yours stand out. Let's dive into the nuts and bolts of "Easy Apply" and learn how to make it work for you in this high-volume, high-speed job market.

How "Easy Apply" Works: The One-Click Wonder

"Easy Apply" is LinkedIn's answer to the collective groan of job seekers everywhere. Here's the lowdown:

- **One-Click Magic:** With just a few taps, you can submit your application without ever leaving LinkedIn. It's like teleporting your résumé directly to the recruiter's desk.

- **Profile Power:** "Easy Apply" harnesses the information from your LinkedIn profile to auto-fill application details. It's like having a personal assistant who knows your professional life inside out.

- **Résumé on the Go:** You can attach your résumé in a snap, either by uploading a new one or using one you've previously saved on LinkedIn. It's your professional calling card, ready to be dealt at a moment's notice.

- **Quick Questions:** Some postings might include a few brief screening questions. Think of these as your chance to slip the recruiter a note saying, "Pick me!"

- **Application Tracking:** LinkedIn keeps tabs on your "Easy Apply" submissions in your "Jobs" section. It's like having a logbook for your job search journey.

Navigating the Application Crossroads: "Easy Apply" vs. Traditional Methods

When it comes to job applications on LinkedIn, there are two main paths: the express lane of LinkedIn's "Easy Apply" and the more scenic route of traditional applications. Let's break down both to help you choose the right path for each job opportunity.

Easy Apply: The Express Lane

LinkedIn's "Easy Apply" feature offers a streamlined application process that prioritizes speed and convenience. With "Easy Apply," you can submit applications to multiple jobs in minutes, not hours. This method eliminates the need to create accounts on various company websites, saving you valuable time. Your LinkedIn profile ensures your information is presented uniformly across all applications, maintaining consistency. Additionally, some recruiters prefer "Easy Apply" for its seamless integration with LinkedIn's ecosystem, potentially increasing your visibility.

However, "Easy Apply" isn't without its drawbacks. The streamlined nature of this method often limits your ability to customize your application for each specific job. The convenience of "Easy Apply" can also lead to increased competition, as more candidates are likely to apply when the process is simplified. There's also a risk that complex qualifications might not be fully conveyed through this simplified application method.

Traditional Applications: The Scenic Route

Traditional applications involve applying directly through a company's website or applicant tracking system. This process typically requires creating an account on the company's career portal, uploading a tailored résumé and cover letter, filling out detailed application forms, and potentially answering specific questions about your qualifications.

While more time-consuming, traditional applications offer several advantages. They provide the opportunity to customize every aspect of your application, allowing you to tailor your materials specifically to each job. This method also gives you more space to explain complex experiences or career transitions in depth. By investing time in a company's application process, you signal your commitment to the role. Additionally, navigating their system can provide insights into the company's culture and processes.

However, traditional applications have their own set of challenges. They can be significantly more time-consuming than Easy Apply, often requiring you to enter the same information multiple times. Some company systems may also be glitchy or user-unfriendly, potentially causing frustration during the application process.

Choosing between "Easy Apply" and traditional applications depends on various factors, including the specific job, your time constraints, and how much you want to customize each application. Consider each opportunity carefully to determine which approach will best showcase your qualifications and increase your chances of landing an interview. Here are some more guidelines:

When to Choose Easy Apply:

- **Volume Applications:** When you're casting a wide net in your job search.

- **Time-Sensitive Opportunities:** For roles with approaching deadlines.

- **Perfect Profile Match:** When the job description closely aligns with your LinkedIn profile.

- **Supplementary Applications:** Use it alongside more detailed applications to increase your chances.

- **Networking Boost:** If you have connections at the company who can vouch for you internally.

When to Go Traditional:

- **Dream Jobs:** For positions you're particularly passionate about.

- **Highly Competitive Roles:** Where standing out is crucial.

- **Career Transitions:** When you need to explain shifts in your professional journey.

- **Specific Requirements:** If the job asks for detailed information not covered in your LinkedIn profile.

- **Writing-Intensive Roles:** To showcase your communication skills through a cover letter.

- **Executive Positions:** Higher-level roles often require more detailed applications.

The Hybrid Approach: Best of Both Worlds

In many cases, a combined strategy works best. Here are the three steps to a hybrid approach:

1. Use "Easy Apply" to get your application in quickly.

2. Follow up with a more detailed application or email to the recruiter.

3. Connect with employees or recruiters at the company to complement your "Easy Apply" submission.

Remember, the goal is to present yourself in the best light possible. Sometimes that means taking the express lane, and other times, it's worth the scenic route to showcase all you have to offer. Assess each opportunity individually, and choose the application method that best allows you to shine.

AI PROMPTS TO TAILOR YOUR APPLICATIONS

Keyword Analysis Prompt: "I'm applying for a [Job Title] position at [Company Name] through LinkedIn Easy Apply. Here's the job description: [paste job description]. Can you identify the top 10 keywords or phrases that seem most important for this role and explain why each is crucial?"

- **Profile Optimization Prompt:** "Based on these key terms for a [Job Title] position: [list 5-7 key terms], please suggest 3-5 ways I could naturally incorporate them into my LinkedIn profile summary and experience sections without sounding forced."

- **Résumé Tailoring Prompt:** "I'm customizing my résumé for a [Job Title] role. Here are the top requirements from the job posting: [list 3-5 key requirements]. Can you suggest how I might reword or reorganize my existing experience to highlight these skills? Here's a brief overview of my current résumé: [provide brief résumé summary]."

- **Cover Note Crafting Prompt:** "I'm applying for a [Job Title] at [Company Name] using LinkedIn Easy Apply. The job requires [mention 2-3 key requirements]. Can you help me draft a brief (100 words max) cover note that highlights my relevant experience and expresses my enthusiasm for the role? Here's a summary of my background: [provide brief background]."

- **Skills Highlight Prompt:** "For a [Job Title] application, the job posting emphasizes these skills: [list 3-5 skills]. Can you suggest 2-3 specific examples or achievements from my experience that would demonstrate each of these skills effectively? My background includes: [provide brief work history]."

- **Company Research Prompt:** "I'm applying to [Company Name] for a [Job Title] position. Can you suggest 3-5 recent news items, company values, or initiatives about this company that I could mention in my application to show I've done my research?"

- **Follow-Up Message Prompt:** "I applied for a [Job Title] position at [Company Name] through LinkedIn "Easy Apply" [X] days ago. Can you help me draft a brief, professional follow-up message to send to the recruiter? I want to reiterate my interest and ask about the status of my application."

- **Connection Request Prompt:** "I've just applied for a [Job Title] role at [Company Name] using Easy Apply. Can you help me write a short, personalized connection request to send to the hiring manager or a team member in the department? I want to express my interest in the role and the company without being pushy."

Standing Out in the "Easy Apply" Fast Lane

Just because it's easy doesn't mean you can't make it exceptional. Here's how to shine:

- **Profile Polish:** Your LinkedIn profile is your "Easy Apply" résumé. Make sure it's spotless, complete, and dazzling. Every section should sing your professional praises.

- **Keyword Wizardry:** Sprinkle relevant keywords from the job description throughout your profile. It's like leaving a trail of professional breadcrumbs for recruiters to follow.

- **Tailored Résumés:** Even with Easy Apply, upload a résumé tailored to the specific job. It shows you're not just clicking apply on everything that moves.

- **The Power of the Note:** If there's an option to add a note with your application, use it! It's your chance to make a personal connection and explain why you're perfect for the role.

- **Follow-Up Finesse:** After applying, connect with the recruiter or someone at the company. A simple statement like "I just applied for X position, and I'm really excited about the opportunity" can work wonders.

- **Quality Over Quantity:** Be selective. Applying to every job with "Easy Apply" can dilute your efforts. Focus on roles where you're a strong match.

- **Track and Learn:** Keep an eye on which "Easy Apply" applications get responses. Use this data to refine your strategy over time.

Remember, "Easy Apply" is a tool in your job search toolkit, not the entire toolbox. Use it wisely, and it can be your secret weapon in landing your next great role. But don't forget the power of a well-crafted cover letter or a personalized application for those jobs that really make your heart sing. So, next time you see that "Easy Apply" button, you'll know exactly when to click it and how to make your application stand out, even in the fast lane.

Your Action Plan to Ignite Your LinkedIn Presence

Remember, knowledge is power, but action transforms that power into results. Everything you've learned in this chapter is your toolkit for LinkedIn success. Now, it's time to put these tools to work and watch your professional presence come alive. Don't wait for the 'perfect' moment - the best time to optimize your LinkedIn profile and supercharge your job search is right now. Let's turn those insights into action!

Ready to activate your optimized LinkedIn profile? Here's your action plan:

- Review and adjust your profile's visibility settings. Ensure key sections are visible to everyone, and customize your LinkedIn URL to your name or professional brand.

- Set up your job preferences in the LinkedIn Jobs section, specifying desired roles, industries, and locations. Activate the "Open to Work" feature, customizing it to your job search needs.

- Upload your current résumé to LinkedIn and enable sharing with recruiters.

- Identify and follow 15-20 companies you're interested in working for. Set up at least three job alerts using variations of your target job titles and relevant keywords.

- Practice using the "Easy Apply" feature for 3-5 job postings that match your criteria. Follow up each application with a connection request or message to the recruiter.

- Review your profile through the lens of the "Easy Apply" feature, ensuring it tells a compelling story at a glance.

- Set a monthly reminder to review and refresh your profile, job preferences, and company follows to keep your presence current and active.

Remember, activating your LinkedIn presence is an ongoing process, not a one-time task. Commit to these actions, and you'll be well on your way to standing out in the competitive job market. Your next great opportunity could be just a click away – so let's get started!

Chapter Twelve

Maximizing Your Profile's Impact

Leveraging AI to Amplify Your Influence

C ongratulations! You've optimized your LinkedIn profile, mastered the art of networking and job searching, and learned how to navigate the platform like a pro. But are you truly maximizing your LinkedIn presence? It's time to take your profile from *great* to *extraordinary*, and AI is here to help you do just that.

Now, we're going to dive into how you can use AI tools to elevate your LinkedIn presence from simply impressive to genuinely influential. Whether you are looking to create thought-provoking content, curate and share valuable insights, engage meaningfully with your network, or build a powerful professional community, AI can help you become a LinkedIn superstar!

Building Your Professional Network

You may have heard it said that "your network is your net worth." This adage rings more true than ever in today's interconnected world. LinkedIn, as the world's largest professional network, offers unparalleled opportunities to build and nurture valuable connections.

But here's the key: building a network isn't just about collecting connections. It's about cultivating meaningful relationships that can propel your career forward. In the following sections, we'll explore how you can leverage LinkedIn's networking features, with a bit of help from our AI assistant, to create a powerful professional community that truly enriches your career "net worth."

Why Your LinkedIn Network Matters

Think of your LinkedIn network as your personal advisory board, job search team, and industry insight panel all rolled into one. A robust network can:

- Provide access to hidden job opportunities

- Offer insights into industry trends and best practices

- Connect you with mentors and thought leaders

- Boost your visibility within your industry

- Provide social proof of your professional standing

For job seekers, a strong LinkedIn network is particularly crucial. It can be your secret weapon in landing that dream job, often before it's even advertised.

Strategies for Building a Powerful LinkedIn Network

As we've already discussed, building a powerful LinkedIn network isn't about amassing a vast collection of random connections. It's about strategically cultivating a community of professionals who can support your career growth, provide valuable insights, and open doors to new opportunities.

But how do you go about creating such a network? It's not as daunting as it might seem, especially with a few AI-powered tricks up your sleeve. In this section, we'll explore proven strategies to expand and strengthen your LinkedIn network, turning it into a dynamic career asset that's not just wide but also deep and meaningful.

PRO TIP

Want to make connecting easier? When you follow someone first and engage with their content for a couple of weeks or months, LinkedIn's algorithm is more likely to suggest you as a connection to them. Plus, you'll have specific posts to reference when you finally send that connection request, increasing your acceptance rate.

Start with Your Existing Contacts

Begin by connecting with people you already know - colleagues, classmates, friends, and family. These connections form the foundation of your network and can provide a springboard for further growth. Here's how to make the most of this strategy:

- **Sync Your Contacts:** LinkedIn offers a feature that allows you to sync your email contacts. This can quickly identify people you know who are already on the platform.

- **Explore Your Past:** Connect with former colleagues, classmates, and teachers. Don't forget about people from previous jobs, internships, or volunteer experiences.

- **Consider Your Personal Circles:** Friends, family members, and acquaintances can be valuable connections, especially if they work in industries or companies of interest to you.

- **Use LinkedIn's 'People You May Know' Feature:** This AI-powered tool suggests connections based on your profile information and existing network. Review these regularly to find relevant professionals to connect with.

- **Be Thorough But Selective:** While it's good to connect broadly, focus on quality connections that could potentially add value to your professional life.

AI PROMPT FOR NETWORK BUILDING

"Generate a list of 15 categories of people from my personal and professional life that I should connect with on LinkedIn. Then, suggest 3 actions I can take to find and connect with people in each category."

Personalize Your Connection Requests

Generic "I'd like to add you to my network on LinkedIn" requests often get ignored. A personalized request shows that you value the potential connection and have put thought into reaching out. It sets the tone for future interactions and can open doors to meaningful professional relationships.

PRO TIP

Think of your LinkedIn connections as an evolving story - keep a "relationship log" (in Evernote, a spreadsheet, or your preferred tool) to track details about your connections' journeys. Note key career moves, shared conversations, their big wins, and professional interests. For example, if a connection mentions they're working on an AI implementation project, jot it down. Six months later, you can ask about the project's outcome. These personal details help you maintain authentic relationships and make your future interactions more meaningful. "I saw you completed that AI project you mentioned - would love to hear how it went!" is more engaging than a generic "Hope you're doing well!"

Before sending any connection request, take a moment to craft a personalized message. Even if you're using LinkedIn's mobile app, which doesn't always show the option to add a note, you can cancel the automatic request and use the 'More' option to find 'Personalize invite.'

AI PROMPT FOR CONNECTION REQUEST MESSAGES

"Help me craft a personalized LinkedIn connection request to [Name], who is a [Their Job Title] at [Their Company]. I'm a [Your Profession] in [Your Industry], and I want to connect because [reason for connection]. Consider our shared [interests/background/mutual connections] if any. Suggest a concise, friendly message (300 characters max) that includes a personalized opening, a brief explanation of why I want to connect, and a relevant icebreaker. Ensure the message is genuine and professionally appropriate for LinkedIn."

This extra step can make a significant difference in your networking success. Here's how to make your connection requests stand out:

- **Research First:** Before sending a request, review the person's profile. Look for shared interests, mutual connections, or recent achievements you can mention.

- **Explain the 'Why':** Clearly state your reason for connecting. Whether it's admiration for their work, a shared industry, or a mutual acquaintance, giving context helps the recipient understand your intentions.

- **Reference a Shared Experience:** If you met at an event or worked together in the past, remind them of this shared experience. It immediately establishes a connection.

- **Mention Mutual Connections:** If you have connections in common, mentioning this can add credibility to your request.

- **Keep it Concise:** LinkedIn limits connection notes to 300 characters, so be brief but impactful.

- **Add Value:** If possible, suggest how the connection could be mutually beneficial. Perhaps you have insights to share or a common professional goal.

- **Be Authentic:** While it's essential to be professional, let your personality shine through. Authenticity can make your request more appealing.

- **Proofread:** A typo-free message shows attention to detail and respect for the recipient's time.

Join and Engage in LinkedIn Groups

While LinkedIn groups may not always be as lively as forums on other platforms, they still offer valuable networking opportunities. Find groups related to your industry or interests, but be selective – quality matters more than quantity.

Joining relevant LinkedIn groups can significantly expand your professional network beyond your direct connections. As a group member, you can engage in discussions, share insights, and connect with industry peers who share your interests. This not only increases your visibility but also allows you to message other group members directly, even if you're not connected, opening up new opportunities for networking and potential job leads.

AI PROMPT FOR LINKEDIN GROUPS

"Based on my profile as a [your profession] in [your industry], suggest 5 types of LinkedIn groups I should join and 3 engagement strategies for each."

Leverage Alumni Networks

Connect with alumni from your educational institutions. Shared alma maters can be a great conversation starter and foundation for professional relationships. Fellow alumni often have a built-in sense of camaraderie and are more likely to respond to connection requests or help requests. They can provide industry insights, job leads, or even become mentors or business partners.

AI PROMPT FOR ALUMNI NETWORKING

"I'm an alumnus of [Your University] working in [Your Industry]. Generate 5 personalized connection request templates I could use to reach out to fellow alumni in my field or at companies I'm interested in. Include a way to reference our shared university experience in each."

Attend Virtual Events and Webinars

Virtual events provide a low-pressure environment to learn and connect with professionals in your field. They're often more accessible than in-person events, allowing you to expand your network beyond geographical limitations. Many offer networking opportunities, and you can connect with fellow attendees on LinkedIn afterward.

AI PROMPTS FOR EVENT FOLLOW-UPS

"Create a follow-up message template I can use to connect on LinkedIn with someone I met at a virtual industry event."

- "Based on my profile as a [your profession] in [your industry], suggest 5 types of virtual events or webinars I should look for and where I might find them. For each, provide a strategy to maximize networking opportunities before, during, and after the event."

Connect with Recruiters and HR Professionals

Recruiters and HR professionals are often the gatekeepers to job opportunities. Building genuine relationships with them can give you insider knowledge about job openings, company culture, and hiring processes. They can become valuable allies in your job search. Here's how to approach this strategically:

- **Target the Right People:** Use LinkedIn's search function to find recruiters and HR professionals in your target industries and companies. Look for those who specialize in your field or level of experience.

- **Engage Before Connecting:** Before sending a connection request, interact with their content. Like, comment on, or share their posts to get on their radar.

- **Personalize Your Approach:** When reaching out, mention specific aspects of their work or recent company news that are of interest to you. Show you've done your homework.

- **Highlight Mutual Interests:** If you share any groups, skills, or educational background, mention this in your connection request.

- **Be Clear About Your Intentions:** Explain why you're reaching out, but avoid directly asking for a job. Instead, express interest in learning more about their company or industry.

- **Offer Value:** Consider how you might help them. Maybe you know potential candidates for other roles, or you have insights about industry trends.

- **Follow Company Pages:** Many companies post job openings on their LinkedIn pages. Following these pages can alert you to opportunities and provide talking points.

- **Join Relevant Groups:** Many recruiters are active in industry-specific LinkedIn groups. Joining these can increase your visibility.

- **Be Patient and Professional:** Building these relationships takes time. Don't get discouraged if you don't get an immediate response.

AI PROMPT FOR RECRUITER CONNECTIONS

"As a job seeker in [Industry], help me craft a connection request to a recruiter at [Target Company]. Include a brief introduction, mention a recent company achievement or news item, express my interest in the company's work, and suggest a way we might have a mutually beneficial professional relationship. Keep it under 300 characters."

Make connecting with relevant recruiters and HR professionals a regular part of your job search routine. Set a goal to reach out to a certain number each week. Keep track of your interactions and follow up periodically with those who respond. Remember, the goal is to build a relationship, not to ask for a job immediately.

Leverage Second-Degree Connections

Second-degree connections are a goldmine of networking opportunities, especially when job hunting or exploring new career paths. Here's how to effectively leverage these connections:

Identify Strategic Second-Degree Connections:

- Use LinkedIn's advanced search to find people working at your target companies.

- Filter results to show second-degree connections.

- Look for roles or departments that align with your career goals.

Analyze Mutual Connections:

- Review which of your first-degree connections know the person you want to reach.

- Consider which of your mutual connections might be most likely to facilitate an introduction.

Prepare Your Approach:

- Research the second-degree connection's profile thoroughly.

- Identify specific reasons why connecting would be mutually beneficial.

- Prepare a clear, concise explanation of why you're seeking the introduction.

Reach Out to Your Mutual Connection:

- Choose the right mutual connection to ask for an introduction.

- Explain why you're interested in connecting with their contact.

- Make it easy for them by drafting a brief introduction they can use or modify.

Follow Up and Show Gratitude:

- If your mutual connection agrees to introduce you, follow up promptly with the new contact.

- Always thank your mutual connection for their help, regardless of the outcome.

Nurture the New Connection:

- Once introduced, focus on building a genuine relationship, not just asking for favors.

- Offer value to your new connection where possible.

AI PROMPT FOR REACHING DEEPER INTO YOUR NETWORK

"I'm interested in connecting with [Name], a [Job Title] at [Target Company], who is a second-degree connection through my contact [Mutual Connection's Name]. Help me draft two messages. First, create a polite, concise message (max 200 words) to [Mutual Connection's Name] asking for an introduction. This message should explain why I'm interested in connecting with [Name] and how this connection could be mutually beneficial. It should also include a brief, ready-to-use introduction they can send to [Name]. Second, draft a follow-up message (max 150 words) that I can send to [Name] after the introduction. This message should thank them for connecting, briefly explain my interest in their work or company, suggest a specific way we might help each other professionally, and propose a next step (like a brief call or coffee chat). Ensure both messages are professional, genuine, and respectful of everyone's time."

Engage in Informational Interviews

Informational interviews are powerful tools for career exploration and network building. They allow you to gain insider knowledge about roles, companies, and industries while establishing valuable professional connections.

Start by identifying professionals in roles or companies you're interested in through LinkedIn. When reaching out, be clear that you're seeking information, not a job, and suggest a brief 15-20 minute call. Prepare thoroughly by researching the person and their company, and develop thoughtful questions about their role and industry. During the interview, listen more than you talk, take notes, and show genuine interest.

After the conversation, send a thank-you note within 24 hours, mentioning specific insights you found valuable. Keep the door open for future communication by periodically sharing relevant articles or congratulating them on their achievements.

AI PROMPT FOR INFORMATIONAL INTERVIEWS

"I'm interested in conducting an informational interview with [Name], a [Job Title] at [Target Company]. Help me craft a concise LinkedIn message (max 150 words) requesting the informational interview. Include a brief introduction of myself, why I'm specifically interested in speaking with them, a clear request for a 15-20 minute call, and flexibility in scheduling. Ensure the message is professional and demonstrates that I've done my research on their role and company."

Remember, building a strong LinkedIn network is a marathon, not a sprint. It's about quality over quantity and nurturing relationships over time. With these strategies and a little help from AI, you'll be well on your way to creating a powerful professional network that can open doors and accelerate your career growth. So, start connecting and engaging, and watch your professional opportunities multiply!

Using AI Writing Tools for Thought Leadership Content

Think of your LinkedIn profile as the storefront for your Business of One. Remember when we talked about being the CEO of your own career back in Chapter 1? Well, this is where that mindset really comes into play. Your LinkedIn profile isn't just a digital résumé; it's the hub of your professional brand, your marketing platform, your networking central, and your career catalyst all rolled into one.

But here's the kicker: in the world of Business of One, a static storefront doesn't cut it. To truly stand out in the crowded digital marketplace, you need to keep your storefront fresh, engaging, and valuable to your audience. This is where thought leadership comes into play.

Now, let's talk about the invisible force that's constantly at work on LinkedIn: the algorithm. LinkedIn's algorithm, powered by sophisticated machine learning and AI, is like a discerning customer constantly browsing through the professional marketplace. It's looking for quality, relevance, and engagement. Every post you make, every article you write, every interaction you have – it all feeds into this AI-driven system.

The more active and valuable your contributions are, the more the algorithm favors your content, increasing your visibility to potential employers, clients, and collaborators. It's a virtuous cycle: quality content leads to more engagement, which leads to more visibility, which in turn can lead to more opportunities.

The problem for most of us is that consistently creating high-quality, engaging content while managing all other aspects of your 'Business of One' can feel like a Herculean task. That's where AI tools come in, ready to be your tireless assistant in this endeavor.

LinkedIn offers multiple avenues for sharing your expertise and insights. Whether it's long-form articles, shorter posts, or even multimedia content, each format presents unique opportunities to showcase your thought leadership. Let's explore how AI can help you create compelling content across these different formats:

- **LinkedIn Articles:** These are long-form pieces, ideal for in-depth analysis, case studies, or comprehensive guides. They appear on your profile and can be shared with your network.

- **LinkedIn Posts:** These are shorter updates that appear in your connections' feeds. They're great for sharing quick insights, asking questions, or sparking discussions.

- **LinkedIn Documents:** You can share PDFs, PowerPoint presentations, or other documents, which can be an effective way to share visual information or detailed reports.

- **LinkedIn Video:** Short video content can be a powerful way to engage your audience and showcase your personality along with your expertise.

Identifying Trending Topics in Your Industry

Before creating content, you need to know what topics will resonate with your audience. But how do you keep your finger on the pulse when information is constantly flowing? This is where AI becomes your personal trend analyst. Let's dive into how you can leverage AI tools to identify hot topics that will resonate with your LinkedIn audience:

Utilize AI-Powered Chatbots

Think of AI chatbots as your 24/7 industry research assistants. Tools like ChatGPT, Claude, or Perplexity can process vast amounts of information and provide you with concise, relevant insights.

AI PROMPTS TO IDENTIFY TRENDS

Ask for recent developments to get a quick snapshot of what's buzzing in your field:

- Try prompts like, "What are the top 5 trending topics in [your industry] for this month?"

Uncover professional pain points to help you address real issues your audience is grappling with:

- Use queries such as, "Identify the most pressing challenges professionals in [your field] are currently facing."

Explore technological shifts to stay ahead of the curve and position you as a forward-thinking professional:

- Ask, "What emerging technologies are making waves in [your industry] right now?"

Harness AI Search Engines

AI-enhanced search engines like Perplexity or Bing Chat are like having a team of research assistants at your fingertips. They can sift through recent news articles, reports, and studies, giving you a bird's-eye view of your industry landscape.

AI PROMPTS FOR CURRENT NEWS AND DATA

Get a comprehensive overview to gain a broader perspective on what's trending:

- Try prompts like, "Show me the most discussed [industry] topics in reputable publications over the last 30 days."

Dive into research to back up your content with solid data and insights:

- Ask, "Summarize the main findings from recent [industry] reports published by leading research firms."

Generate Article Ideas with AI

Once you've identified key trends, harness AI as your creative partner to generate compelling content ideas. The following are some prompts to get you started.

AI PROMPTS TO GENERATE CONTENT IDEAS

Trend-Based Brainstorming: "Based on [identified trend], suggest 5 article topics that provide actionable insights for [your field] professionals."

- **Unique Perspectives:** "Propose a fresh angle on [current industry challenge] suitable for a thought-provoking LinkedIn post."

- **Engaging Formats:** "Outline a listicle addressing the top 3 [industry] trends, including potential subheadings and key points."

- **Counterintuitive Ideas:** "Generate 3 counterintuitive viewpoints on [industry topic] that could spark meaningful discussions."

- **Trending Topic Article:** "Based on LinkedIn's current trending topics in [your industry], suggest an outline for a 500-word article that offers unique insights."

- **Viral Post Structure:** "Analyze recent viral posts in [your field] on LinkedIn and propose a structure for a post that could achieve similar engagement."

- **Expert Interview Post:** "Generate 5 thought-provoking questions for a LinkedIn post featuring a Q&A with an industry expert in [your field]."

- **Data Visualization Article:** "Suggest 3 key statistics about [industry trend] and describe how to present them visually in a compelling LinkedIn article."

- **Personal Experience Narrative:** "Outline a structure for a LinkedIn post that shares a personal career challenge in [your field] and the lessons learned from overcoming it."

Validate and Refine Topics

While AI is a powerful tool, remember that you're the industry expert. Use your professional judgment to refine and validate the AI-generated suggestions:

- Cross-reference AI insights with reputable industry sources to ensure accuracy.

- Consider your unique expertise and how it can add value to the identified trends.

- Reflect on your audience's specific needs and interests when selecting final topics.

Remember, AI is a springboard for your expertise, enhancing your thought leadership rather than replacing it. While AI can provide valuable insights, it's not infallible and may occasionally generate inaccurate information or "hallucinate" facts. Always verify key points against reputable industry sources and your personal experience before incorporating them into your strategy.

By combining AI-powered trend identification with your professional insights, you'll be able to consistently produce content that's not just relevant but truly valuable to your LinkedIn network.

PRO TIP

Set up a regular "trend check" session with your AI assistants. Maybe it's every Monday morning or the first of each month. This habit will keep you consistently informed and inspired, making content creation a breeze.

AI-Assisted Content Creation and Editing

Once you've identified your trending topic, AI can be your trusty sidekick throughout the content creation process. Let's explore how AI can assist you in crafting compelling content across various LinkedIn formats:

LinkedIn Articles

Articles provide an opportunity to explore topics in depth. With AI as your assistant, you can streamline your writing process from start to finish. Begin by asking the AI to create a detailed outline for your article, complete with an introduction, main points, and a conclusion.

AI PROMPT FOR OUTLINING A LINKEDIN ARTICLE

"Create a detailed outline for a LinkedIn article about [your chosen topic]. Include an introduction, 3-4 main points, and a conclusion."

As you flesh out your content, use AI to expand on specific sections, providing additional insights or examples. Once your draft is complete, leverage AI's editing capabilities to refine your work, enhancing clarity and coherence. This comprehensive approach ensures your LinkedIn article is well-structured, thorough, and polished.

LinkedIn Posts

Posts offer a platform for sharing concise, impactful thoughts with your network. AI can be invaluable in crafting these bite-sized pieces of content. Start by asking the AI to distill your chosen topic into a compelling 2-3 sentence summary, capturing the essence of your message.

To make your post stand out in busy feeds, use AI to generate multiple attention-grabbing opening lines. You can then select the one that best resonates with your voice and audience. This approach allows you to quickly create engaging posts that spark interest and encourage interaction among your LinkedIn connections.

AI PROMPT FOR LINKEDIN POST CREATION

"Summarize the key takeaway from [your chosen topic] in a compelling 2-3 sentence LinkedIn post."

LinkedIn Documents

Documents offer a versatile way to share visual and detailed content with your LinkedIn network. AI can be a valuable ally in creating compelling, informative documents that capture your audience's attention.

Start by asking the AI to generate an outline for a one-page infographic or multi-page document about your chosen topic. This provides a solid structure upon which to build.

As you develop your content, leverage AI to suggest effective ways to visualize your data or key points. Whether it's proposing chart types, info-graphic layouts, or creative ways to present statistics, AI can help transform complex information into easily digestible visual content.

AI PROMPT FOR INFOGRAPHIC IDEAS

"Create an outline for a one-page infographic about [your topic], and suggest 3 creative ways to represent the key statistics or main points visually."

LinkedIn Video

Video content offers a powerful way to connect with your audience visually and aurally. AI can assist you throughout the video creation process, from conceptualization to final scripting. Begin by asking the AI to write a 60-second script for your LinkedIn video, ensuring it includes an attention-grabbing opening and a clear call-to-action at the end. To enhance your video's visual appeal, prompt the AI to suggest key scenes or visuals that will effectively illustrate your main points. This collaboration with AI helps you create well-structured, visually engaging video content that resonates with your LinkedIn audience and conveys your message effectively.

AI PROMPT TO CREATE A VIDEO SCRIPT

"Write a 60-second script for a LinkedIn video about [your topic], including an attention-grabbing opening and a clear call-to-action. Also, suggest 5 key visuals or scenes to illustrate the main points."

Optimizing Content for LinkedIn's Algorithm

Creating great content is only half the battle; ensuring it reaches your target audience is equally crucial. LinkedIn's algorithm plays a pivotal role in determining the visibility and reach of your posts. By leveraging AI, you can fine-tune your content to align with the algorithm's preferences, potentially boosting your post's performance. Here are some AI-assisted strategies to optimize your content for maximum impact on LinkedIn.

AI PROMPTS TO OPTIMIZE CONTENT

Use AI to suggest relevant keywords for your article. Try:

- "What are 10 relevant keywords or phrases for an article about [your topic] in the [your industry] industry?"

Ask AI to help craft an engaging headline. For example:

- "Generate 5 attention-grabbing headlines for my LinkedIn article about [your topic]. The headlines should be compelling and professional."

Use AI to suggest ways to break up your content for better readability. Try:

- "How can I improve the structure of this article to make it more engaging on LinkedIn? [paste your article]"

Optimizing Your Profile for Voice Search

As technology evolves, so do the ways people search for information and connections. Voice search is rapidly gaining traction, making it essential to adapt your LinkedIn profile for this emerging trend. By optimizing your profile for voice search, you can increase your discoverability and stay ahead of the curve in the digital professional landscape. Let's explore how AI can help you tailor your profile to be more voice-search-friendly.

AI PROMPTS TO OPTIMIZE FOR VOICE SEARCH

Ask AI to help you identify voice-search-friendly terms:

- "What are 10 conversational phrases or questions someone might use in a voice search to find a professional like me? I'm a [your profession] specializing in [your niche]."

Use AI to help you incorporate Q&As into your profile:

- "How can I rephrase my key skills and experiences in a question-and-answer format that might align with voice search queries?"

More AI Prompts to Help with Content Creation

Here are some additional prompts you can use with AI chatbots to assist in your article creation

AI PROMPTS FOR CONTENT CREATION

"Can you suggest a powerful opening paragraph for an article about [your topic] that will grab the reader's attention?"

- "What are some effective ways to conclude an article about [your topic] that will encourage engagement from LinkedIn readers?"

- "How can I incorporate data or statistics into my article about [your topic] to make it more compelling?"

- "What are some potential objections or counterarguments to my main points about [your topic], and how might I address them in my article?"

- "How can I repurpose my LinkedIn article about [your topic] into a series of shorter posts?"

- "Suggest 5 visually engaging ways to present statistics about [your topic] in a LinkedIn document."

- "What are some best practices for creating engaging LinkedIn video content about [your topic]?"

Remember, while AI is a powerful tool in your content creation arsenal, the most valuable content will always showcase your unique professional perspective. Use AI to overcome writer's block, generate ideas, and polish your work - but always let your authentic voice shine through.

By leveraging AI across these different content formats, you're not just creating content; you're building a diverse and engaging presence on LinkedIn that establishes you as a thought leader in your field. And the best part? With AI as your assistant, you can maintain this high-quality content production consistently, keeping your audience engaged and coming back for more.

AI-Powered Content Curation and Sharing

In the world of LinkedIn, you're not just what you create—you're also what you share. Curating and sharing valuable content is like hosting a fantastic dinner party for your professional network. You're not just serving up your own dishes (original content) but also bringing in some gourmet takeout (curated content) to create a feast of insights.

However, there's more to content curation than just broadcasting to your entire network. Sending carefully selected content directly to individual contacts is like offering them a personalized gift basket of professional insights. It's a subtle yet powerful way to stay on their radar, demonstrate your industry knowledge, and provide value without asking for anything in return.

Whether it's a cutting-edge article that aligns with a contact's recent project, or an insightful report relevant to their business challenges, these targeted shares can spark meaningful conversations and strengthen your professional relationships. And guess what? AI can help you match the right content to the right contact, making this personalized approach both impactful and efficient.

Using AI to Find Relevant Industry News and Insights to Share

While we've already covered how to use AI to identify trending topics, you can also set up news aggregators such as Feedly or Flipboard, which use AI to learn your preferences and serve up relevant articles. Of course, you may also use AI search engines such as Perplexity for real-time updates.

AI PROMPTS FOR CONTENT CURATION

"What are the top 3 breaking news stories in [your industry] from the past 24 hours?"

- "Summarize the key points of the latest report on [industry trend] in bullet points."

- "Based on recent news articles, what emerging trend in [your field] should professionals be paying attention to?"

- "Find an article relevant to my colleague's recent project on [topic]. Summarize why it would be valuable to them."

Strategies for Effective Content Sharing

Simply curating content isn't enough; how you share it can significantly impact its reach and engagement. Effective content sharing is a nuanced skill that combines timing, presentation, and audience understanding.

Here are some ways in which AI can help you craft more compelling, audience-tailored, and personalized content shares that resonate with your LinkedIn network:

AI PROMPTS FOR CONTENT SHARING

Use AI to help you write compelling intros for shared content. Try:

- "Write 3 engaging one-sentence introductions for this article I'm sharing on LinkedIn: [paste article title and brief summary]"

Tailor content to your audience. Ask AI:

- "Based on my LinkedIn audience of [describe your connections], how can I frame this article to make it most relevant to them?"

Use AI to craft personalized messages when sharing content directly:

- "Write a brief, friendly message to [contact name] explaining why I think this article on [topic] would be interesting to them."

Here are more AI prompts to help with curation and sharing:

- "Find 5 recent articles about [specific topic] that would be valuable to my LinkedIn network of [describe your audience]. For each, write a brief, engaging summary I could use when sharing."

- "I want to position myself as a thought leader in [your field]. Suggest a weekly content-sharing schedule that balances industry news, trend analysis, and my own insights."

- "How can I use the 5-3-2 rule (5 pieces of content from others, 3 pieces of original content, 2 pieces of personal content) in my LinkedIn sharing strategy? Provide specific examples for each category based on my industry: [your industry]."

- "I'm sharing an article that challenges a common belief in my industry. How can I present this contrarian view in a way that encourages thoughtful discussion rather than controversy?"

- "Analyze these 3 articles I'm considering sharing: [paste titles/links]. Which would be most valuable to my network, and why? How can I add my own insights when sharing the chosen article?"

- "I want to reach out to [contact name] who works in [their field]. Find a recent, insightful article relevant to their work and draft a brief message explaining why I think they'd find it interesting."

Remember, the goal of content curation isn't just to fill your feed—it's to provide value to your network while reinforcing your own expertise. This applies both to your general posts and to the personalized content you share with individual contacts. Use AI as your assistant in this process, but always apply your own professional judgment to ensure that what you're sharing aligns with your personal brand and resonates with your audience or the specific contact you're reaching out to.

By mastering the art of AI-powered content curation and sharing, you're not just participating in your industry's conversation—you're helping to guide it. And by using this strategy for personalized networking, you're nurturing meaningful professional relationships. This combination of broad influence and targeted connection is what sets apart true LinkedIn superstars. So, start serving up that content feast, and watch your professional influence grow!

Engaging with Other Content: Your Key to Visibility

Active engagement on LinkedIn is a crucial component of building a strong professional presence. It's not just about broadcasting your own thoughts—it's about being an active, interested participant in your professional community.

Why Engagement Matters

Engagement is the lifeblood of your LinkedIn presence, serving as a powerful catalyst for professional growth and visibility. By actively participating in discussions and interacting with others' content, you're doing far more than simply clicking buttons or typing responses—you're strategically positioning yourself within your professional ecosystem.

Think of each comment or reaction as a networking opportunity. Every thoughtful interaction opens the door to new connections and deepens existing relationships, all without the pressure of face-to-face small talk. These digital exchanges showcase your expertise and personality, subtly but effectively reinforcing your personal brand with each engagement.

Moreover, your active participation catches the eye of LinkedIn's algorithm. The platform rewards engaged users with increased visibility, meaning that the more you interact, the more likely your own content is to be seen and shared. This creates a virtuous cycle of visibility and engagement.

Perhaps most importantly, consistent engagement keeps you present in your connections' minds. It's a gentle, professional way to maintain relationships and stay relevant in your network without resorting to pushy tactics or overt self-promotion.

In essence, engagement on LinkedIn is not just about being active—it's about being strategically, consistently, and authentically present in your professional community. This intentional engagement is what transforms a basic profile into a robust, dynamic professional presence.

AI-Powered Engagement Strategies

Now, let's explore how AI can help you engage more effectively and efficiently.

AI PROMPTS TO BOOST ENGAGEMENT

Use AI to help you identify posts that align with your professional interests and goals. Try prompts like:

- "Based on my professional background as a [your role] in [your industry], suggest 5 types of LinkedIn posts I should be looking to engage with regularly."

- "I want to connect on LinkedIn with thought leaders in [specific industry]. What are some trending hashtags or topics I should be following and engaging with?"

AI can help you draft engaging, insightful comments. Here are some prompts to try:

- "I want to comment on this LinkedIn post: [paste post content]. Generate 3 thoughtful comment ideas that showcase my expertise in [your field] while adding value to the discussion."

- "How can I respectfully disagree with this LinkedIn post [paste content] in a way that opens up a constructive dialogue?"

Remember, while AI can suggest comment ideas, always review and personalize them to maintain authenticity.

Strategically Using Reactions

Engaging effectively on LinkedIn isn't just about quantity—it's about quality and strategy. By using AI to guide your engagement efforts, you can ensure that each interaction contributes to your professional goals, whether that's expanding your network, positioning yourself as a thought leader, or opening doors to new opportunities.

AI PROMPTS TO IMPROVE INTERACTIONS

"Create a weekly engagement plan for me to interact with content from 1) My close professional network, 2) Industry thought leaders, 3) Potential clients or employers, and 4) My current colleagues and company."

- "I've been regularly engaging with posts from [Company Name], a company I'd love to work for. Suggest 3 ways I could leverage this engagement history to explore job opportunities there."

- "I've had a great comment exchange with [Name], a thought leader in my industry. Draft a connection request message that references our interaction and suggests continuing the conversation."

Engagement Etiquette

While AI can help you engage more effectively, remember that authentic, respectful interaction is key.

By thoughtfully engaging with others' content, you're not just boosting your own visibility—you're contributing to the vibrancy of your professional community. It's a win-win that positions you as an active, insightful member of your industry.

Remember, at the end of the day, LinkedIn is about building relationships. You can use these AI-powered strategies to engage meaningfully and watch as your professional network—and opportunities—grow.

Expressing a Consistent Personal Brand

In the digital marketplace of professionals, your personal brand is your unique selling proposition. It's what sets you apart from the millions of other LinkedIn users vying for attention. But here's the challenge: maintaining a consistent brand across your profile, posts, articles, and interactions can feel like juggling while riding a unicycle. It requires constant attention, creativity, and a clear vision of who you are professionally.

Luckily, AI can serve as your brand manager, helping you craft and maintain a compelling, consistent personal brand that resonates with your target audience. Let's explore how you can leverage AI to ensure every aspect of your LinkedIn presence is working in harmony to showcase the best professional version of you.

Aligning Your Profile Elements with Your Brand

Your LinkedIn profile is like a puzzle - each piece should fit together to create a cohesive picture of your professional self. Here's how AI can help you ensure all elements are singing the same tune.

AI PROMPTS TO ENSURE BRAND ALIGNMENT

Profile Audit: Start by asking AI to analyze your current profile.

- "I'll paste my LinkedIn profile sections below. Can you analyze them for consistency in tone, messaging, and personal brand? Identify any areas that seem out of sync."

Tone Alignment: Ensure your writing style is consistent.

- "Analyze the tone of my About section: [paste section]. How can I adjust the tone in my Experience descriptions to match this while still sounding natural and professional?"

Brand-Reinforcing Content: Your content is the ongoing conversation you have with your professional world. Make sure it's consistently on-brand.

- "Based on my expertise in [your field] and my personal brand as [brand description], suggest 5 content pillars I should focus on in my LinkedIn posts and articles. For each pillar, provide 3 specific topic ideas."

Maintaining Brand Consistency Across Platforms

Your LinkedIn brand should harmonize with your broader online presence.

AI PROMPTS FOR CROSS-PLATFORM CONSISTENCY

Use AI to ensure consistency:
- "I'll paste the bios from my LinkedIn, Twitter, and personal website. Can you analyze them for brand consistency and suggest how to align them better while optimizing for each platform's unique features?"

Let AI help you adapt content for different platforms:
- "I have a LinkedIn article about [topic]. How can I repurpose this content for Twitter, Instagram, and my personal blog while maintaining my brand voice and key messages?"

Remember, your personal brand isn't just what you say about yourself - it's the consistent experience others have when they interact with you professionally. Use these AI-powered strategies to ensure that every element of your LinkedIn presence is working in harmony to present the best, most authentic version of your professional self. Here are some more prompts to try.

MORE PERSONAL BRANDING AI PROMPTS

"Based on my LinkedIn profile, what are 5 unique selling points that set me apart in my industry? How can I emphasize these more throughout my profile and content?"

- "Analyze my recent LinkedIn posts: [paste 3-5 posts]. Are they consistently reflecting my personal brand? Suggest improvements to make them more aligned with my professional identity."

- "I want to be known for [your desired professional reputation]. What are 3 concrete actions I can take on LinkedIn to reinforce this perception?"

- "How can I use storytelling techniques in my LinkedIn content to reinforce my personal brand? Suggest 3 types of stories I could share and how they would strengthen my professional image."

- "Review my LinkedIn recommendations. Do they reinforce my personal brand? Suggest how I could request future recommendations that better align with my professional identity."

By maintaining this consistency, you're not just building a brand - you're creating a memorable, impactful presence that will make you stand out in the crowded professional landscape. And with AI as your branding assistant, you can maintain this high level of consistency with efficiency and ease.

Measuring Your LinkedIn Impact with AI Analytics

You've optimized your profile, created compelling content, and engaged with your network. But how do you know if all this effort is paying off? Enter the world of analytics. It's time to put on your data scientist hat (don't worry, AI will be your lab assistant) and dig into the numbers behind your LinkedIn success.

Key Metrics to Track

In the vast sea of LinkedIn data, here are the lighthouses you should be watching:

Profile Views

Who's checking you out? This is your basic measure of visibility.

- **How to learn:** Go to your profile and click on "Analytics" near the top. You'll see who's viewed your profile in the last 90 days, including their job titles and companies (if they're not in private mode).

- **Why it matters:** An increase in profile views could indicate that your optimized profile or recent activity is attracting more attention.

- **How to use it:** If you notice an increase in profile views, it's a sign that your recent activities are drawing attention. Keep up what you're doing! If views are low, consider updating your headline, adding new skills, or increasing your posting frequency.

Post Impressions:

How far is your content reaching?

- **How to learn:** For each post, LinkedIn shows you the number of views. For a broader picture, go to your Activity section and click on "See all posts" to view impressions for all your recent posts.

- **Why it matters:** This metric shows the potential reach of your content. More impressions mean more people are seeing what you share.

- **How to use it:** High impression numbers mean your content is reaching a wide audience. If a particular post gets significantly more impressions, analyze what made it special – perhaps the topic, format, or posting time – and try to replicate that success.

Engagement Rate

Are people interacting with your posts? This includes likes, comments, and shares.

- **How to learn:** Divide the total number of interactions (likes + comments + shares) by the number of impressions, then multiply by 100 for a percentage.

- **Why it matters:** A high engagement rate indicates that your content resonates with your audience and prompts them to interact.

- **How to use it:** This tells you how interesting or valuable your audience finds your content. If certain posts get more likes, comments, or shares, focus on creating similar content. Low engagement might mean it's time to experiment with different types of posts or more compelling topics.

Connection Growth

Is your network expanding?

- **How to learn:** LinkedIn doesn't provide a direct metric for this, but you can track your total number of connections over time to calculate growth.

- **Why it matters:** A growing network means more potential opportunities and a wider reach for your content.

- **How to use it:** A steadily growing network opens more opportunities. If growth is slow, be more active in joining discussions, commenting on others' posts, or reaching out to relevant professionals in your industry.

Content Performance

Which types of posts resonate most with your audience?

- **How to learn:** Analyze the engagement rates of different types of content (text, images, videos, articles) to see which perform best.

- **Why it matters:** Understanding what your audience prefers helps you tailor your content strategy for maximum impact.

- **How to use it:** Pay attention to which types of posts (text, images, videos, articles) get the most engagement. Double down on what works best for your audience.

Profile Rank

How do you stack up against others in your industry for profile views?
- **How to learn:** LinkedIn shows your profile rank for viewers from your current company, as well as viewers from your current company's industry.

- **Why it matters:** A high rank indicates strong visibility within your professional sphere.

- **How to use it:** If your rank is high, you're on the right track. If it's lower than you'd like, focus on optimizing your profile and increasing your activity on the platform.

SSI (Social Selling Index)

LinkedIn's measure of how effective you are at establishing your professional brand, finding the right people, engaging with insights, and building relationships.
- **How to learn:** Go to linkedin.com/sales/ssi to see your score. It's updated daily and gives you a score out of 100.

- **Why it matters:** A high SSI score indicates that you're effectively using LinkedIn for professional networking and engagement.

- **How to use it:** This score gives you a good overall picture of your LinkedIn effectiveness. Look at which of the four elements (establishing your professional brand, finding the right people, engaging with insights, and building relationships) has the lowest score and focus on improving that area.

Follower Growth

Are more people choosing to see your content in their feeds?

- **How to learn:** If you have LinkedIn creator mode turned on, you can track your follower count over time.

- **Why it matters:** More followers mean a potentially wider organic reach for your content.

- **How to use it:** If your follower count is steadily increasing, your content strategy is working. Keep creating valuable content that resonates with your audience. If growth is slow, consider diversifying your content types or topics to attract a broader audience.

Click-Through Rate (CTR)

Are people clicking on the links you share?

- **How to learn:** If you use URL shorteners or tracking links, you can calculate CTR by dividing clicks by impressions.

- **Why it matters:** A high CTR indicates that your content is not just seen but compelling enough for people to want to learn more.

- **How to use it:** A high CTR suggests your content titles and descriptions are enticing. Analyze which posts have the highest CTR and try to replicate those elements in future posts. If CTR is low, work on crafting more compelling headlines and clearer calls to action.

Dwell Time

How long are people spending on your posts or articles?

- **How to learn:** LinkedIn doesn't provide this directly, but you can get an idea from the "Views" vs "Reads" metrics for articles.

- **Why it matters:** Longer dwell times suggest that your content is engaging and valuable to your audience.

- **How to use it:** If you notice a high ratio of "Reads" to "Views" on your articles, it means people are finding your content worth their time. Focus on creating more in-depth, valuable content. If dwell time seems low, consider ways to make your content more engaging, such as adding visuals or breaking up text into more digestible sections.

In the Reader Resources, I've provided a downloadable tracking sheet that you can use to keep tabs on the movement of your LinkedIn metrics.

Remember, the goal isn't to obsess over numbers but to use them as a guide for improvement. If you notice your engagement dropping, maybe it's time to refresh your content strategy. If your profile views are increasing but not leading to connections, perhaps your profile needs some tweaking to showcase your value better.

Treat your LinkedIn presence as an ongoing experiment. Try new things, see how they affect your metrics and adjust accordingly. Over time, you'll develop a strategy that works best for you and your career goals. And don't forget – behind every number is a real person. While metrics are valuable, building genuine professional relationships should always be your ultimate aim on LinkedIn.

Your Action Plan for Thought Leadership and Network Building

You've learned how to leverage AI to create compelling content, curate valuable insights, and engage meaningfully with your network. Now, it's time to put these strategies into action and transform your LinkedIn presence from a static profile to a dynamic hub of thought leadership. Let's turn your LinkedIn profile into a powerful career catalyst! Here's your action plan:

- **Establish a content strategy:** Create a monthly content calendar mixing original posts, articles, and shared content. Use AI to identify trends and develop content ideas.

- **Expand your network strategically:** Use AI to draft personalized connection requests to 5 relevant professionals in your industry each week.

- **Engage consistently:** Interact with at least 10 posts from your network weekly, using AI to help draft thoughtful comments.

- **Publish thought leadership content:** Write and publish one long-form LinkedIn article monthly, using AI for outlining and editing.

- **Curate valuable content:** Use AI to find and share 3 relevant articles with your network weekly, adding your insights.

- **Leverage second-degree connections:** Identify 3 strategic second-degree connections monthly and use AI to craft introduction requests through mutual connections.

- **Participate in groups:** Join 2-3 relevant LinkedIn groups and contribute to discussions at least twice a week.

- **Conduct informational interviews:** Reach out to one professional in your desired role or company monthly for an informational interview, using AI to craft your request.

- **Analyze and adjust:** Review your LinkedIn analytics monthly. Use AI to interpret the data and suggest strategy improvements.

Remember, consistency is key. Implement these actions regularly, always infusing them with your unique voice and expertise. Your goal is to create a LinkedIn presence that not only attracts opportunities but also adds genuine value to your professional community.

Your AI-Enhanced LinkedIn Journey Begins

More Links, Tips, and Resources

C ongratulations! You've reached the end of "The AI-Savvy Job Seeker: Transform Your LinkedIn Profile and Outshine the Competition." By now, you're equipped with powerful AI-driven strategies to elevate your LinkedIn presence and stand out in today's competitive job market. But remember, this isn't the end—it's just the beginning of your journey towards a more impactful and engaging professional online presence.

Putting Your Knowledge into Action

As you've learned throughout this book, the key to a successful LinkedIn profile lies in the perfect blend of your unique professional story and strategic optimization. The AI tools and techniques we've explored are designed to enhance your profile, making it more visible, compelling, and aligned with your career goals.

Now, it's time to put all this knowledge into practice. Revisit each chapter, implement the strategies, and use the AI prompts to refine your profile. Remember, the most effective LinkedIn profiles are those that evolve with your career. Make it a habit to update and optimize your profile regularly, leveraging the AI techniques you've learned to stay ahead of the curve.

For readers ready to take their LinkedIn profile transformation to the next level, **"The AI-Savvy Job Seeker Workbook: Your Interactive Guide to LinkedIn Profile Transformation,"** available on Amazon, offers a hands-on approach to implementing the strategies outlined in this guide.

Packed with over 25 interactive worksheets, exercises, and templates, the workbook provides step-by-step guidance to help you craft a standout LinkedIn profile and apply AI-powered techniques effectively. Whether you're refining your personal brand, optimizing for keywords, or creating compelling content, this workbook is your go-to resource for turning insights into action.

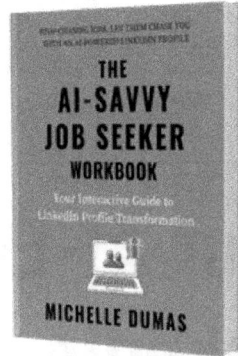

Leveraging Online Resources

To support you in your ongoing LinkedIn journey, I encourage you to take full advantage of the online resources I've prepared for you.

Visit **www.distinctiveweb.com/linkedin-book-resources** to access:

- A comprehensive compilation of AI prompts discussed in the book

- A curated collection of symbols and emojis to enhance your profile's visual appeal

- An easy reference to the many profile formulas in this book

These resources are designed to make the implementation of the strategies in this book as seamless as possible.

The Power of Professional Résumé Templates

While your LinkedIn profile is a crucial part of your professional online presence, don't forget about the importance of a well-crafted résumé. To complement your newly optimized LinkedIn profile, I invite you to explore our collection of professionally designed ATS-friendly résumé templates at **www.distinctiveresumetemplates.com.**

These templates were crafted personally by me with the same level of expertise and attention to detail that went into this book. They're designed to help you create a résumé that not only passes through ATS but also impresses human recruiters. By using these templates in conjunction with your enhanced LinkedIn profile, you'll present a cohesive and powerful professional brand across all platforms.

To take your résumé writing journey even further, I've created comprehensive Resume Writing Toolkits that give you everything you need to craft a powerful, modern résumé quickly and easily. Each toolkit includes four professionally designed, ATS-friendly résumé templates, plus extensive digital guidebooks packed with expert professional résumé, bio, and LinkedIn profile writing tips. With more than 125 pages of indispensable advice, expert guidance, and professionally written examples, these toolkits offer insights you won't find anywhere else—all crafted for immediate application. Access these resources at **www.distinctiveresumetemplates.com/toolkits/.**

By using these templates and toolkits in conjunction with your enhanced LinkedIn profile, you'll present a cohesive and powerful professional brand across all platforms.

The Value of Expert Support

While this book has armed you with valuable tools and strategies to optimize your LinkedIn profile using AI, I understand that some situations call for personalized, expert assistance. Perhaps you're facing a career transition, aiming for an executive position, or simply want the assurance of a professional touch. In such cases, I invite you to reach out to us at Distinctive Career Services.

Our team of professional résumé and LinkedIn profile writers brings decades of experience and a deep understanding of current job market trends. We offer:

- Personalized LinkedIn profile optimization

- Expert résumé writing services

- Career coaching and strategy sessions

- Complete career marketing packages

Whether you need a complete overhaul of your professional branding or just want an expert review of your AI-enhanced profile, we're here to help. Visit our website at **www.distinctiveweb.com** to learn more about our services and how we can support your career goals.

Expanding Your AI-Powered Job Search

While this book has equipped you with powerful AI strategies for LinkedIn optimization, your career journey encompasses much more. That's why I've created The Ultimate AI-Powered Job Search Playbook, available at **www .ai-powered-playbook.com**. This comprehensive guide takes AI-driven job searching to the next level, offering over 1,000 specialized prompts designed to support every aspect of your career journey.

The playbook helps you harness AI's potential for countless career tasks, including:

- Crafting compelling cover letters and elevator pitches

- Preparing for job interviews

- Planning career transitions and advancement

- Managing your job search effectively

- Accessing the hidden job market

- Building your professional network

- Negotiating job offers

Whether you're exploring new career paths, preparing for interviews, or negotiating salary, these prompts serve as your personal career coach, helping you navigate each challenge with confidence. The playbook complements the LinkedIn strategies you've learned here, creating a complete AI-powered approach to modern job searching.

For Career Professionals: Elevate Your LinkedIn Expertise

If you're a professional résumé writer or career coach working with job-seeking clients, I highly recommend pursuing the Nationally Certified Online Profile Expert (NCOPE) certification through the National Resume Writers Association (NRWA). As someone who has earned this certification myself, I consider it the gold standard for LinkedIn profile writing and coaching expertise.

You can learn more about this valuable certification at www.thenrwa. org/. While I have no formal association with the program beyond holding the certification myself, I've found it invaluable in elevating my LinkedIn expertise and the quality of service I provide to my clients.

The Journey Continues

As we conclude this book, I want to emphasize that your career success is our shared goal. Whether you're using the AI techniques from this book, leveraging our online resources, using our résumé templates, or engaging our professional services, we're committed to empowering you to achieve your highest career aspirations.

Remember, in today's digital age, your LinkedIn profile is often the first impression you make on potential employers, clients, or networking contacts. By investing time and effort into optimizing your profile, you're not just improving your online presence—you're opening doors to new opportunities and positioning yourself for career success.

As you move forward with your newly acquired knowledge and tools, keep in mind that the world of AI and professional networking is constantly evolving. Stay curious, keep learning, and don't hesitate to experiment with new strategies.

I encourage you to connect with me on LinkedIn [www.linkedin.com/in/michelledumas/] for ongoing tips, insights, and updates in the world of career development and AI-driven strategies. Share your success stories, ask questions, and join a community of forward-thinking professionals who are leveraging AI to advance their careers.

Thank you for joining me on this journey to transform your LinkedIn profile. Here's to your continued success and the exciting opportunities that await you. Remember, your dream career is out there—now you have the tools to pursue it with confidence.

About the Author

M ichelle Dumas is a pioneering force in the professional résumé writing and career services industry. With over 25 years of experience, she has established herself as one of the foremost experts in career development and personal branding.

In 1996, Michelle founded Distinctive Career Services, driven by her passion for helping individuals design careers and lives on their own terms. Her mission: to empower as many people as possible with the tools, resources, and confidence they need to pursue and achieve their dream careers.

Throughout her career, Michelle has:

- Supported well over 10,000 professionals across all 50 U.S. states and internationally

- Earned multiple certifications, including Nationally Certified Online Profile Expert, Nationally Certified Resume Writer, and Certified Personal Branding Strategist, among others

- Won numerous awards for her résumé-writing expertise

- Been recognized as the National Resume Writers Association's 2021 "Industry Hero," recognizing leading-edge career services providers who are passionate about the profession's advancement

- Authored and contributed to dozens of books and articles on job searching and résumé writing

Michelle's expertise extends beyond résumé writing. As an early adopter of LinkedIn, joining when the platform first launched, she quickly recognized its potential and began incorporating LinkedIn profile writing into her services. This foresight has positioned her as a thought leader in online professional branding.

Michelle's approach to career services is characterized by her dedication to personalized service, intensive exploration of each client's unique strengths, and an unwavering commitment to world-class quality. She believes in the power of storytelling and has a natural talent for identifying and articulating each individual's personal brand and career narrative.

In addition to her work with individual clients, Michelle is committed to supporting both her industry peers and job seekers at large. She created Distinctive Resume Templates to help career industry professionals enhance their services with expertly designed, modern, and ATS-friendly résumé templates. Now, with "The AI-Savvy Job Seeker: Transform Your LinkedIn Profile and Outshine the Competition," Michelle combines her decades of expertise with cutting-edge AI technology to empower professionals at all stages of their careers. These initiatives reflect her mission to make high-quality career tools and advice accessible to everyone, whether they're working with a professional career coach or navigating their job search independently.

When not revolutionizing the career services industry, Michelle enjoys the tranquility of her rural New Hampshire home. She cherishes time spent with her family, including her husband of over 37 years and their daughter and grandson. Michelle's passion for exploration extends beyond careers; she loves traveling throughout the U.S. and internationally, embracing new experiences and learning about different cultures. An outdoor enthusiast, she can often be found gardening, kayaking, biking, hiking, ATVing, or camping in the beautiful New Hampshire wilderness. Michelle also nurtures a deep interest in genealogy, finding joy in uncovering and telling the stories of her ancestors. Through it all, she continues to lead Distinctive Career Services, continuously seeking innovative ways to help professionals design careers they love, drawing inspiration from her rich personal life and diverse interests.

Did You Enjoy This Book?

Dear Reader,

Thank you for investing your time in "The AI-Savvy Job Seeker: Transform Your LinkedIn Profile and Outshine the Competition." I hope this book has provided you with valuable insights and practical strategies to enhance your professional online presence.

If you've found this book helpful, I would be incredibly grateful if you could take a moment to rate and review it on Amazon. Your feedback not only helps other readers make informed decisions but also assists in improving future editions.

To leave a review, visit the book's review page. This QR code will take you directly to the review page.

Your support means the world to me and helps in the mission of empowering more professionals to achieve their career goals. Thank you again for being part of this journey.

Best wishes for your continued success,
Michelle Dumas
Founder & CEO, Distinctive Career Services